After Welfare

After Welfare

The Culture of Postindustrial Social Policy

Sanford F. Schram

NEW YORK UNIVERSITY PRESS

New York and London

NEW YORK UNIVERSITY PRESS
New York and London

Library of Congress Cataloging-in-Publication Data
Schram, Sanford.
After welfare : the culture of postindustrial social policy /
Sanford F. Schram.
p.   cm.
Includes bibliographical references and index.
ISBN 0-8147-9754-7 (cloth : alk. paper) — ISBN 0-8147-9755-5
(pbk. : alk. paper)
1. United States—Social policy—1993– 2. Public welfare—United
States. I. Title.
HN65 .S426 1999
361.6'1'0973—dc21   99-006916

New York University Press books are printed on acid-free paper,
and their binding materials are chosen for strength and durability.

Manufactured in the United States of America

10 9 8 7 6 5 4 3 2 1

To Joan

Contents

Acknowledgments

Chapter 1 is an expanded and revised version of an earlier piece: Sanford F. Schram, "Contracting America: The House Republicans and the Cycle of Representation," in Sanford F. Schram and Philip T. Neisser, eds., *Tales of the State: Narrative in U.S. Politics and Public Policy* (Lanham, Md.: Rowman & Littlefield, 1997), pp. 63–86. Chapter 3 is a revised and longer version of Sanford F. Schram, "In the Clinic: The Medicalization of Welfare," *Social Text* 62 (spring 2000). Chapter 4 is a revision of material used in Sanford F. Schram and Joe Soss, "Making Something Out of Nothing: Welfare Reform and A New Race to the Bottom," *Publius: The Journal of Federalism* 28 (spring 1998): 67–88; Sanford Schram and Joe Soss, "The Real Value of Welfare: Why Poor Families Do Not Migrate," *Politics & Society* 27 (March 1999): 39–66; and Sanford F. Schram and Carol S. Weissert, "The State of American Federalism, 1996–1997," *Publius: The Journal of Federalism* 27 (spring 1997): 1–31. Chapter 6 is a revised version of Sanford F. Schram and R. Scott Daniels, "'Poor' Statistical Accounting: Welfare Policy Research in Cyberspace and Public Sphere," *Theory & Event* 2 (http://muse.jhu.edu/journals/theory_and_event/).

Numerous people advised me on the issues I address in this book, others commented on selected chapters, and still others read the entire manuscript. For very helpful discussions, I thank Raymond Albert, Leslie Alexander, Jeffrey Applegate, Dana Becker, Jane Bennett, Richard Cloward, Donald Culverson, Karen Curtis, Sheldon Danziger, Joan Davitt, Kathy Ferguson, Nancy Fraser, Marisa Golden, Jack Gunnell, Thomas Hawley, Beverly Keever, Julia Littell, James Martin, Sankar Muthu, Brian Richardson, Todd Swanstrom, John Tambornino, Thomas Vartanian, and Carol Weissert. I greatly appreciate the comments on selected chapters provided by Gregory Acevedo, Bruce Baum, Jim Baumohl, William Connolly, Barbara Cruikshank, Scott Daniels, Tom Dumm, Kennan Ferguson, Jon Goldberg-Hiller, Manfred Henningsen, Henry Kariel, Patrick Kaylor, George Kent, Claudia Krugovoy, Peter Manicas, Neal Milner, Carolyn Needleman, Philip Neisser,

Brian Schmidt, Michael Shapiro, Noenoe Silva, Joe Soss, Clay Steinman, Ellen Szabo, Douglas Torgerson, and Phyllis Turnbull. Barbara Cruikshank, Clay Steinman, and Michael Shapiro provided extensive advice beyond reading selected chapters, for which I am most grateful. I also want to thank the two anonymous reviewers of the original draft manuscript for their very helpful comments. In addition, Frances Fox Piven read the entire manuscript and provided extensive commentary as she has for so many others, proving once again her dedication to welfare scholarship. Whatever relationship social welfare research can hope to have to the cause of social justice has been for some time now largely due to her generous spirit, keen intellect, and impeccable political sensibilities.

Ellen Szabo's very able assistance in preparing the index is also most appreciated. Mary Byers provided extremely helpful suggestions on my writing. I want to express my deep appreciation to Ruth Mayden, Dean of the Graduate School of Social Work and Social Research, Bryn Mawr College, for all the support she has given this project. I also appreciate the support of the Bryn Mawr College Committee on Faculty Awards and Grants and the Louise Hess Miller Modern Media Center at the University of Hawai'i for funding research related to the book. And I want to thank the graduate students in my seminars at Bryn Mawr on social theory and welfare reform and those at the New School for Social Research for engaging me so thoughtfully on issues raised in this book.

At New York University Press, Despina Papazoglou Gimbel, Andrew Katz, and Cecilia Feilla prepared the manuscript with great care and Stephen Magro provided wise advice throughout the process of completing the book. I thank them all.

Ryan Schram was particularly helpful in the numerous discussions we had about this manuscript, and so were Joan and Jack Schram who had to live with this book if for no other reason than that it was written at home. I thank them from the bottom of my heart for not just tolerating this intrusion into our home but helping to make it a most enjoyable experience.

Introduction

The chapters that follow offer a cultural critique of social welfare policy in the United States at the end of the twentieth century. While historically social welfare policy has reflected cultural norms, *fin de siècle* social welfare policy has proved to be a flash point for struggle over the fundamental cultural categories that undergird the social order. The end of the century has seen intensified concerns about the end of the industrial social order and the emergence of a new postindustrial set of social relations.[1] In the process, social welfare policy has become unusually freighted with cultural significance and has been enlisted in the effort to deny the changes that are occurring in work and family relations. Along with persistent poverty, growing inequality, and the collapse of the manual labor market, the traditional two-parent family has continued to dissolve and gender relations have undergone wholesale revision. Social welfare policy has been enlisted in what seems to be an eleventh-hour attempt to enforce the traditional values of work and family that have propped up what Nancy Fraser, Linda Gordon, and others have called the industrial "family-wage system" that is based on the traditional two-parent family in which the male "breadwinner" earns enough to support his wife the "homemaker," and their children.[2] The ideal of the traditional family was never realizable for most families in the industrial era; with postindustrialism, it is no longer sustainable as an ideal. However, social policy has been enlisted to deny this reality and insist on the maintenance of the ideal. It is very much part of what Lawrence M. Mead has touted as the "New Paternalism."[3] In the face of social change, this desperate new paternalism seeks to reassert the traditional values of work and family as if insisting on the old values would suffice to maintain the old arrangements. At the same time, this new paternalism denies that social changes in work and family have helped highlight the profound inequities of the old system, especially for women and minorities.[4]

While recent debates in social theory have often divided those who want to emphasize material issues of redistribution from those who put the stress

1

on cultural issues of recognition, in this book I pursue a path that assumes these are interrelated.[5] I agree with Andrew Ross when he writes:

> The vast economic forces that take their daily toll on our labour, communities, and natural habitats are the most powerful elements in our social lives. The power with which they work on our world is exercised through cultural forms: legal, educational, political, and religious institutions; valued artifacts and documents; social identities; codes of moral sanctity; prevailing ideas about the good life; and fears of ruination, among many others. Without these forms, economic activity remains a lifeless abstraction in the ledgers and databases of financial record.[6]

The economy allocates material value in good part on the basis of what culture marks as valuable. In turn, the culture gets to assign symbolic value in good part on the basis of its relationship to the way the economy has allocated material value.[7] This interplay between the material and symbolic dimensions of life plays out in public policy in a variety of ways. "Guns or butter": the aesthetics of materialism suggest the material consequences of aesthetics. Symbolism matters. The "welfare queen," for instance, not only instigates the marginalization of public assistance recipients but enacts that marginalization in ways that have real material effects in the form of lower benefits, increased surveillance, and reduced economic opportunities. Identity matters.

My approach assumes that cultural contests have always been a significant dimension of social welfare policy. This approach takes seriously the idea that social welfare policy can be effectively understood as a hybrid, like everything else in the real world. Its hybridity comes from its being situated between culture and political economy. Social policies provide material assistance to people but are intended to reproduce cultural norms.[8] Therefore, in what follows I pay attention to the way the Defense of Marriage Act of 1996 has sought to maintain the legal privileges of the traditional family and heterosexual marriage even as I focus on the way the Personal Responsibility and Work Opportunity Reconciliation Act of 1996 reformed public assistance for low-income families.

My critique employs culture in its own distinctive way. In invoking culture, I make the following assumptions: (1) culture is a critical ingredient making social interaction possible; (2) culture is manifested in the interpretive categories we use to make sense of the world; (3) these categories are grounded in oppositions; (4) a culture grows and develops through the linking of interpretive categories in one area to another; (5) new and unsettling social developments, such as same-sex marriage or the increase of single-parent families, tend to be understood in terms of preexisting interpretive categories and conceptual oppositions, often by way of borrowed metaphors that link new developments to old practices; (6) while the process of cultural elaboration is necessarily biased and ideological, it can be reworked to create the conditions for positive social change; and (7) contesting the ways in which metaphors are applied from one area to another is an important cultural struggle that can have significant material consequences.

For me, therefore, culture is not so much a set of shared rituals, traditions, and values as it is shared ways of communicating, coding, and categorizing. It is akin to what J. M. Balkin calls "cultural software." Balkin emphasizes that "people make sense of the cultural world not through isolated conceptual oppositions but through networks of linked conceptual oppositions."[9] From this perspective, culture is an ideologically selective set of interrelated, nested oppositions that are often linked in unanticipated ways, as suggested by the homology of nature : culture :: reason : passion :: male : female. Each dichotomy operates through interdependent relationships with the other.[10] A culture's nested oppositions operate ideologically as selective forms of power that reinforce hierarchies of privilege, often in unintended but nonetheless powerful ways.

In examining the culture of postindustrial social policy in this specific way, I ask how cultural anxieties leave their traces in the texts of social welfare policy. I find evidence for these cultural traces in unexpected connections between policy and culture, across various social practices, in the relationships of one discourse to another, on the relays between text and image, and through multiple levels of consciousness.

My analysis starts with the Republicans' 1994 Contract with America as a critical document laden with its own cultural significance which provided the impetus for the changes that followed. I end with an examination of how the struggle for more socially responsible welfare policies can survive the current onslaught. These essays emphasize in particular that cultural power is manifested in established ways of expressing reality in discourse and that this not only affects social reality but is a force for making social welfare policy what it is. Whether it is "contract" or "dependency" or "insurance," the ascendant cultural categories limit the possibilities of social welfare policy. Throughout, I emphasize that while the existing conceptual oppositions operate in conservative ways, they remain vulnerable to a deconstruction that suggests they can be reworked in order to better accommodate change and make possible a more inclusive, tolerant, and caring social welfare policy. My intent is to show that this is a form of "word play" that can do important "norm work," encouraging us to rethink what our social standards should be and how they should be applied. I hope to successfully demonstrate that this form of postmodern cultural theory constitutes an important way to combat the cultural biases empowering the current retrograde changes in social welfare policy.

1

Contracting America
The Cycle of Representation and the Contagion of Policy Discourse

Since I took office, I have worked to craft a new social contract.
—President Bill Clinton, July 14, 1999

The "Contract with America" was proposed by Republican congressional candidates during the 1994 elections. A superficial campaign device, this conservative document became the basis for rewriting the liberal social contract that has served as the foundation of the social welfare state since the New Deal of the 1930s. Within the framework of the ephemeral "Contract," Congress passed and President Clinton signed into law the Personal Responsibility and Work Opportunity Reconciliation Act of 1996. This law abolished the federal entitlement for poor families by repealing the Aid to Families with Dependent Children program that was originally enacted with the Social Security Act of 1935.[1]

While the significance of the 1996 welfare reform law is not to be underestimated, in many important respects the problems of the conservative Contract lie not with the fact that it promoted legislation that rescinded a program of sixty years' standing but rather with the way it has reinscribed the relations of power implicit in liberal discourse more generally. As reproduced in the *New York Times* shortly after the November 1994 elections, the "Contract with America" put forth ten promises made by Republican congressional candidates concerning legislative action they would undertake during the first hundred days of the 104th Congress. Here are the Republicans' promises "in their own words," to quote the *New York Times:*

1. *The Fiscal Responsibility Act:* A balanced budget/tax limitation amendment and a legislative line-item veto to restore fiscal responsibility to an

out-of-control Congress, requiring them to live under the same budget constraints as families and business.

2. *The Taking Back Our Streets Act:* An anti-crime package including stronger truth-in-sentencing, "good faith" exclusionary rule exemptions, effective death penalty provisions, and cuts in social spending from this summer's "crime" bill to fund prison construction and additional law enforcement to keep people secure in their neighborhoods and kids safe in their schools.

3. *The Personal Responsibility Act:* Discourage illegitimacy and teen pregnancy by prohibiting welfare to minor mothers and denying increased AFDC for additional children while on welfare, cut spending for welfare programs, and enact a tough two-years-and-out provision with work requirements to promote individual responsibility.

4. *The Family Reinforcement Act:* Child support enforcement, tax incentives for adoption, strengthening rights of parents in their children's education, stronger child pornography laws, and an elderly dependent care tax credit to reinforce the central role of families in American society.

5. *The American Dream Restoration Act:* A $5,000 per child tax credit, begin repeal of the marriage tax penalty, and creation of American Dream Savings Accounts to provide middle-class tax relief.

6. *The National Security Restoration Act:* No U.S. troops under U.N. command and restoration of the essential parts of our national security funding to strengthen our national defense and maintain our credibility around the world.

7. *The Senior Citizens Fairness Act:* Raise the Social Security earnings limit which currently forces seniors out of the work force, repeal the 1993 tax hikes on Social Security benefits and provide tax incentives for private long-term care insurance to let older Americans keep more of what they have earned over the years.

8. *The Job Creation and Wage Enhancement Act:* Small business incentives, capital gains cut and indexation, neutral cost recovery, risk assessment/cost-benefit analysis, strengthening the Regulatory Flexibility Act and unfunded mandate reform to create jobs and raise worker wages.

9. *The Common Sense Legal Reform Act:* "Loser pays" laws, reasonable limits on punitive damages and reform of product liability laws to stem the endless tide of litigation.

10. *The Citizen Legislature Act:* A first ever vote on term limits to replace career politicians with citizen legislators.[2]

The Republicans stressed that these measures would impose standards of "common sense," "business," "family," and "personal responsibility" on some future "out-of-control Congress" in order to reinforce and restore the

"American Dream." By the end of 1996, parts of the Contract had become law, including welfare reform, which was enacted in full force. Yet, as the rhetoric surrounding the ten points suggests, the ultimate power of the Contract may be determined by more than its limited policy success.

The Contract was probably more successful in terms of what it represented—whether as electoral politics or policy agenda, as symbolic or material practice. Although there may have been a time when such distinctions were meaningful, the Contract's ambiguous status as a "hybrid imagined agreement" highlights the way binaries such as politics/policy, symbolic/material, and the like fail to adequately represent what they describe.[3] In fact, the Contract's ambiguous representational status as something between elite political posturing and popular policy agenda highlights the problem of representation in politics. In the case of the Contract, its politics lie in the terms it used to represent a policy agenda.

The Contract's power and therefore its politics were to be found most especially in its relationship to the term "contract" as used in liberal policy, as well as legal and business, discourses. In what follows, I focus in particular on the "Contract with America" as a prime example of what J. M. Balkin calls "cultural software."[4] My discussion illustrates Balkin's argument that a culture develops by borrowing key metaphors and other interpretive practices and that these key devices arise out of and establish the ground for categorical distinctions. I suggest that the process of mimetic transmission in the Contract with America operates like a virus infecting one area with the biases associated with the metaphors and interpretive practices of another area.[5] I emphasize how the "contract" in the Contract with America has operated as a contagion of policy discourse.[6] I examine how the "contract" in the Contract with America has reinforced the idea that welfare recipients have failed to meet the basic threshold requirement of personal responsibility expected of full citizens of the contractual order.[7]

In particular, the concept of contract was especially important because it reinscribed a distinctive self as the kind of person assumed by a liberal society to be needed in so many settings: the contractual person.[8] The contractual person was the implicit standard used to enforce the idea of "personal responsibility" upon welfare recipients. The preoccupation with personal responsibility in turn has led to punitive results for welfare recipients, such as requiring all employable recipients, including even single mothers of young children, to find work and cutting off aid to families after five years regardless of how young their children are. The Contract has narrowed down the meaning of personal responsibility to not taking welfare and having paid employment instead, regardless of mitigating circumstances.

Therefore, irrespective of its inability to achieve its entire agenda, the Contract is an important contemporary illustration of how liberal theory has become the "common sense" of the United States and how this common sense operates as a lexicon of signs, symbols, and images used to reinforce prevailing relationships of power. The liberal "common sense" of the conservative Contract, therefore, becomes a political subtext that needs to be questioned. This is not an apolitical literary exercise. Anne Norton has emphasized the political value of such analysis in her examination of liberalism's unquestioned authority as the common sense of the contemporary United States:

> Silence concerning the authority of language over the constitution of the self, the realization and expression of the will, permits liberal regimes to maintain the myth of the word, particularly the spoken word, as a neutral instrument for the utterance and realization of the individual will. It enables liberal regimes to maintain established hierarchies by predicating the achievement of equality and the establishment and maintenance of cultural difference on involvement in practices that obstruct or preclude these ends.[9]

The following analysis seeks to break that silence about the liberal politics of allegedly neutral contractual language by discussing its role in the conservative Contract with America. In the process, we can begin to see that even the conservative Contract with America has strengthened liberal contractual discourse and that that discourse has perpetuated biased notions of personal responsibility that reinforce the marginalization of people in need of public assistance.

Contracts and Diaries: Linguistic Dispatches to the Self

April 7, 1995: Dear Diary, I promised you (or did I promise myself?) that I would log in the status of the Contract with America after the United States House of Representatives had voted on all its components.[10] Before I do that I cannot help but relay my reactions to this idea of "the contract." I am struck by the many meanings of "contract," especially for Americans living in the late twentieth century. "Contracting America,"[11] as the activity engendered by the contract, is unavoidably a multidimensional practice. Once we start contracting America, the question immediately arises as to whether we will go all the way: privatize the country to subcontractors, retrench to a "two-thirds society," or contract the disease that the contagion of policy discourse spreads.[12]

"Contracting America" is at least trebled in meaning—legally binding exchange, welfare state rollback, or disease.[13] The idea of contract serves the politics of today in various convenient ways: (1) the reassurances that come with business transactions between ostensibly free and equal parties; (2) the insistences derived from persistent political pressures to reduce the welfare state; and (3) the anxieties attached to contagious diseases, given the decline of immunology in a postantibiotic age. At a time when the modernist impulse to insist on airtight distinctions between nature and culture has broken down, contract becomes a hybrid simultaneously implying the symbolic and the material, if not the cultural and the natural.[14] It is a multipurpose term whose multiple resonances suggest a variety of possible responses, each of which can be said to "process" the idea of contract in a distinctive way.[15]

"Contract" in America, therefore, is a potent if unstable metaphor. In the United States contract is the metaphor of choice for legitimating much of what we do publicly and privately, in marriage, business, law, and social policy. Contract is a live metaphor (i.e., is used so often) because it is a dead metaphor (i.e., it has lost its figurative character and is seen as literal). Yet the power of contract lies in its articulation—that is, the extent to which it can be connected with so many different things as an expressed representation.[16] In the contractual society so much is about contract, even if diversely so, and the Contract with America is a quintessentially American discursive practice.

From campaign spectacle to policy agenda, this act of contracting America becomes, then, a paradigmatic example of the dangers associated with borrowing a metaphor across the overlapping, discontinuous discourses of business, law, and politics. Contracting America underscores how one discourse must of necessity invoke another, given the pervasive impossibility of getting beyond intertextuality. In the quest to use discourse as an attempt to make coherent the incoherences of public life or of life generally, one discourse trades on another, borrowing metaphors for justification, creating an inevitable layering of meaning. Contractarians would probably prefer the formulation that one discourse must inevitably contract with other discourses in order to create meaning. The "metaphors of contract" highlight the "contracts of metaphor." Meaning becomes contingent upon the deferred promise of representation.

To "Contract with America" is therefore also unavoidably vexed as a linguistic act. The "Contract with America" is not just what J. L. Austin calls a "constative" (i.e., a descriptive) statement.[17] Constatives include descriptive statements even if they are dramatic declarations of fact, as in "You are guilty of murder and are sentenced to death." In name and deed, the "Contract with America" would also be for Austin a "performative" statement (i.e., a statement that is itself an act). Performatives include commands and proclamations, as in "I hereby pronounce you guilty of murder and sentence you to death." A performative can have more than what Austin calls the "locutionary" force of referencing the world beyond itself. It can have the greater "illocutionary" force of being something that in the act of being spoken becomes a deed. Illocutionary acts, for Austin, are statements that are also deeds.[18] To make the statement is to enact the deed, as in a judge "pronouncing a sentence." Performatives can also have what Austin calls "perlocutionary force," whereby the statement has consequences. Here the statement is not itself the deed but is a condition that leads to "certain effects that are not the same as the speech act itself,"[19] as in a judge pronouncing a death sentence that leads to the convicted person's execution. This example highlights how speech acts can have both a performative and a constative dimension and be locutionary, illocutionary, and perlocutionary all at the same time.

So it is with the "Contract with America." In the case of the term "Contract with America," the simultaneity of speech acts leads to multiple confusions, because "Contract with America" can mean many different things depending on how this speech act is interpreted. If it is a constative, then it is a representation of some previously agreed upon arrangement. But this would be a dangerous position to take because it would suggest that there was some other process by which the people of the country and the House Republicans made an agreement. Beyond the low-turnout elections of 1994, which brought Republican majorities to both houses of Congress, there seems to be no process, other than perhaps the massaging of polling data, for suggesting mass support for the Contract. And in hindsight that seems exactly how the Contract was to be challenged as a false constative that failed to register what the "real" American people would endorse.[20]

The Contract's linguistic confusion points to the fact that it provided the background for its own creation. The Contract concealed how it constructed its signatories, rather than the other way around.[21] The opening lies in the idea of signature itself. Signature connotes an absent authorizing agent whose signature is thereby required. The idea of signature has proved to be a historic problem for the liberal social contract. Whether founding the American or other liberal political systems, the contract had to construct the "People" of that nation-state ahead of time, and they were then posthoc taken to comprise the consenting parties to the agreement.[22] The state constructs the nation rather than the people constructing the state—as when the leaders of the American Revolution claimed to be acting in the name of the "American People" who had yet to consent to the formation of a new government. The Contract with America trades on the social contract of liberal political discourse with its assumptions of signature and consent as well as related notions of fiduciary responsibility and reciprocal rights and obligations associated with business and marriage contracts.

The way "contract" operates in the Contract with America therefore demonstrates that contagion rather than communication best characterizes liberal policy discourse today.[23] Borrowing the contractual metaphors of catachresis (i.e., metaphors about contract that make the dissimilar similar) from business practice to legal document to policy prescription results in its own linguistic subversion.[24] The Contract with America undermined the critical subject position that was its central object of inquiry—"personal responsibility." The Contract with America sought to legislate personal responsibility, especially for people in need of public assistance, while denying the extent to which the people represented by the symbol of "America" actually got to be real signatories responsible for a contract made in their name. In the parlance of liberal political discourse, "contracting America" inevitably means converting America into a form of property to be bought and sold on the open market.[25] The commodity sold here is the reified, repackaged, already preprocessed entity known as the "American People." Accepting this transaction would imply condoning a form of property theft—the stealing of the American people for the purpose of "forging" national public policy in the name of the people who are alleged to have made those policies. Of necessity, then, resisting the theft associated with the Contract with America involves interpretive practices that challenge in particular how the Contract appropriates the "American People" for its own political purposes.

Contesting the Contract with America therefore starts by challenging the way it operates as a conservative discursive practice whose liberal silences are tied to the prevailing common sense about that exchangeable commodity called the "American People." More to the point, political struggle over the Contract with America involves contesting both the commodification associated with contracting America and the possessiveness implied by the snatching of that (body) politic. The right to take possession of that *proper* name and to treat it like one's own personal *property* is like other *property* rights and is therefore constructed out of law. Who has title to the American people, and to what extent and under what conditions are the people who comprise that populace entitled to benefits from the state? To what extent does the power to name the "American People" in the linguistic sense promote the power to disentitle some of those people in the political sense?

In response, I would suggest that the corporealization of "America" implied by the Contract inaugurated an imperialistic, if contemporary, form of top-down ventriloquism. After one hundred days of legislating in order to fulfill the promise of the Contract, Newt Gingrich, the then-Speaker of the House, pronounced that the House had upheld its end of the bargain, all the while denying that he had positioned members of the American polity as contractors in his discourse. In his House, the "Contract with America" became the "Discourse on America"—the one and only promise that needed to be kept. Never mind that his was but one House and that policy promises cannot be fulfilled in this country unless they are affirmed in at least two houses and gain the signature of the resident of the White House. Nonetheless, the Speaker of the House at least got to keep his promise to himself, even as his pronouncements denied the ways in which his discourse on America contracts it.

The Contract with America was therefore very much like a diary entry; it was a memo that Gingrich and other House Republicans had written to themselves. Furthermore, however, it was a diary entry meant to be read as if it were a letter posted to someone else. By supplying a subtext that assumed its audience, it anticipated being read, and it did so by implicating that audience in the text. In so doing, this textual practice denied readers their readership. It was more like O. J. Simpson's *I Want to Tell You* than the *Bob Packwood Diaries*. To read the Contract with America was to be denied the opportunity to supply what was missing from the text—that is, the very act of supplementation that Paul de Man suggests defines readership. Specifically, de Man defines reading as a negative process that highlights the indeterminacy of texts. Such an act must of necessity create a new text that is also in need of supplementation. This suggests that all readings should be open-ended and not foreclose the possibility of additional readings.[26] But reading the Contract was a close-ended pact Newt Gingrich had made with himself only in order to claim that it was a pact he had made with the "American People." Reading the Contract, the American people found out what that text was supposed to mean for them.

The Contract with America was therefore not just the public equivalent of a bedside diary, it was also the political equivalent of a draft notice—if not a form of conscription, then a coercive form of enlistment.[27] Enlistment is supposedly voluntary whereas conscription forcibly enrolls individuals. That is what can be so insidious about enlistments like the Contract with America. It enlisted the "American People" as signatories without their actually signing anything. The Republican Party made the American people into a "party"—that is, the other side of the negotiations that produced the Contract.

The Political Signal

The Contract therefore was what Jacques Derrida has called a "simulacrum"—a model that is its own referent.[28] It was a representation that referred to itself. Yet it is not a simulacrum in the sense that Jean Baudrillard has used the term.[29] For Baudrillard, a simulacrum is an act of signification based on the autonomous "signal" rather than the context-dependent "sign." Baudrillard uses simulacrum as a signifier liberated from its referent, divested from history and disconnected from meaning.[30] "Baudrillard characterizes the sign as the increasing separation of signifier and signified. In the twentieth century the sign has been replaced by the signal. With the signal, words are structured to have reflexlike responses."[31] Signals send messages that receivers cannot challenge on the grounds that they misrepresent their referent. In this "mode of signification," simulacra operate as decontextualized signifiers that invert the process of referentiality. Simulacra become models that precede that on which they are modeled. The model precedes the referent, and the referent is modeled after the model to the point where models are all that there is. Shopping districts come to be modeled after the shopping malls that simulated shopping districts to the point where there are only shopping malls. Public opinion is modeled after the polls to the point where polls alone need to be anticipated irrespective of what opinions the public might otherwise formulate.[32] Simulacra point to themselves without context and do not suggest anything other than themselves.

But, the Contract with America was arguably not so decontextualized. As a term of liberal political discourse, the word contract was subsumed under the established liberal lexicon. Like so many signs of liberalism, the Contract was integrated into the prevailing common sense. Like the dense, if mute, imagery associated with the liberal order (whether it be the U.S. flag or the Constitution), liberal metaphors like contract immediately invoked the mythology of the liberal sense of place and time (i.e., how things came to be the way they are in the here and now). In this sense, contract is more mythology than simulation. It does point somewhere, but its referent is not a real referent—instead it is the mythology with which it is associated. As a semiliberated signifier, contract points to the preexisting understandings of liberal mythology. It is therefore conservative in its political effects, preserving the existing liberal cosmology on which liberal relations rely for their justification.[33] Contract, then, is an inevitably conservative simulacrum destined to invoke the commodifying properties of a contractual society. The Contract with America may have pointed nowhere but to itself, but when it did so it reinscribed the terms for living in that contractual society. It asked us to imagine people embodying the characteristics of contractual persons who participate in contractual relations to the extent that they can demonstrate that they are self-made persons responsible for their personal property. Right conduct became an issue of representation. The Contract with America did not so much represent the American people as represent how the American people ought to be represented.

Contracting the Liberal Origin Story

The Contract with America could be said to have exploited the Achilles' heel of its namesake—the idea of consent in contract theories of traditional liberal political thought. The persistent problem of all contract theories is, how can people actively consent to membership in a political order before they are constituted as the members of a political order?[34] The flip side of this problem is that people who confront the problem of state legitimacy are often born into that state system, one to which they have never explicitly consented. The solution to the question of active consent that comes either too early or too late is to assume that consent to state rule can be taken as a given if people are silent. Active consent can be inferred from tacit consent. Asking for consent from those born into a state that has already allegedly been legitimated according to the idea of popular consent requires a thought-experiment of intense reversibility. This thought-experiment takes the form of a story about how the state came into being. For this story to legitimate the contemporary state, it only needs to be believed as a theoretical possibility with relevance to the present state of affairs. We are asked to imagine if we would have consented to this state if we had been there at its inception or if we were forced to start all over again. The liberal state is legitimated by a narrative that constructs the populace as people who would have had every reason to have consented to the state if they had had the chance to do so.

Liberal stories of origin comprise just one distinctive set of stories about how the nation-state was legitimated in the name of a nation that constitutes a state.[35] Many nation-state narratives stress that the state was fashioned out of a preexisting nation while deemphasizing how the nation was developed by the state.[36] Nation-state legitimation narratives resist the "continental drift" that would destabilize the idea that the state stands in for the nation that precedes and authorizes it.[37]

Bonnie Honig argues that such fables are critical to the performative politics associated with "declarations of independence" that imagine the citizenry as signatories to a contract authorizing the state to act on its behalf.[38] In the American instance, the Declaration of Independence asserts the existence of the citizenry in a linguistic performance that imposes the idea of an imagined preexisting people. This performative speech act comes at the outset of the Declaration: "We hold these truths to be self-evident." Truths are asserted, not proved. The "We" similarly so.[39]

The story of the origin of the American polity rehearses the account implicit in liberal contract theory and in particular trades on the irony of signature.[40] The Declaration of Independence is signed and so it is authorized by those who are not present. Signature as a signifying act is just that: it stands in for that which it represents. But, if the document in question is the originating text, the signatories do not have the authority to sign, as the American people or whoever, until after they have signed and the "American People" become a legitimated entity.[41] Signatures must of necessity become self-legitimating performances.

For Anne Norton, contract has played a special role in the American self-constitution as a nation: "America was constituted in the space between law and outlawry, between legitimacy and rebellion, between the immediacy of the spoken word and the endurance of the written text."[42] As a negotiated promise between consenting parties, contract helps construct this middle ground between law and outlawry. Contractual space becomes a place where the volitional subjects of liberal discourse can stabilize their relationships in ways that are neither preset in law nor contingent upon anarchical interaction. The contractual society is constituted through promises whereby people commit to be true and consistent with the way they have been constituted in contractual discourse.[43]

Othering Government

The Contract with America not only confused the issue of who the "American People" were who were signing the imagined document; it also confounded the issue of the government that was to be the other party to this agreement. After the 1994 elections, an issue arose: was this a contract with the House Republicans who in an act of electoral posturing had signed the document on the steps of the Capitol at the height of the 1994 elections? Was it a contract that bound all House Republicans? Or the entire House now ruled by a Republican majority? Both houses of Congress? The government overall? The Contract did not specify; however, it did seem that the government was somehow, if unclearly, to be implicated in this agreement, both as a party to it and as an object of its scrutiny.

This double move need not be duplicitous; in fact, it could represent a moment of ethicality in contractual discourse in general and in the Contract with America in particular. As with constructions of the represented, the construction of the representative (government) need not in and of itself constitute an indefensible misappropriation. To view the government as an ongoing construction is to resist the notion of the government as a fixed alien "other" that is to be essentialized and endowed with certain qualities from which it cannot divest itself.

Frequently, for members of Congress particularly, "the government" is an essentialized "other" that they promise to attack in the name of the people they, as elected officials, represent. As the political scientist Richard Fenno has suggested, candidates run for Congress by running against it.[44] Government is made out to be something other than itself. Congress as a collection of representatives is against Congress as an institution. The Contract with America unfortunately reinforced the fixation on government as that which is to be treated as alien. The Contract's confusing positioning of the government promoted the idea that rather than the government remaking itself, the Republicans would remake the government. The government was the despised entity that could only be remade from the outside. It may not have been the ZOG (Zionist Occupation Government) of the Illuminati of Freemason British bankers who are imagined by survivalist militia around the United States to be taking over the U.S. political system on behalf of a conspiracy to achieve a brave new world order of global governance.[45] But this demonized government has been consistently depicted as a dangerous abuser of power in the mainstream stories that circulate in electoral politics. The Contract with America traded on these narratives and reinforced the demonization of the federal government in particular as the alien other bent on destroying "America" and "the American Way of Life."

The Silent Majority Is Given Personal Responsibility

Republican campaign strategists themselves emphasized this symbolic dimension of the Contract.[46] Early in 1994, pollster Frank Luntz and other Republican strategists had at first referred to the Contract in experimental focus groups as the G.O.P. Contract with America, without much resonance.[47] But when they renamed it the Contract with America, they struck a chord that registered in public opinion polls. Now polls could be framed so as to construct a public opinion that could be quantified as supporting a Republican takeover of Congress, while simultaneously naming that public the "American People." This well-established process of constructing public opinion out of the study of it made plausible the notion that essentially the "American People" had signed the Contract with America.

A populace that had experienced Ross Perot's "United We Stand America" was already primed for being constituted as a coherent entity imagined as being a signatory to this new Contract with America. By 1992 Perot had helped intensify the reliance in political discourse on business metaphors to legitimate his "common sense, no-nonsense, all-business, businesslike" approach to putting government on a sound managerial foundation.[48] While the Contract with America continued the nostalgic and fantastic cosmology of the Reagan revolution of the 1980s, it was also tied to a growing movement to reenact the age-old American practice of evaluating political issues in economic terms. In these terms, the primary business of government was not so much business as it was to run government as if it were a business.

Embodying the Contractual Person

The significance of the Contract with America therefore lay less in its precise policy prescriptions than in its ability to symbolize prevailing notions about the relationships of citizens to the state. In fact, as the Republicans in the Senate moved to enact parts of the Contract, polls began to indicate that a growing number of citizens were becoming increasingly uneasy about what the Contract, still largely unread, would actually mean for public policy.[49] However, these growing doubts about the specifics of the Contract emerged even as the Republican Party remained popular enough to retain control of Congress after the 1996 elections. The Contract continued to succeed symbolically even as it began to founder materially.

The Contract with America reinscribed the idea of social contract even as it rewrote it. In doing so, it reprivileged what might be called "contractual persons"—those people who are of the right frame of mind, habit, and behavior to fulfill positions of responsibility in a contractual order. It reminded its audience that their contractual society was a social order in which people were expected to meet certain specific behavioral prerequisites in the form of adherence to work and family norms. William Reddy has shown that contractual discourse even calls for a contractual body—one appropriate to contractual relations.[50] Liberal political discourse describes the actors of the public sphere as commercial persons, contractual bodies. The public sphere is inscribed by a liberal contractual discourse that develops hierarchies of value for appraising the worthiness of participants. This appraisal is based on their ability to adhere to the regime of contribution and need that contractual discourse designates as appropriate for the contractual body.

Contractual discourse as a disciplinary knowledge affirms certain needs and particular ways of managing them. It also delegitimates other needs and alternative need-coping practices as inappropriate or as not worthy of consideration for determining the requirements of the contractual body. The work ethic of self-discipline, delayed gratification, and modulated pursuit of self-interest becomes the ethos of the contractual body. This ethos promotes the successful management of one's own body as a piece of property worthy of investment and available for positioning within the public sphere of individuated exchanges. Failure to attend to one's commercial person as understood in contractual discourse, regardless of mitigating circumstances such as single motherhood, now marks one as possessing a deficient contractual body that is open to state regulation in the name of maintaining the conditions necessary for the contractual public sphere.

Rewriting Contract: Reinscribing Personal Responsibility

The Contract with America is a contemporary instance of how power operates in politics not so much to regulate citizens as to produce them in particular ways. For Barbara Cruikshank, "citizens are also subjects."[51] They are empowered to act but in ways that are limiting and confining. This interest in promoting the contractual subject was behind the Contract with America's emphasis on welfare reform. That this becomes a state interest in public assistance programs gives new meaning to the phrase "promoting the general welfare." In these terms, it therefore becomes possible to provide social welfare by regulating public assistance recipients.[52] The Contract's welfare proposals followed through on this logic, emphasizing the need to enforce "personal responsibility" not only to promote individual well-being but also for the good of the whole country. In the nationalistic, individualistic, capitalist idiom of the Contract's ten-point program, people who met traditional work and family standards were personally responsible, self-sufficient selves who ought to be rewarded for their behavior and accorded full status as citizens with the rights and entitlements to which U.S. citizens had become accustomed. Others were at best second-class citizens not entitled to the status of full citizens with contractual rights. Immigrants were to have limited access to the country and its welfare benefits. Welfare recipients were to receive assistance only for a limited time and only if they made progress in replacing welfare with work, defined as paid employment.

The Contract's Personal Responsibility Act was finally enacted in the summer of 1996 after twice being vetoed by President Clinton. He finally reversed himself because he too had been advised how to make public policy in order to achieve electoral success. The disentitlement of the needy was the exorbitant price the president was willing to pay in order to make good on his 1992 campaign promise to "end welfare as we know it" and achieve a reelection that by the summer of 1996 was basically assured. He signed the law on August 22, 1996, and his lead in the polls remained intact right through to election day. From that point on, Clinton assumed from Gingrich primary responsibility for rewriting the social contract.

By then the law was named the Personal Responsibility and Work Opportunity Reconciliation Act of 1996.[53] But the change in name to include the notion of work opportunity did not signal an improvement. While the law has been amended to fund the creation of more jobs, it still does not guarantee paid employment; it only expects it and penalizes people for not getting it. Most significantly, welfare as an entitlement—Aid to Families with Dependent Children (AFDC)—was abolished and replaced with Temporary Assistance for Needy Families (TANF)—a block grant that states could administer much more arbitrarily, without as many legal safeguards, and with many more punitive requirements. In fact, states did not have to provide cash assistance any more if they chose not to. Instead the money could be used to fund shelters, soup kitchens, and other forms of in kind assistance or services. Significantly, the law also required states to meet work quotas that mandated that by 1997 25 percent of the single mothers receiving aid be working twenty hours a week, and that by 2002 50 percent of them be working thirty hours a week. Recipients could not receive federally funded TANF assistance for more than two years unless they were participating in "work-related activities," and they could not receive assistance for more than five years in a lifetime. They had to make the transition to paid employment within that time frame regardless of circumstances.

The new law gave states the option of requiring recipients to sign "individual responsibility plans" or what some states called "contracts of mutual responsibility" whereby they promise to move toward paid employment.[54] The social contract has been inverted. Whereas under AFDC recipients were entitled to aid on the basis of a "social contract," now they could get aid only if they first signed a contract that promised they were becoming personally responsible in the narrow sense of being willing to take paid employment. Welfare recipients have been disentitled and moving from welfare to work, regardless of mitigating circumstances such as single motherhood, has become the primary characteristic of the personally responsible contractual person.

The Personal Responsibility and Work Opportunity Reconciliation Act therefore reinforced the Contract with America's version of the contractual person as privileged in the social order. The act allowed states to make welfare conditional upon signed agreements. The use of the word "contract" here was not coincidental. States wanted people to now first prove that they are personally responsible, by signing a contract that committed them to taking paid employment regardless of other circumstances.[55] The "individual responsibility plans" or "contracts of mutual responsibility" spawned by the 1996 welfare reform law were in keeping with a new Contract with America. In the process, a new inverted contract has been written and with it a new regime for getting welfare recipients to embody the contractual person. As Lawrence M. Mead puts it: "The idea of a social contract in benefit programs should be seen as an enforcement device. . . . Society says to clients, in effect, 'we will support you in need, but only if you behave in ways society routinely expects.'"[56] Unfortunately "routine expectations" have come to involve applying standards for the privileged to the disadvantaged. Single mothers must act as if they are heads of traditional two-parent families. Not surprisingly there is not much evidence that the inverted social contracts of this "new paternalism" actually increase welfare recipients' chances of escaping poverty.[57]

The Contractual Self in the Family-Wage System

In welfare, the social contract has changed to being an enforcement device designed to instill "personal responsibility" by exchanging public assistance for a commitment to becoming "self-sufficient," largely construed to mean taking paid employment. Therefore, the idea of contract in the system of social provision is designed primarily to reinforce the social conditions necessary for contractual relations in the existing political and economic order. Political relations are embedded in economic relations and vice versa. These prevailing practices also include assumptions about the families in whose name people are expected to practice "personal responsibility." In this sense personal responsibility is familial as well as individual. Today, the common sense of liberal society is that the personally responsible individual is one who does not create a family unless he or she can support it according to the prevailing economic realities of the market-based society. "Personal responsibility" therefore cannot but be understood as something that grows out of traditional work and family values. The use of contract in welfare highlights the fact that contractual liberalism only makes sense in the context of a particular social and economic configuration, which we might call the "family-wage/breadwinning system."

Under this system, the personally responsible family traditionally provides for itself through the efforts of a breadwinner who earns a wage sufficient to support a family.[58] The modal family is assumed to be a two-parent, male-headed family with the husband-father as breadwinner and the wife-mother as homemaker. As Stephanie Coontz and others have noted, however, this modal family may never have been the norm statistically, although it was for many years the moral norm.[59] However, although the family-wage system has become harder to sustain in the face of postindustrial economic change, the rise of families with two wage earners, increased single motherhood, and other changes, the welfare system continues to be tied to reinforcing this idealized breadwinner model. Consequently families have increasingly been judged as failing to meet the threshold requirements of "personal responsibility."[60]

Social provision continues to be articulated in terms of the standards associated with promoting people who are thought to have needs associated with liberal contractual relations. Welfare therefore continues to be provided in ways designed to promote personal commitment by recipients and others to achieve self-sufficiency largely through the opportunities made available by the market system. The assistance provided by welfare is therefore highly constrained in ways designed to shore up traditional work and family values and to enforce prevailing understandings of personal responsibility. But it does so by ignoring the social and economic realities that make it difficult for many families to conform to those standards. As a result, welfare operates to punish families that fail to meet these standards and to penalize recipients who fail to behave as contractual persons rather than helping them meet those standards and assume that identity. The social contract explicitly becomes an enforcement device and nothing more. The idea of contract consequently loses much of its sense of reciprocity.

The primary goal of contract in welfare is to enforce standards associated with meeting the threshold requirements to demonstrate that one qualifies as a contractual person. The contract exists to enforce standards of personal responsibility narrowly construed according to traditional work and family values and the family-wage system. Needs beyond this regime are considered extraneous. Paradoxically this creates real gaps in the system's assistance to its main beneficiaries—single women with children. Welfare is a genuine alternative resource for them, but since they represent a transgression of the normative ideal they are provided only limited benefits in highly demeaning ways.[61] Nancy Fraser has argued that the discourse of what she calls the "juridical-administrative-therapeutic state apparatus" (JAT) ascribes an identity to poor women and serves a "politics of need interpretation."[62] The JAT defines women as deficient and in need of treatment and rehabilitation so that they can better fill the gendered role positions of wife and mother that society has slated for them. This often means encouraging all women on welfare—who usually receive low benefits under demeaning conditions—to think about getting married, and failing that, of working in the paid-labor market, even in the face of consequent loss of child care, health benefits, and other social supports. The JAT "imposes monological, administrative definitions of situation and need and so preempts dialogically achieved self-definition and self-determination."[63] As a result, welfare reinforces the positioning of public assistance recipients as second-class citizens in the public sphere of contractual relations.

Historically, the political rights of citizenship in the United States were granted prior to and independent of economic rights. The separation of political and economic rights has been a somewhat "exceptional" feature of the U.S. political economy, making it harder to achieve social democracy and build a welfare state.[64] Yet the welfare reform politics of recent years has solidified the reality that not only do political rights still offer only limited protection from economic adversity, but economic performance is an assumed critical feature for establishing political rights. In the new contractual order welfare recipients get to be full citizens only if they demonstrate that they meet the implied threshold requirements. First they must work, which will prove they are personally responsible; only then can they get the benefits they need from the state.

Disentitling the Unentitled

The contractual person in the late 1990s is one who practices "personal responsibility." The welfare state has been founded on the assumption that the modal citizen is such a person; however, welfare has been constructed as a program for people who are deficient as contractual persons and who therefore are not really entitled. In fact, for much of its history, welfare—or cash assistance to the needy—has never been an entitlement, even after the Social Security Act of 1935 initiated the program that became AFDC. Only in response to welfare rights litigation in the 1960s did welfare benefits become a form of "property" that could not be denied due process.[65] States even then still retained the discretion to set benefits. For most of its history welfare has not been a federal entitlement, and when it was, it was so only in name.

Welfare's questionable entitlement status is underscored by its problematic relationship to the "social contract." Contract has always been an important metaphor for narrating the origin not just of the state but of the social policies of the state as well.[66] Even the Social Security Act of 1935 was narrated effectively for political effect in terms of a social contract between the state and its working citizens for security in their older, nonworking years.[67] The narrative about Social Security retirement insurance and to some extent other programs as well—perhaps even unemployment compensation—was that they were born of a contract between the government and citizens. Benefits from these programs thereby acquired the status of entitlements that could not be taken away without violating the original agreement. However, welfare has usually been narrated as being bereft of any such origin. Often depicted as an anachronism, it is said to have no origins in contract and therefore to be a lesser entitlement, if at all. Consequently, benefits from this program can be taken away without abrogating any binding agreement. Because it is a contract society, social policy in the United States is narrated in terms of contract discourse. The major consequence is a two-tiered welfare state in which public assistance benefits for poor single mothers are relegated to the second tier as an inferior program for inferior persons.

Therefore, even before the new inverted welfare contracts showed how welfare recipients were not really part of the "social contract," contract discourse had primed the relevant publics to the plausibility of the idea that the less than fully entitled ought to be at risk of disentitlement. Linda Gordon has pointed out that welfare was never fully an entitlement like Social Security pensions. It was not included in the "legal fiction that contracts had been established between government and citizen, or more specifically between government and worker."[68] This was in good part because a maternalist politics had reinforced the idea that women were second-class citizens and that a program—such as welfare—that focused on mothers was a form of special protection to dependents rather than a form of rights to citizens.[69] While the maternalism of the early part of the century may have helped relegate welfare to a secondary status, the paternalism of the latter part of the century has done the same, if in a different way.

The paternalism in the Contract with America reinforced the tie between public assistance's weak contractual status and the alleged failure of welfare recipients to fulfill contractual society's standard of personal responsibility. As Gordon suggests, women on welfare were to be "pitied but not entitled."[70] The unentitled could be disentitled. The second-class status of welfare as a program for second-class citizens makes it more vulnerable to further retrenchment. As is often noted: "Programs for poor people make for poor programs."

The Contract with America reiterated the undeserving status of welfare recipients in spite of their poverty and need. The welfare reform law that followed was a symbolic act in that it ended an entitlement program that had only recently become one and was an entitlement in name only. Nevertheless, reaffirming an already suspect population as undeserving and ending an entitlement that had existed only in name are significant acts that will ensure that the real needs of single mothers will continue to go unrecognized in liberal contractual discourse and unmet by the contracting welfare state.

These circumstances pose intensified obstacles for welfare advocacy at this point in time. Cruikshank discusses what she calls the "political trap" of welfare advocacy, which parallels what I would call the broader trap of welfare receipt.[71] The trap of welfare receipt is the double bind of work and family commitments for single mothers who are damned for taking welfare while trying to fulfill their roles as good mothers and are equally damned when they go to work if their children end up neglected. The political trap of welfare advocacy is the double bind of being critical of a punitive welfare system while advocating for the extensions of that system. For Cruikshank, the political trap of welfare advocacy highlights how welfare is not simply a form of social control that regulates people but is better understood as a "technology of citizenship" that empowers people to be citizens but in ways that also disable them.[72] At this point, welfare advocacy may need to begin emphasizing that the problem it confronts is not so much how the liberal order has excluded welfare recipients as citizens, but rather how it has included them.

Conclusion

It may be time to reconsider the unnecessary violence done in the name of regimenting people in the contractual society. The idea of a social contract has been an important one for building the welfare state. Yet the terms of contract have historically been exclusionary and it has been necessary to continually reconsider how they have marginalized people who are considered unqualified to participate in the agreement. In good part, this is because historically "the people" have been party to the social contract in theory only. They have been positioned as party to an agreement they did not actually sign even if, ironically, the agreement constructs them as autonomous agents personally responsible for their own actions.

The Contract with America is only a contemporary instance of such regimentation. It exemplifies how even, or how especially, antistate conservative symbolization can reinforce the prejudices of traditional liberal political discourse. In the process, the contract intensifies the violence done in the name of identifying who qualifies for participation in that contractual society. It exercises its linguistic power over the title the "American People" so as to promote the political power to disentitle some of those people. Symbolic and material disentitlement reinforce each other. It unilaterally invokes the name of the "American People," deprives them of their capacity to act for themselves, and defines them as people who do so act (contractual persons) for the purpose of penalizing those who cannot (welfare recipients).

In this as in other instances, contractual discourse favors those who are already seen as fulfilling the obligations of contract in a market-centered society. Contractual discourse does this by stealth as it silently privileges male whiteness while masquerading as liberal, neutral standards that androgynously treat everyone alike. This masquerade even allows those breaking their contract to be seen as honoring them, while welfare recipients must be held accountable to theirs. Women on welfare face new contractual obligations that often put their children at increased risk of not getting the financial support and parental attention they need. "Deadbeat dads," on the other hand, though much talked about, will not be pursued quite as aggressively as some had hoped under the reforms stemming from the Contract with America. The argument is that aggressive enforcement of child support orders, even if they are contracts, would prejudice the rights of individuals involved in divorce and child custody proceedings.[73] Although child support enforcement has been strengthened under the Personal Responsibility and Work Opportunity Reconciliation Act of 1996, interstate cooperation to track fathers who move out of state is still lacking and is not being developed as effectively as it could.[74] Such problems with men do not invalidate them as contractual persons; but problems with women who have been deserted and left to raise children on their own do. The needs and rights of some people are better recognized in liberal contractual discourse than those of others. Some people are considered in need of constant monitoring, others are not. Not all contracts are the same in the contractual society. In the process, social policy becomes its own cause, slaying its own dragons as it creates its own welfare queens.

2

Where the Welfare Queen Resides

The Subtext of Personal Responsibility

The Personal Responsibility and Work Opportunity Reconciliation Act of 1996 (PRWORA) requires welfare recipients to take paid employment in order to receive aid and imposes a five-year lifetime limit on eligibility. After this time recipients are expected to be supporting themselves. Welfare reform is predicated on the assumption that staying home and caring for one's children is not work, and that the primary, and perhaps only, way an individual can demonstrate "personal responsibility" is by taking paid employment. In what follows, I argue that not only is this emphasis on "personal responsibility" prejudiced against mothers who stay at home with their children, but that it operates to allow dominant gender, race, and class biases to infiltrate allegedly neutral welfare policy and ensure the continued subordination of poor families. In other words, the contemporary welfare policy discourse of "personal responsibility" might sound fair in the abstract; however, in late-twentieth-century America, it has become a way to blame the poor for their poverty without ever having to say so. "Personal responsibility" allows the cultural biases of welfare reform to be "hidden in plain sight."[1]

Is this controversial? For some, the 1996 reform law obviously intensifies the unfairness of welfare toward recipients by allowing the broader social biases of gender, race, and class relations to structure the system of welfare provision.[2] Making low-income single mothers work for poverty wages while having to care for their children on their own amounts to punishing them for being at the bottom of the gender-race-class system, sometimes euphemistically referred to as the socioeconomic order. The existing political economy is rationalized according to a family-wage logic that incorrectly assumes that families tend to have two parents, one of whom, "the breadwinner," is able to earn enough to support the family while the other, "the homemaker," provides the necessary nurturance at home.[3] The family-wage system is biased in favor of middle- and upper-class, male-headed, white families that tend to be able to conform to this model. While most families, white ones included, have found it difficult to succeed in a political economy structured according to this logic, they find it even more difficult in the changing postindustrial economy. Poor single mothers of color are the least likely to be able to participate effectively in such a biased system. Welfare compensates families who face extreme financial hardship, but it has historically been constrained to provide aid in limited amounts and under strict conditions so as not to conflict with the family-wage logic. The 1996 law has adjusted welfare to reinforce this, thereby reinscribing the gender, race, and class biases of the dominant culture.

Other commentators find it irresponsible to suggest that the 1996 law does anything beyond trying to get welfare recipients to be "self-sufficient" and not depend on the government for assistance.[4] Insisting on "personal responsibility" is good for recipients. It does not perpetuate their subordination in the existing political economy. In fact, it increases their chances of being treated as equal citizens in a society where the cardinal threshold criteria for establishing one's legitimacy as a fully entitled citizen are having paid employment, being "self-sufficient," and practicing "personal responsibility." The way to overcome any biases is to demonstrate "personal responsibility," which shows that you are no different from the "modal citizen."

These competing positions reflect debates about welfare that have gone on for centuries. Michael Katz has noted that the debates have a dreary familiarity to them, reflecting the competing tendencies of either blaming society or blaming "the poor" for their poverty.[5] However, while the contemporary debate continues to stress these themes, I would suggest that the terrain has changed significantly, if subtly. Not only has the debate moved to focus specifically on "personal responsibility," but cultural values now infiltrate welfare policy more by stealth. These two developments are related. In an era in which discriminatory ideologies are encoded in euphemistic language, blaming the victim gets legitimated by way of the seemingly neutral category of "personal responsibility." Replacing the already bland "family values," the ostensibly neutral language of "personal responsibility" provides cover for more blatant gender, race, and class biases to be insinuated into welfare policy. Consequently, welfare reform has become a rationalization of poverty rather than an attack on it.

In this critique I highlight how the hidden is in plain sight. I first offer a short genealogy of "personal responsibility," explicating it as a term of contractual discourse. Then I examine how it is being transformed today in welfare policy discourse.[6] I suggest that "personal responsibility" is being transformed in ways that make it more vulnerable to being encoded with biases. My point is not that the term "personal responsibility" was previously unbiased. I accept that as a term of liberal contractual discourse, "personal responsibility" was always culturally encoded with particular biases. But when placed within the context of contemporary welfare policy in the late 1990s it tends more readily to be culturally encoded in ways that specifically reinforce gender, race, and class biases.

In the context of welfare reform, "personal responsibility" has come to be limited to a narrow focus on escaping "welfare dependency" and achieving "self-sufficiency" by taking paid employment.[7] This tunnel vision does not bode well for single mothers on welfare. It devalues mothering. It also neglects the fact that the work world has a long way to go before it can be said to accommodate all people regardless of class, race, and gender.[8] *Fin de siècle* welfare policy discourse sounds neutral but it often fails to account for the work-related disadvantages posed by class, race, and gender, especially for single mothers. Insisting on "personal responsibility" therefore risks reinforcing the tendencies already built into welfare to stigmatize, demonize, and even criminalize poor single mothers.

After discussing how "personal responsibility" becomes a site for encoding cultural biases, I make explicit the specific mechanisms by which this transmission occurs. I suggest that a series of "relays" provides opportunities for the ostensibly neutral concept of "personal responsibility" to reflect cultural biases: text and subtext, conscious and unconscious, word and image.[9] As a result, the behavior implied by "personal responsibility" can be said to suggest an identity. The text of "personal responsibility" implies multiple identities available from the iconography of the dominant culture, among them the middle-class man of virtue and the so-called "welfare queen" as the embodiments of what "personal responsibility" represents and what it does not. The welfare queen is the implied, visualizable "other" of the contemporary welfare policy discourse of "personal responsibility."

I conclude this analysis by considering that the welfare queen is an artifact produced by discourse rather than a preexisting reality.[10] The welfare queen is real only in the sense that she is a reified creature of the discourse of "personal responsibility." The welfare queen is not homeless but is lodged inside the discourse of "personal responsibility." To turn a phrase: since there is no welfare queen, welfare discourse has to create her. We see this most especially when we turn to the way "personal responsibility" is administered by welfare agencies. The welfare queen is needed both to delegitimize welfare use by single mothers and to perpetuate the ideal of the traditional two-parent family and the maintenance of the family-wage system. We will therefore reduce the presence of the welfare queen in our lives not by changing the behavior of women receiving public assistance but only by changing the discourse of "personal responsibility."

A Short Genealogy of Personal Responsibility

Since the welfare reform law was passed in 1996, welfare recipients can only get federally funded welfare benefits for two years after which they must participate in "work-related activities." Furthermore, they can only receive these benefits for five years over a lifetime after which they are expected to have made the transition to paid employment.[11] States can set stricter requirements. Arguably, welfare's emphasis on work requirements makes it a critical policy in which the work ethic is being held up as a universal standard to prove that one meets the threshold requirements for citizenship in late-twentieth-century America.[12] The social contract is thus being rewritten to help buttress the increasingly beleaguered family-wage system. In the face of declining economic prospects for low-income families in a changing postindustrial economy, imposing a work requirement becomes a last-ditch effort to stave off the need to recognize that work and family values are untenable for many low-income individuals.[13] Instead of confronting the postindustrial collapse of economic opportunities for working families at the lower end of the socioeconomic structure, welfare reform tries to deny that collapse. People must demonstrate "personal responsibility" narrowly defined as working in paid employment in order to prove that they qualify as full citizens deserving of entitlements. But this threshold is being imposed just when it is becoming harder to meet.

"Personal responsibility," however, is not a new idea—it derives from the lexicon of liberal contractual society.[14] For several hundred years, Western liberal discourse has focused on articulating the particular type of self needed for the liberal social order.[15] This self can be counted on to use the freedom available under liberalism in orderly ways. This, then, is the paradoxical creature who gets to be seen as "self-made" and "self-sufficient," but only insofar as she can demonstrate that she is "self-regulating." Until the second half of the twentieth century this self-sufficient person was rarely a woman, as it was near impossible for a woman to be credible in the role of a self-sufficient self.

For Friedrich Nietzsche, the problem was not the exclusive male focus of liberal contractual discourse. Instead, Nietzsche saw the personally responsible individual in the liberal contractual order as a paradox. Such an individual was not a "promising animal" as much as a promising animal of a particular predictive sort:

> To breed an animal with the right to make promises—is not this the paradoxical task that nature has set itself in the case of man? Is it not the real problem regarding man? . . . [T]he ripest fruit is the sovereign individual, like only to himself, liberated again from morality of custom, autonomous and supramoral, in short, the man who has his own independent, protracted will and the right to make promises.[16]

However, Nietzsche castigated the liberal order that created "last men" who were incapable of making and keeping promises on their own.[17] Slavoj Žižek extends this idea of preconstructed choice to all social orders:

> Every belonging to a society involves a paradoxical point at which the subject is ordered to embrace freely, as the result of his choice, what is anyway imposed on him (we *must* all love our country, our parents. . .) . This paradox of willing (choosing freely) what is in any case necessary, of pretending (maintaining the appearance) that there is a free choice although in fact there isn't, is strictly co-dependent with the notion of an empty symbolic gesture, a gesture—an offer—which is meant to be rejected: what the empty gesture offers is the opportunity to choose the impossible, that which inevitably will *not* happen.[18]

Nietzsche's paradox was that to be free, to exercise one's free will, to make a choice, is to do all those things in ways that the culture recognizes, which in a sense invalidates one's free will to do those things. In the liberal contractual society that particularly valorizes choice, "personal responsibility" is therefore especially paradoxical. It implies being willing to take responsibility for what the dominant culture has already assigned as one's responsibility, and on terms predetermined by the culture.

"Personal responsibility" only makes sense according to the way the culture distinguishes it from other things. We learn to live the paradox culture creates for us. J. M. Balkin suggests that we do this by learning how to work with the available "cultural software"—the dominant conceptual oppositions that are built up over time and that are used for interpretive purposes.[19] For instance, liberal contractual discourse has distinguished personal responsibility from state responsibility. Yet liberal discourse has also juxtaposed personal responsibility against individual freedom, as in rights versus responsibilities, suggesting that there be more government involvement to monitor people's behavior so as to ensure they do the right thing. Libertarian and paternalistic definitions of personal responsibility clash. The paradoxes of liberal contractual discourse are carried over to personal responsibility. The paradox of the self-regulating self implies a nested understanding of personal responsibility that is both consistent and inconsistent with increased personal freedom. Working within the culture's oppositions, we learn to negotiate this paradox, though not always successfully and in ways that favor some people over others. In this sense, personal responsibility is not a rational, coherent, objective, neutral idea so much as a culturally acquired, and culturally biased, understanding of what it means to be a person in a given social order.

The Contemporary Welfare Policy Discourse of Personal Responsibility

When placed within the context of contemporary welfare policy discourse, personal responsibility reflects even more specific ties to the liberal order. Welfare reform refers explicitly to personal responsibility as it relates to economic as well as therapeutic matters.[20] In the economic register, welfare reform's emphasis on personal responsibility is a reference to the idea of less government involvement in the lives of and less support for low-income families. In the therapeutic register, the notion of personal responsibility implies owning up to bad personal habits and disciplining oneself to avoid them. In either case, it becomes less likely that single mothers receiving welfare will be seen as personally responsible. The discourse of personal responsibility fails to account for the fact that existing social relations are structured so as to make it harder for welfare mothers to be seen as achieving "self-sufficiency," especially when this term is narrowly defined as taking paid employment.

As its very title suggests, the Personal Responsibility and Work Opportunity Reconciliation Act (PRWORA) of 1996 dramatically vaulted the discourse of "personal responsibility" to center stage in welfare policy. The 1996 law abolished the federal welfare entitlement established under Aid to Families with Dependent Children (AFDC) and replaced it with Temporary Assistance for Needy Families (TANF), the block-grant program that gives states funding for time-limited welfare benefits coupled with work requirements.[21] The goal is to get families to use welfare for only a short period of time and, regardless of circumstances, to make the transition to paid employment.

While PRWORA is premised on the idea that "marriage is the foundation of a successful society" and is dedicated to reducing welfare dependency—which it sees as a cause for the increase in single parenthood—the law is more focused on enforcing personal responsibility among single mothers by getting them to work than it is on ensuring adherence to family values and preventing family breakup.[22] Yet, given the difficulties facing poor single mothers who must work and raise their children on their own, requiring a single mother to work seems more to be designed to discourage her from setting up a household separate from the father of her children rather than enforcing the work ethic. Whether an emphasis on work requirements will produce more two-parent families, let alone families based on sound relationships, however, is very doubtful.[23]

Whether it seeks to promote family values or the work ethic, the 1996 welfare reform law has defined "personal responsibility" primarily as achieving "self-sufficiency" by taking paid employment. By offering states the option of having recipients sign "individual responsibility plans" or "contracts of mutual responsibility" the law makes it explicit that recipients are expected to promise to try to achieve "self-sufficiency."[24] But even when so defined, "personal responsibility" is simply a "cultural placeholder" that the culture can fill as it deems appropriate. In a culture that valorizes individual choice, personal responsibility inevitably becomes incapable of accounting for the fact that culture, social relations, and institutional practices favor some people over others—that is, that some people are deemed more responsible and self-sufficient than others.

The willful ignorance of welfare reform is becoming more visible over time. Numerous recipients have already been "sanctioned" for not fulfilling the promises they made in their individual responsibility plans. The growing use of such sanctions has contributed to the reduction in the number of recipients, from 14.2 million in 1993 to 9.8 million in 1997, and 7.955 million by September 1998.[25] Also, according to initial reports, as many as one-quarter to forty percent of the people who had left the rolls were not working after one year and, having neither welfare nor work, were trying to get by with more informal means of support.[26] Most remained poor; many returned to the rolls to use up more of their limited eligibility even in a growing economy. While personal responsibility may once have referred to someone who "kept a promise" (like a mother who promised her children she would take care of them), now it has been reduced to indicating someone who can "hold a job" (like a mother forced to work in a low-wage, dead-end job even though her children were being neglected).[27] In the context of welfare policy "personal responsibility" is a trap for poor single mothers. It sets them up to be evaluated according to standards that are often inappropriate for them, their circumstances, and their prospects for achieving "self-sufficiency" as conventionally understood.

Equal Citizenship and the Orgy of Victimhood

As culturally encoded, "personal responsibility" encourages individualistic explanations for the causes of poverty. This individualistic approach to poverty is no accident. For years, proponents of welfare reform such as Charles Murray and Lawrence Mead have railed against liberals for caving in to the demands of women and the "nonworking" poor, with the result that standards of personal responsibility were no longer being enforced.[28] The cultural biases Murray, Mead, and others represent are explicitly defended in their published works. They have criticized liberals for dealing with their guilt by relaxing societal standards to allow poor minorities and women to get welfare rights without having to fulfill the social obligation to try to work or practice traditional family values.

Welfare reform has therefore been quite explicitly aimed at stopping liberal practices that "coddle people" and make "special allowances" for them, based on their race and gender.[29] Welfare reform with its cutbacks may be about saving money but it is also about saving the cultural values of work and family. It tries to put an end to the idea that race and gender ought to be grounds for claiming victim status and thereby exempting some people from having to adhere to these values. It insists on personal responsibility narrowly construed, without accounting for the race and gender biases of society.

Lest there be any mistake about this, think back to the Los Angeles riots after the acquittal of the policemen who beat Rodney King. The Bush administration, Vice President Dan Quayle in particular, spread the word that the riots were caused by the permissive welfare policies started by the liberals in the 1960s.[30] This remark went largely unchallenged, lost in the confusion that followed. But it was no idle comment. Welfare policies from the 1960s and riots in the 1990s are not easily connected.[31] The circuitry that has been constructed in the attempt to connect these poles is elaborate.[32] It draws its charge from the wider cultural war afflicting this country as exemplified in events as apparently disparate as the impeachment of President William Jefferson Clinton and welfare reform. It is tied to the growing concern among some segments of society that making special allowances for persons of color and women in particular, is not only wrong but has been destructive of the very fabric of society since it got started in the 1960s. Social disorder results when we start excusing the behavior of those who are not complying with societal norms. Black single mothers especially become a flash point, sometimes implicitly, other times explicitly, as if to remind us what the argument is really about. Well before the Los Angeles riots, Murray wrote:

> White confusion and guilt over the turn of events in the civil rights movement created what [Daniel P.] Moynihan has called "a near-obsessive concern to locate the 'blame' for poverty, especially Negro poverty, on forces and institutions outside the community concerned."[33]

According to Gertrude Himmelfarb, since the 1960s welfare reform has led to the "demoralization of society."[34] Mead has added:

> The struggle with [welfare] dependency could lead to a general demoralization. . . . Morale could spiral downward in an orgy of competitive victimhood. . . . Personal responsibility must be willed, precisely because it can no longer be assumed. It must become an explicit policy because it is no longer, as in the progressive era, the unspoken ground of the political culture.[35]

The phrase "an orgy of victimhood" is freighted with much of the subtext of the culture wars and finds its own place in welfare reform as well. "Orgy" is used to delegitimize the claims of recipients by suggesting that their behavior is promiscuous and generally irresponsible, and that their claims are overblown. "Victimhood" suggests an undeserved permanent status—like an undeserved entitlement—for those who have been wronged. Mead is implying that what he calls the "unspoken ground of the political culture" justifies coercion to stop these groups from seeking unfair allowances for their welfare dependency. He insists that we impose the cultural standards of work and family upon them and make them behave as everyone else allegedly does. In this interpretation, personal responsibility is an ideal idiom for denying that gender, race, and class play a role in creating the need for public assistance.

Working for Equal Citizenship

Mead in particular is explicit that the well-being of the social order is contingent on universal work norms being imposed on all adult citizens other than the disabled. For Mead, the existing order desperately needs to adopt a system whereby full citizenship with rights and entitlements is contingent upon demonstrated social competence, a willingness to practice prosocial behavior, and, most important, working in paid employment.[36] The social risks of the "competent," so defined, must be protected, and the rest must submit to a welfare regime dedicated to realizing the goals of the "new paternalism." In exchange, they will receive the reduced benefits of welfare—but only temporarily, until they start to work and become part of the competent class. "Competence" is central to Mead's "personal responsibility." This new transformed "personal responsibility" must be enforced if the existing political economy is to survive. For Mead, "personal responsibility" makes the "unspoken ground of the political culture" explicit:

> The final option for antipoverty policy represents a return to a citizenship rationale, but this time with the emphasis on obligations rather than rights. The argument is that, if nonwork and other incivilities have weakened the welfare state, then work and other duties should be enforced. . . . Community among citizens can only be built on the basis where individuals show enough self-command to merit the esteem of others. The danger raised by poverty is not that the poor will make excessive demands. . . . It is rather that the new social minorities no longer display the *personal* organization that makes a community of equal citizens imaginable. . . . Today, there is less poverty, but the separation of the poor from the economy makes integration more doubtful. Therefore, social programs must promote work, and even enforce it, assuming the function that the workplace did before. . . . The prospect is for a long struggle to restore the self-reliance assumed in Western politics. Only if order is restored in cities, and especially if work levels rise, could the poor become more self-respecting. Only then could they stake claims on the collectivity as equals, rather than seeking charity as dependents. In restoring some coherence to the lives of the poor, the new paternalist social policies, if well-implemented, could make a critical contribution.[37]

Mead understands that the political economy of citizenship is culturally constituted. To be a citizen is not to assume some disembodied position in the political order, or to be a universal subject evaluated according to neutral standards of justice. It is to be a political being within an economic order. It is to assume a culturally encoded subject position reflective of the biases of the existing political economy. Mead understands that the culture war has implications for the political economy and has sought to have these implications registered in the battle over citizen entitlements. To ensure the maintenance of the existing political economy, he nonetheless embraces universal standards of citizenship that apply a transformed definition of personal responsibility to all. Now work is the threshold criterion for achieving full citizenship. But while the standard is universal, it is bound to have discriminatory effects. All must work regardless of circumstances—regardless of the lack of preparation, a shortage of economic opportunities, and an excess of family responsibilities.[38] Cultural bias still drives political and economic decision making regarding citizen entitlements and welfare reform reflects those culturally encoded political and economic biases.

The New Isms: Discrimination by Stealth

However, the infiltration of the concept of personal responsibility with culturally dominant biases is usually less explicit than Mead's rhetoric. It is generally an instance of what some have called "new" forms of discrimination that discriminate without explicitly saying so.[39] In this way, contemporary welfare policy discourse fails to account for race, gender, and class privileges. Some people get to be seen as self-sufficient without doing anything whereas others cannot be seen that way regardless of effort. Inner-city black homeowners and working single mothers may be seen as having failed to acquire assets and an income according to the accepted standards of self-sufficiency even if they work harder than suburban couples. The latter, meanwhile, reap the benefit of being the right people in the right place at the right time and allow their assets to accrue in value without much effort at all.[40]

The language of personal responsibility as a new form of discrimination therefore tends to privatize these issues of self-sufficiency by silencing references to "social capital" and the broader context that helps people be self-sufficient.[41] Segregation in the United States today ensures that access to housing, schools, and jobs is implicitly still allocated by race to a large extent.[42] Public policies and market practices continue to systematically disadvantage mother-only families by failing to account for their special needs for income support, child care, and flexible schedules.[43]

Public opinion tends to exaggerate the percentages of nonwhites receiving public assistance.[44] Yet, over 60 percent of adult welfare recipients are nonwhite single mothers with children, and about three-quarters of this group are African-American.[45] The percentages are even higher for long-term welfare recipients and persistently poor families.[46] While the public exaggerates the numbers of African-Americans on welfare, African-Americans are overrepresented among the poor. But ostensibly neutral discourse on personal responsibility is enforced on all regardless of recipients' economic circumstances and the uneven allocation of social capital.[47] As a result, welfare becomes its own self-fulfilling prophecy making real the claims about racial minorities on welfare. Because the 1996 legislation has hit the poorest communities the hardest, the demographic composition of the recipient population now reflects popular stereotypes.[48] By default, the welfare population is now composed largely of nonwhite, unmarried, inner-city mothers.[49]

Gender

There is in particular a troubling gendered subtext to the discourse of personal responsibility. Part of the problem is that "personal responsibility" is a patriarchal term. Women have often found themselves in relations in which they demonstrated care or connectedness, in which they showed the ability to be supportive of others, whether these be their families, their spouses, their friends, or their community. Yet, "personal responsibility" is traditionally expected of men—who were taught to be autonomous, self-disciplined, and able to act on their own. It is not that there are natural differences between men and women on these issues, but rather that by holding women to the traditional male standard of "personal responsibility" we overlook what women have contributed as caregivers and as collaborators in creating a more supportive set of social relations inside the family and out in the community. "Personal responsibility" immediately stacks the deck against women and undervalues the traditional women's work they have to do.[50] "Personal responsibility" however furthers the problem because it pretends to accord women equality by ostensibly holding them to the same gender-neutral standards—but in a way that is covertly biased against them.

The quest for women's equality has been volatile. Feminism's calls for equal treatment have accompanied tumultuous changes in sexual relations, marriage, family, work, and the culture more broadly. Most troubling for many people has been the precipitous increase in the proportion of children born to unmarried mothers. While not all these changes have been the result of women's push for equality, feminism has helped women become more independent. But the backlash has been real. Much of the resistance to women's equality is grounded in a patriarchal ideology. Women's continued subordination as a "second sex" is reflected in persistently high rates of male violence against women which is often the product of male dysfunction—an inability to control anger, oversocialization to a culture of violence and aggression, and other social and psychological problems.[51]

However, patriarchal ideology is no longer as dominant as it once was and today professional and nonprofessional white women can benefit from numerous opportunities for economic independence long denied them. Sexism is now often encountered in a new form—less ideological and more implicit, less the product of intent than the consequence of neglect. To varying degrees all women still confront a patriarchal ideology that promotes a conscious attempt to position them in subordinate social roles. Yet now, allegedly neutral discursive practices will also reinscribe their subordination. This is the real problem with "personal responsibility" for women on welfare.

Women confront a new double bind. In the early part of the century maternalist policies were enacted to provide special protections for women as wives and mothers, which reinforced their subordinate status as dependents.[52] Now the new paternalism is insisting that they be treated equally with men but in ways that fail to account for their special circumstances. For women on welfare this bind is intensified. In welfare, the discourse of personal responsibility neutrally applies a work test for two-parent families to the attempts by single mothers to achieve self-sufficiency. Neutral standards of personal responsibility—paid employment—ignore the fact that many single mothers want to work but find it difficult to do so. The jobs that suit their special circumstances may not be available; they may not pay enough to support a family; or they may require leaving young children at home without sufficient parental attention and adequate care.

Single mothers are judged unfairly by the standards applied to two-parent families and have to do double duty as both "homemaker" and "breadwinner." While this is difficult for any single mother, it is even more so for low-income, low-skilled single mothers with young children. They are sorely tested to make ends meet even when they combine incomes from a variety of sources—child support, payments from relatives and friends, public assistance, as well as paid employment.[53] Single mothers on welfare are damned if they do and damned if they don't, whether they emphasize care at the expense of work or vice versa. The intensity of this double bind results from gender bias infiltrating the ostensibly neutral welfare policy discourse of personal responsibility. Mothers who work and do not give their children sufficient attention are not "real" mothers, while women who do not work reinforce the idea that they are not fit to take on the traditional male role of provider.

The push to require single mothers receiving welfare to work highlights gender bias in another regard as well. As mentioned earlier, the 1996 law is prefaced with a concern about the deterioration of the traditional two-parent family, which it calls "the foundation of a successful society." Its major response to this problem has been to require single mothers receiving welfare to work. This seemingly odd connection is made possible by a gendered subtext. The reformers ostensibly want to save the family but they have chosen to do so by requiring single mothers to work because the women are available. Because women need to rely on welfare when the men do not support the family sufficiently, they become convenient targets.

Their greater availability is a sign of their vulnerability, which often stems from their being left to care for the children. They are more vulnerable to state regulation than men. Requiring them to work and limiting their access to welfare sends the signal that traditional families rather than welfare should be responsible for caring for children. While the law allows states to require noncustodial, usually male, parents of children receiving welfare to work, and encourages states to collect child support from fathers, the lack of employment for poor low-skilled males has made both these measures far less significant as sources of welfare receipt than the work requirements and time limits imposed on single mothers.[54]

The unstated reality, then, is that women are being used to punish both male and female parents for not forming traditional two-parent families and not avoiding the use of welfare. The sins of the fathers are visited not on the sons but on the mothers. As Frances Fox Piven and Richard A. Cloward have suggested, requiring single mothers to work is legitimated in part by their "deviant" sexual and family lives. However, the work requirement is also being used to enforce the traditional two-parent family, both among these women and others.[55] Requiring noncustodial fathers to work has become an option under welfare reform but it remains a minor one. Welfare reform may initially be largely about getting single mothers to work, but as those jobs fail to produce a livable wage, the policy's focus logically shifts to getting women to marry men.

Requiring women to work in order to increase marriage rates does not make much sense, however, if the result is that families remain poor. It might make sense if the goal of welfare is to enforce the two-parent family regardless of circumstances. Yet if welfare is supposed to combat the underlying poverty that destroys the two-parent family, then welfare reform is a non sequitur. Instead, contemporary welfare policy is accelerating the "feminization of poverty"—a phrase coined by Diana Pearce to refer to the fact that a growing number of the families living in poverty are headed by women.[56] By forcing women into low-wage work and cutting them off from needed assistance, the 1996 legislation is likely to increase this statistical trend.

The "feminization of poverty" also implies a double coding between welfare and the broader culture whereby the discourse of personal responsibility encodes poverty as female, and vice versa. The "feminization of poverty" implies that low income and female gender reinforce each other as a lack or deficiency. We come to think of poverty as a feminized state, just as we see the female as a lack, like a form of impoverishment. As Balkin writes, "Jeanne Schroeder has summed up this phenomenon aptly when she states that in patriarchal thought, a thing is privileged not because it is male, but is called 'male' because it is privileged."[57] Poverty is seen as a state of personal deficiency not because it is female; rather, it is made out to be female because it is seen as a state of personal deficiency. Therefore, while there is much value in highlighting the "feminization of poverty" as a statistical trend, it is also important to note that poverty is being feminized today in this other sense of being made out to be a female-like state of being. The nesting of the oppositions in male : female :: abundance : lack :: wealth : poverty encourages the formulation that women are more likely to be poor and the poor are more likely to act in a female-like fashion. Given its failure to account for the way these gender biases operate, "personal responsibility" is not only likely to reinforce the "feminization of poverty" as a statistical trend but also to accelerate the tendency to see poverty as a feminized state of being. In the process, not only does poverty get feminized but personal responsibility is again reinscribed as a male phenomenon that women lack.

Race

The 1996 law is also a dramatic recent example of what a growing number of scholars are calling the "new racism."[58] Lawrence Bobo and associates refer to the decline of "Jim Crow racism" and the rise of "laissez-faire racism."[59] Without making explicit distinctions based on race, this newer form of discrimination reinscribes race privileges implicitly through a euphemistic, encoded discourse.[60] According to Amy Ansell, the economic and social discourses of the new right encode these newer forms of discrimination even while ostensibly focusing on allegedly race-neutral issues such as personal responsibility.[61] In fact, the allegedly neutral categories of universal rights may always have had racial biases.[62] The problem of encoding shows exactly how the dominant categories of rights, entitlements, deservingness, and the like latently carry a racial subtext that implies that blacks are less deserving. The false neutrality of encoded categories reinforces the false neutralism that ignores variations in the broader social and economic context and the way that variation disproportionately works against blacks being able to demonstrate self-sufficiency and personal responsibility as well as whites.

Some might want to argue that there is nothing new about the new racism. The old racism infiltrated neutral social categories, while contemporary racism is often explicit in its castigation of people of color. Still others might want to suggest that since racism now has to be encoded to be used, racism must be on the decline. But perhaps the practice of racism has simply changed rather than declined, given a legal and social climate that makes it less legitimate to be explicitly racist.

While the old racism was ideological, the new racism is discursive.[63] The old racism was grounded in an obfuscating ideology of racial superiority; the new racism is an artifact of allegedly neutral discourse reinscribing racial privilege without ever arguing for it explicitly. While the old racism has not entirely gone away—as the high rates of hate crimes indicate—it is being outflanked by a less virulent, if more insidious, new racism. The old racism was grounded primarily in an ideology that infiltrated one's consciousness and argued for white superiority. The new racism eschews blatant theories of racial hierarchy and operates surreptitiously, perhaps even subtly without intention, by being insinuated into allegedly neutral practices that just happen to disproportionately disadvantage people according to race.

"Black" today does not mean inferior as much as it did twenty-five years ago. Instead, today it more often denotes risk. "Black" alerts the economically wary to stay away. Black is still a significant marker but now more as a signal of economic danger than racial inferiority. It is a hollowed out discursive practice rather than a thick ideological symbol. It does not refer to the biology or culture of race as much as to the economics of it. If working with "blacks" does not decrease your job prospects then that is acceptable, but if blacks move into your neighborhood your investment goes down and that is not. But as an institutionalized practice to signal economic danger, race is institutionalized racism. Used as a marker, race continues to systematically disadvantage blacks. As long as African-Americans are treated differently— even if not on account of their biology or culture—the conditions for their subordination are re-created.

Therefore, William Julius Wilson is both right and wrong when he argues that race is less significant as a source of discrimination and we should deemphasize politically counterproductive and divisive race-based social policies like affirmative action.[64] He is right that explicit racial discrimination is less tolerated; however, he is wrong if he is understood to suggest that race is not significant for privileging some over others. The difference is that now whites discriminate on the basis of economics rather than biology or culture. Therefore, race today is most significantly encoded with economic danger. To mark someone in terms of race in the market society is to constitute that person as a subject worthy of marginalization.

Black is a self-legitimating signifier. As long as African-American represents black economic disadvantage, being black will be a marker that can be used in ways that work against African-Americans, and as long as it disadvantages African-Americans black will imply economic disadvantage. African-Americans will not be treated equally until black is equal to white. In a segregated society, the redistribution of social and economic capital to equalize access to critical resources, housing, schools, jobs, and so forth will have to come first if African-Americans are to be treated equally.[65] Treating black equal to white, however, will help bring about the equalization of resources. Only then will black no longer be the critically distinctive signal that it is currently. Until then, it will continue to be encoded in economic anxiety.

In the "new racism," black is encoded with economic danger as opposed to explicit references to inferiority. What then explains the popularity of the very controversial book *The Bell Curve* by Richard Herrnstein and Charles Murray?[66] I would argue that it provides a strikingly public example of how the socially anxious periodically seek recourse to a more explicit subtext in order to reaffirm the meaning of the main social text. *The Bell Curve* is ostensibly about intelligence; in fact, it is about social policy. Many of its later sections argue that social policies designed to improve the condition of the poor, who belong disproportionately to ethnic and racial minorities, are futile because there is a genetic basis for their inferior state. These social programs are wasteful because they are trying to change the unchangeable. The money would be better spent on other things or not at all. This book could do much to reinvigorate the age-old and long-held prejudice that African-Americans in particular are genetically inferior.

The popularity of the book's argument that blacks are less intelligent is surprising in a society that claims to be increasingly successful in vanquishing racial prejudice. Part of the answer lies in the fact that racism is still embedded in our unconscious even as public discourse discourages racist ideas. Sometimes a segment of the population want to be reminded that the neutral categories favor whites. Race privilege still contributes to the structuring of everyday life; people half-know this and many are anxious that that might change. They want to be reassured that racial privilege will not only continue, but that it is justified. The notion that race undergirds the neutral categories of public discourse reassures them that their racial resentments are legitimate. For these reasons, racial bias that is hidden in the subtext of public discourse is periodically made explicit.

The subtext of narrative operates like an unconscious space where anxieties referenced by the conscious narrative are made explicit. Žižek suggests that the subtext serves as a relay, just as pornography can for civilized discourse.[67] It is here in the subliminal passage that implicit meaning is made explicit. The more explicit implications of the word are made visible in this subterranean state. That which is encoded for public presentation is decoded to reassure the reader as to its implications. The off-the-record nonpublic transcript provides explicit details for those who need such reassurance. Ironically, while the unconscious is an imaginary, it has less need for imagination. In this way, the "symbolic" and the "real" supplement each other.

The Bell Curve can thus be seen as the pornography of the "new racism." Its popularity serves to remind us that some whites still want the old racial biases of public discourse spelled out. Disturbing though it sounds, *The Bell Curve* was a source of reassurance to some. It was its own form of reconciliation. It was a gesture designed to underscore the need to state in explicitly clear language that the implicit assumption of racial superiority still informs public discourse. It reduced the anxiety caused by the rhetoric of equality and personal responsibility that insists on not taking race into account. It was time to explicitly recognize that the old racial prejudice is still legitimate in the public realm, if only a subtextual dirty little secret most of the time.

The Holocaust offers a striking parallel to the way the vulgar subtext buttresses the abstract public text. Žižek shows how the Nazis relied on an interplay between public pronouncements on the Jewish Question and the hidden subtext of bureaucrats. How else would people know that the Eichmanns of the regime were "doing their real job" and not "just following orders"? I offer this example not to confuse the racial discrimination of welfare reform with the genocidal discourse of Nazism but to highlight how the vulgar subtext is critically involved in supplementing public discourse. According to Žižek, this process of supplementation was the dirty little secret of the Holocaust that could not be acknowledged but which helped translate the impersonal, abstract public language into concrete acts of genocide. For Žižek, the subtext added the extra charge to public pronouncements and created "surplus obedience":

> The fact remains, however, that the execution of the Holocaust was treated *by the Nazi apparatus itself* as a kind of obscene dirty secret, not publicly acknowledged, resisting simple and direct translation into the anonymous bureaucratic machine. In order to account for the way executioners carried out the Holocaust measures, one should thus supplement the purely *symbolic* bureaucratic logic involved in the notion of the "banality of Evil". . . . One should fully agree with [Daniel Goldhagen] that [Hannah] Arendt's notion of the "banality of Evil" is insufficient, in so far as—to use Lacanian terms—it does not take into account the obscene, publicly unacknowledged surplus-enjoyment provided by executing orders, manifested in the "unnecessary excesses in this execution." . . . [Y]et [o]bscene unwritten rules sustain Power as long as they remain in the shadows; the moment they are publicly recognized, the edifice of Power is thrown into disarray.[68]

That the problem of personal responsibility in welfare reform is not of the magnitude of the Nazi Holocaust does not negate the distinct possibility of a parallel in the way they are structured. Both have their dirty little secrets, their subtextual pornography, which if revealed undermine the pretense that legitimates them.

Individuation: Social Capital as the Surplus Whiteness of Class

The subtextual processes that inform the discourse of "personal responsibility" are a site for a particularly invidious form of individuation.[69] Individuation is the process which reduces people to atomistic selves whose particular differentiating circumstances need not be taken into account. The race and gender of an individuated self do not matter. Class relations are not taken into consideration either. The way these factors have impacted a person is deemed irrelevant and not to be compensated for in public policy and institutional practices.

This false neutrality makes invisible what Charles Tilly calls the "categorical inequalities" which influence the way gender, race, and class prefigure the allocation of economic opportunities across and within various institutional settings ranging from the family to community, schools, employment, housing, and the like.[70] For Tilly, categorical inequalities are "durable inequalities" because they create the prearranged institutionalized practices that slot social capital and access to resources on the basis of gender, race, and class distinctions. Once these distinctions are privileged, persons identified with them can exploit their material advantages, emulate their gains in one area after the next, and adapt to change in ways that maintain and build on the initial categorical privileges. Tilly finds that neglect of these built-in categorical inequalities leads to an incorrect emphasis on individual differences as the explanation for inequalities:

> We should find that once categories are fixed in place they greatly attenuate the effects of individual variation in knowledge, skill, attitude, and performance on either side of categorical divides. We should also find that categorical organization helps produce individual differences as a consequence of structured differentials in contacts, experiences, opportunities, and assistance or resistance from others. . . . Categorical inequality actually accounts for a major share of interindividual and interhousehold inequality in material welfare. Production of qualifications for, and connections to, different kinds of work—human capital, broadly defined—operates categorically, with systematic differences by race, gender, ethnicity, and citizenship. Since human-capital differences themselves result to an important degree from categorical processes, categorical inequality actually lies behind much of what economists now measure as interindividual or interhousehold inequality. Once we consider both indirect and direct effects of categorically organized inequality, we discover that a large share of the variation in rewards and resources commonly attributed to individual differences in capacity and effort actually results from the categorical organization of production and reproduction. If so, we should reverse the conventional procedure for analyzing discrimination: instead of treating it as the residual difference between categories once all possible sources of individual variation are taken into account, treat it as the portion of inequality that corresponds to locally relevant categories, and then see how much of the residual can be explained by variation in human capital, effort, and similar individual-level factors.[71]

In this way, personal responsibility organizes discrimination. Without accounting for preexisting categorical inequality, it becomes a vacated space where the class, race, and gender of the embodied self-sufficient self is not accounted for. It is a site where we construct a moonscape with no recognizable social context. The variation in people's circumstances does not rise to the level of visibility in the predominant discourse of personal responsibility that drives the reform legislation.[72] In title and text, therefore, the Personal Responsibility Act has its own "surplus whiteness" that erases the social and economic context of welfare receipt and makes invisible the way those contextual factors contribute to the reliance on welfare by poor women, in particular poor black women.[73]

The growing gap between skilled and unskilled workers exacerbates the consequences of not taking organized class relations into account.[74] Unskilled workers are increasingly unable to keep up with skilled workers in wages, benefits, and work conditions. In recent years, it has become more common for unskilled workers to settle for low-wage jobs. In 1982, workers in the top one-tenth of the labor force made in wages 3.95 times what workers in the bottom tenth made; however, in 1996 they made 4.72 times as much. There is evidence that unskilled workers are also less likely to receive benefits than skilled workers. Whereas benefits were once what made low-wage jobs worth taking, they are less and less available to serve that purpose. In 1982, the total compensation of the top one-tenth of workers was 4.56 times that of workers in the bottom tenth; by 1996, the top tenth received 5.43 times as much compensation as the bottom tenth. Additional evidence indicates that unskilled workers, especially temporary ones, are more likely than before to be put in risky work environments.[75] Going to work is quite different for the unskilled, and so is practicing "personal responsibility." For single mothers with children, it means little more than participating in the rapidly emerging global sweatshop economy or more established forms of economic exploitation.[76]

Rereading and Reencoding Personal Responsibility

Given the foregoing, it is imperative that we consider the possibility that gender, race, and class biases infiltrate the contemporary discourse of "personal responsibility" by a variety of covert means—by a series of tacit relays. One such tacit relay is the aforementioned relationship of text to subtext. It is there that cultural encoding takes place. Personal responsibility as an allegedly neutral category can undoubtedly be read in many ways: no more government handouts; no more collective responsibility for social problems; poverty is a private issue; private virtue is the basis for personal success; each poor person needs to accept responsibility for her or his own poverty, and so on. It can also more explicitly and crudely mean: "get over it; no more whining; no more claiming victim status; stop blaming other people for your own failures."

In addition, however, the discourse of personal responsibility can be used anew to imply other, more empowering approaches to addressing poverty. We might even recognize that victims are often "heroes of their own lives." Linda Gordon has used this phrase effectively to highlight the courage of female victims of domestic violence who step forward and take action to protect themselves and their children, often by being willing to go on public assistance.[77] In spite of all the social opprobrium and risks to their personal safety, these women come forward to achieve their independence from those who have wronged them. Yet such courageous acts of personal responsibility are not what the phrase means today.

Paul de Man has been said to suggest that reading "performs that which is in the text but always escapes us."[78] Reading is an act of supplementation, supplying what is missing from a text. A new reading can make for a different text, different from the way it was read previously. Yet this is also to suggest that the cultural reserve that readers draw on to interpret texts gets imbricated in them. What the text signifies is therefore not entirely autonomous, and whether such a reading is active or passive, performative or not, is not entirely clear.

De Man's definition of reading suggests it is like remembering, wherein the previous event is remembered in terms of the way it was experienced rather than in isolation.[79] The written word is also never read on its own but in terms of its cultural codes, which are nested in the related interpretive distinctions supplied by the culture. Personal responsibility is linked to conceptual oppositions like strong and weak, active and passive, culture and nature, reason and passion, male and female, and white and black.

Then again, if reading is like remembering, it is also like misreading. Take the case of Dan Quayle. As was widely publicized, as Vice President Quayle misstated the Negro College Fund's slogan "a mind is terrible thing to waste." He restated it as "what a waste it is to lose one's mind, or to not have a mind."[80] The text read, "invest in education for deserving African-American children," but Quayle's statement reads as if "those kids wasted their opportunities and wasted them by getting wasted." Whether it was bad memory, bad public speaking skills, or a case of letting the culture do the interpreting we will probably never know; however, the example serves three times over to indicate how context can infiltrate the reading of texts.

"Personal responsibility" is therefore most often read or misread in the context of the rich cultural reserve of the biases and prejudices of the existing social order. It is a dead metaphor—tethered tightly to the existing culture of liberal capitalism and its commitments to limited definitions of work and family. No matter how neutral it sounds, personal responsibility is at best a semiliberated sign, still tied to the culture that supplies it with meaning. It is mythical in the sense that it easily can be used to invoke widely shared myths of the prevailing cultural heritage such as the myths of self-sufficiency and dependency.

The discourse of personal responsibility is a culturally loaded one that excludes alternative points of view and makes invisible many other types of personal responsibility. The increasing evidence that suggests that women who rely on welfare are indeed often—more often than previously thought—trying to escape from abusive relationships underscores the way the discourse of personal responsibility is encoded. At any point in time roughly one-fifth of welfare recipients are suffering from abuse at the hands of a partner, and about two-thirds of recipients have at some point in their lives been victims of abuse.[81] Women who choose to go on welfare to escape domestic abuse are therefore inverting the prevailing discourse of personal responsibility: They are engaged not in a passive act of dependency but in an active move to achieve independence. In refusing to account for the special circumstances of many welfare recipients, the discourse of personal responsibility thus neglects the fact that what it depicts as deplorable acts of passive dependency are often laudable acts of active independence. With these contextual silences embedded in the discourse of personal responsibility, women on welfare are evaluated according to the liberal standards of a decontextualized individuated self—a self who must always prove herself by being willing to work regardless of whether it puts her or her family at greater physical, emotional, or economic risk. This is the loaded subtext to "personal responsibility," filled with the prevailing cultural biases.

Hidden in Plain Sight

According to Pierre Bourdieu, the encoded meanings of texts like welfare's "personal responsibility" are part of the "unsaid" that accompanies what he calls each person's "*habitus.*"[82] The *habitus* is an unstated sixth sense about how things work—social relations in particular—in a specific cultural setting. People draw on their sense of *habitus* in order to do many things, including even the basic act of reading social policy texts. But it would be misleading to say that such encoded unsaid meanings are hidden below the text. The subtext is still a legible text available for inspection by those who care to read it, although, like all texts, it is open to multiple readings. Instead, as has been suggested by others, the encoded bias of the subtext of welfare policy discourse operates not so much like the *un*conscious as what Freud called the *pre*conscious. It is like the *un*conscious in that it reflects emotions that are not made explicit in conscious activity. Yet it is also like the *sub-* or preconscious in that it is not entirely *un*conscious but is an accessible storehouse of images and messages. Jacques Derrida reminds us that Freud saw even the unconscious as analogous to the wax paper "mystic writing pad" of his youth that left behind traces of what had been written even after it had been erased.[83] "The Unconscious is outside, not hidden in any unfathomable depths."[84]

I want to emphasize that the subtext of welfare policy discourse is similar, in that it is not in the strict sense an inaccessible *un*conscious. Rather, it is *semi*conscious. It is a partially visible and accessible subtext that records the fantasies and dreams, anxieties and fears associated with the publicly muted main text. In this sense, the latent subconscious subtext is an unutterable ground that is "hidden in plain sight."[85] It is readable and recognizable even though we articulate the main text. It tells us that we are still involved in making distinctions based on the embodied identities of race and gender despite the publicly promulgated laws being written in an idiom that denies this. As Žižek writes:

> Fantasy designates this unwritten framework which tells us how we are to understand the letter of the Law. And it is easy to observe today, in our enlightened era of universal rights, racism and sexism reproduce themselves mainly at the level of the phantasmic unwritten rules which sustain and qualify universal ideological proclamations. The lesson of this is that—sometimes, at least—the truly subversive thing is not to disregard the explicit letter of Law on behalf of the underlying fantasies, but to *stick to this letter against the fantasy which sustains it.*[86]

The neutral law is not really neutral. We can see that. It is hidden in plain sight. The radical response, therefore, Žižek suggests, is to insist on the neutrality the law promises but implicitly denies. This is one way to challenge the latent biases of state-sanctioned universalistic discourse such as "personal responsibility."[87]

Visualizing Welfare Policy Discourse

The foregoing suggests that the subtext also includes an imaginary that texts inspire. One means of making this explicit is what W. J. T. Mitchell has called iconology or theories illustrating how texts and image are entwined.[88] Mitchell has also outlined what he calls "picture theory."[89] "Picture theory" builds on the chiasmus that pictures call forth theories and vice versa. For instance, Francis Ford Coppola's 1974 Watergate-era film *The Conversation* shows how text and image are implicated in each other.[90] In *The Conversation*, Gene Hackman plays Harry Caul, a surveillance expert, who surreptitiously tapes a couple's conversation in Union Square in San Francisco. He then uses cutting-edge technology to decipher the conversation embedded in the sounds of the tape, making an innocent lover's conversation take on new meaning as a conspiracy to commit murder. Here *The Conversation* is the audio equivalent of another film, Michelangelo Antonioni's 1966 *Blow-Up* (from the Julio Cortazar short story) in which a photographer uncovers a murder plot when he blows up pictures he shot of a couple in a public park in London.[91]

But it is not the surveillance of things hidden in the plain sight of parks and other public spaces that interests me here, though the issue of how the public transcript, whether a law or a campaign speech, already has hidden messages in it is pertinent to my discussion. Nor am I interested in the old cliché that things are never quite what they seem, though that is what encoding is all about. Instead I want to show how text and image are implicated in each other. In *Blow-Up,* the Rorschach of photographic images gives way to a gunman in the bushes. The continual enlargement of the photo tells a story of murder. In *The Conversation,* the tape recording is played over and over in a way that changes the sound of what is being heard. But the replaying of the tape also changes something else. We are shown the tape but see the conversation. The audio implies the visual, and the image a text. Text and image invoke each other.

This, then, is where we find the "welfare queen"—hidden in plain sight in the text of welfare policy discourse.[92] That is home. The "welfare queen" is not a woman; she is not a she; she is an it, a particular kind of it. It is nonhuman, but not cyborg. Instead, it is another kind of hybrid—a text/image—a phrase that is a picture. We read "personal responsibility" but we see "welfare queen." The "watchword" of "personal responsibility" has its own "optical style."[93] With the contemporary welfare policy discourse of personal responsibility, we express fear of poor neighborhoods and broken families but we see "black women with children." The welfare queen is an oxymoron—a queen of welfare; she cannot be and is not real. She is an it; an artifact of text, a condition whose possibility is made plausible by the discourse of personal responsibility with its implied debts to gender, race, and class. A more reified "Willie Horton" of Republican fearmongering ads about crime during the 1988 presidential campaign, the welfare queen is the implied identity of the contemporary welfare policy discourse of personal responsibility.

Identity Thinking in Personal Responsibility Discourse

These relays of text and subtext, conscious and unconscious, word and image point to the contemporary welfare policy discourse of "personal responsibility" that is prone to create identities to go with the behavior. This additional relay helps the discourse gain much-needed credibility by implying that an abstract category relates to embodied experience. The words of personal responsibility reference the image of the welfare queen. This act of subtextual visual supplementation helps complete the cycle of representation and closes it off from challenge. The universal category of personal responsibility is "sutured" to the embodied, particular identities of real women of color.[94] As Žižek writes:

> In the rejection of the social welfare system by the New Right in the U.S., for example, the universal notion of the welfare system as inefficient is sustained by the pseudo-concrete representation of the notorious African-American single mother, as if, in the last resort, social welfare is a program for black single mothers—the particular case of the "single black mother" is silently conceived as "typical" of social welfare and of what is wrong with it.[95]

Given the way life chances are historically and currently distributed, the subtextual identity of the allegedly neutral and colorless behavioral discourse is easily tinted with gender, race, and class. Text and subtext conspire to entwine behavior and identity, so that narrative and image can work hand in glove.

Nietzsche tells us that discourse conspires to assign agents to the actions described: "[T]here is no being behind the doing, effecting, becoming; 'the doer' is merely a fiction added to the deed; when the deed is everything. . . . [O]ur entire science still lies under the misleading influence of language and has not disposed of that little changeling, the 'subject.'"[96] Language forces us to imply agency where it is not clear if there is any. The Liberal contractual discourse is especially in need of agents, for it implies autonomous, self-made, self-sufficient selves who have made their own promises and can be held accountable for them. Without that constitutive assumption, the order quickly falls into disorder.

Analogously, the text of behavior is in need of a subtext of identity, added after the fact to lend coherence to what is described. As an abstraction disconnected from the real lives of people, personal responsibility desperately needs to be able to associate itself with embodied identities in order to make itself credible. Responsibility in the abstract needs persons in the concrete, for without them "personal responsibility" can be criticized for not offering much guidance to real people. The behavior needs identifiable agents with which it can be associated. Extending the analogy further, welfare discourse calls for its own welfare queens in order to make its criticisms convincing and the behavior it condemns as the product of people's choices.

Thus we read "personal responsibility" and are encouraged to think about a variety of identities, including the "welfare queen." The "welfare queen" serves as the graphic interface of "personal responsibility." The white middle class is provided an opportunity to focus its anxieties on the subtext of welfare policy discourse. The abstraction of personal responsibility is tied to identifiable subject positions based on gender, race, and class prejudices, while real women of color are denigrated in the process. The contradictory relationship of "personal responsibility" to embodied identity reflects the dangers of "identity thinking," as Theodor Adorno calls it, and shows that the process of reification is doubled.[97] Identity thinking reifies both the abstraction and the identity to which it is attached. "Personal responsibility" is given a life it would not otherwise have, and flesh-and-blood single mothers receiving welfare are made out to be welfare queens.

This is what Louis Althusser called the act of interpellation wherein people are assigned an identity according to the way they are positioned as subjects in discourse.[98] Identifying people this way is like calling them "communists." We put a label on people and expect them to live out their lives according to it. When they find that this is their plight—that they have been labeled so as to be marginalized—their refusal to renounce their labeled status only confirms the belief that that is who they were in the first place. By refusing to denounce other communists, the labeled communist proves she is a real one.[99] Anticommunism becomes its own self-fulfilling prophecy. So it is with "personal responsibility" and the "welfare queen," for

Figure 1. Embodying the Welfare Queen.

by refusing to practice "personal responsibility" as defined in welfare policy discourse recipients prove they were irresponsible all along and are sanctioned and eventually liable to be removed from the rolls.

Yet it works both ways, for just as the contemporary welfare policy discourse of personal responsibility creates a space in which we envision the welfare queen, so does the image of the welfare queen reinforce contemporary welfare discourse.[100] The woman depicted in Figure 1 had in 1997 been sanctioned to the point where she was removed from the welfare rolls.[101] Reduced to cooking family meals on an outdoor grill, she sits outside and stares blankly away from the camera while her teenage son looks on. She seems to be an enigma, refusing to work and claiming undetectable maladies, though not even trying to defend herself against a welfare bureaucracy that rejects her story. Her inscrutability creates doubt in our minds, allowing us to decide that she is incorrigible in her insistence on taking welfare. Her passivity becomes a form of active defiance. Her blank face is a blank slate on which welfare discourse can write its stigmatizing story of the welfare queen. Her body language is therefore not of her own making but a discourse that reads her a certain way. Simply by being there, in poverty, on the welfare rolls, in the backyard, cooking on the grill, she is open to being read by welfare policy discourse. Without knowing anything about her life, her personal experiences, or her hopes and fears, welfare policy discourse appropriates her body and judges her passivity as a willfully chosen dependency.

The Administered Welfare Queen

The welfare queen is a textual spectacle and a spectral text. She is not a preexisting reality. Yet she takes on a life of her own beyond the interplay of text and image because welfare regulates recipients in such a way that they cannot but fail to meet imposed standards of personal responsibility. The welfare queen becomes a self-fulfilling prophecy to be restaged by welfare recipients in their daily struggle to make ends meet.[102] Each time a woman on welfare tries to combine unreported income with welfare benefits, she commits fraud according to the state, and no matter how poor she is she becomes the welfare queen all over again.[103] The welfare queen as reenacted is therefore an iterable symbol, designating recipients as undeserving and in need of regulation. Their regulation becomes self-legitimating. As Barbara Cruikshank has emphasized, overly stringent and punitive rules, elaborate procedures for determining eligibility, extensive reporting requirements, surveillance, behavioral standards, work requirements, and the like all combine to create the near-impossibility of being on welfare and not being seen as a rule-violating welfare queen.[104] This is the conspiracy of discourse that covers up its own self-legitimating circuitry. The welfare queen seems to need regulation but only because regulation reinforces the idea that there are welfare queens to be controlled and punished. The welfare queen is an artifact of power and that power is deployed in state administrative practices.

For instance, the individual responsibility plans initiated by the 1996 law have led to massive purges of the welfare rolls, with many single mothers being sanctioned for failure to fulfill all the promises they had made in their plans. Actually, a common reason for being sanctioned seems to be missing scheduled appointments.[105] The welfare queen becomes an artifact of the state's monitoring practices. The individual responsibility plan makes the welfare queen a self-fulfilling prophecy destined to occur, given the high probability that many women on public assistance will not be able to meet the many standards of responsibility imposed on them.

Michel Foucault emphasizes that power creates its own opposition.[106] Power defines what is deviant and then repeatedly hunts it down. Relatedly,

Gilles Delueze has noted how continuous monitoring has replaced periodic surveillance as the technologies of supervision intensify.[107] Power can make the welfare queen a permanent reality as long as a single mother remains on welfare and therefore under suspicion. Welfare regulation therefore continually recreates welfare queens. Women on welfare continually reenact the welfare queen as a self-fulfilling prophecy as they try to make ends meet and of necessity therefore violate their agreements under welfare reform. By going on welfare, not reporting all their income, and doing what they need to do to survive, their attempts to support their children become further evidence of their indolence.

Yet the welfare queen serves ideological purposes that do not just delegitimate welfare use by single mothers; it also buttresses the family-wage system and the traditional two-parent family. For Žižek, power is used not just to thwart social alternatives but also to reproduce existing social relations. Žižek wants to distinguish himself from Foucault by suggesting that power operates on the privileged category as well as the subordinated one. On another subject, Žižek asks:

> One should ask here the naive, but nonetheless crucial question: why does the Army so strongly resist publicly accepting gays into its ranks? There is only one possible consistent answer: not because homosexuality poses a threat to the alleged "phallic and patriarchal" libidinal economy of the Army community, but, on the contrary, because *the Army community itself relies on a thwarted/disavowed homosexuality as the key component of the soldiers' male-bonding.*[108]

Male bonding in the military can only be made acceptable by disassociating it from homosexuality. Military male bonding needs to create homosexuality as a denigrated and deviant practice in order to legitimate itself.[109] And so it is for women's dependence on men in the traditional two-parent family. Dependence on the state is a denigrated deviance that legitimates female dependence on men, especially in a society that valorizes independence. Each discourse beats back a threatening "other" in order to protect its own particular version of that phenomenon. How else is one to distinguish the good from the bad, whether it is male bonding or women's dependence? This is the psychic life of discourse.[110] This is the cultural software that processes social relations.[111] The social relations of male bonding and the traditional marriage are made safe in the process.

Since there is no welfare queen, the family-wage system has to create one not just to discourage the use of welfare but to reinforce the idea of women's dependence on men. It is no surprise that the welfare queen is being ever more intensely sought out at a time when women's dependence on men in the traditional family structure has become suspect. While some religious groups claim that it is God's will that wives submit "graciously" to their husbands and thereby shore up the traditional two-parent family, other institutions manufacture welfare queens in order to get the same result. Thus both God and the welfare queen haunt *fin de siècle* America, working against the odds to reproduce the faltering family-wage system.

Body Knowledge: Real Policy

The harm done by the discourse of personal responsibility begins with the way it misreads the efforts of women on public assistance. It refuses to accept that while some may be irresponsible according to any definition of the term, many others are "heroes of their own lives," and most are victims of circumstances left to fend for themselves by absent partners, poor job prospects, and impoverished neighborhoods.[112]

"Personal responsibility" is a disembodied category, an abstraction that fails to account for the coping practices of people in the real world, real families, and real communities. While "personal responsibility" needs to be attached to an identifiable subject position in order to be credible, it connects to stereotypical identities available in the culture to legitimate its disembodied behavior. Personal responsibility has no use for embodied experience. It is a colorless category that makes no provision for the exigencies of class, race, and gender in the real lives of those who labor under its sign. In real life, personal responsibility is more than an abstraction, it is not a universal category experienced by different people all in the same way.

Putting people's embodied experience into the category of personal responsibility enables us to see how it will be experienced differently by different people. We can then begin to understand how class, race, and gender biases may make it unreasonable to insist on some single mothers practicing personal responsibility, narrowly defined as taking paid employment. We may see that reliance on welfare is a necessity for some single mothers. But the power of "personal responsibility" as a discourse lies in its ability to erase embodied knowledge. It is not interested in the body knowledge that comes from having a "different" body. Everyone is to understand personal responsibility the same way irrespective of that fact that their body has taught them a distinctive set of conditions and consequences. Austere bodily suppression is a requirement if one is to embody personal responsibility. The embodied welfare recipient must regulate her body so that she can achieve the personally responsible body.[113] This goes well beyond the straightening of hair. Poor black single women must act as if they were white, married, middle class, and with substantial job skills, in order to be recognized as personally responsible under welfare reform. The personally responsible body has a surplus whiteness which is called male.

As a cultural icon in the contemporary welfare policy discourse of personal responsibility, the "welfare queen" also remains obtuse to embodied reality. The term is a cipher to be filled with social stigma for the purpose not just of delegitimating welfare use by single mothers but also to legitimate women's dependence on men. By participating in the ongoing recreation of the welfare queen, "personal responsibility" seeks not just to "end welfare as we know it" but also to motivate continued efforts to re-create the traditional two-parent family and shore up the faltering family-wage system. Its cause is huge; its work is never done. For that reason, proponents of "personal responsibility" are not likely anytime soon to admit that the welfare queen is their creation. But, when they do, they will be freed from the growing tendency to use welfare to punish people for the inequities of the existing political economy.

3

In the Clinic
The Medicalization of Welfare

Many features of contemporary welfare reform make it as self-defeating as it is self-legitimating. Welfare reform is busy recreating the problems it attacks while simultaneously rationalizing how it allegedly solves those problems. Prominent among these self-defeating features is its self-legitimating focus on "welfare dependency," which represents a return in social policy to older concerns at the expense of attacking poverty. The country has moved away from the "war on poverty" initiated the 1960s to the "war on welfare" that has become ascendent in the 1990s.[1] It is again assumed—as before the sixties—that reliance on public assistance for anything other than a very short period of time is unquestionably wrong. For people like Newt Gingrich the country's failed welfare policies are a sure sign that a "sick society" is encouraging sickness.[2] Welfare receipt has been transformed from use to abuse, from an active exercise of the legal right to an income to a passive dependency on government. Welfare dependency has returned to its pre-1960s state as a universal deficiency that almost no one can actively support, while poverty is no longer considered a public problem that must be attacked. Unfortunately, the way welfare reform has articulated treatment for welfare dependency in the late 1990s ensures that poverty will persist and intensify.[3]

In what follows, I want to suggest that there is more to this story. While recent changes reflect a return to the focus on welfare dependency, a "new paternalism" is changing welfare administration so that welfare dependency is itself increasingly being transformed from an economic problem to a medicalized one.[4] This medicalization goes further than individualization. The latter locates the problem in the individual; the former likens it to an illness that afflicts the individual. The welfare reform law of 1996 has helped accelerate the tendency to construct welfare dependency as an illness, thereby transforming welfare into a set of therapeutic interventions designed to cure people of that malady. In the process, welfare itself is transformed from a repudiated program of benefit allocation to a socially accepted form of therapy.[5]

While medicalization is different from individualization, particularly in terms of the specific interventions associated with it, its implications are the same. It legitimates new forms of power, procedures, and processes in the administration of welfare that deemphasize the allocation of income and emphasize the treatment of poverty in terms of correcting personal problems and monitoring behavior. To medicalize welfare dependency is to create the conditions for moving welfare from an income redistribution scheme to a behavior modification regime.[6] It is an effective way to locate the problems of low-income families in their behaviors rather than in the broader political economy. Given the growing inequality of economic opportunities in the postindustrial economy,[7] the medicalization of welfare dependency is more than a serious mistake—it is a devastating distraction that diverts much-needed financial and organizational resources away from the creation of economic opportunities.[8] In the process, yet another way has been found to make cultural distinctions that marginalize people who use welfare. The medicalization of welfare dependency proves that in some respects the more things change the more they stay the same.

Nonetheless, the medicalization of welfare dependency is accelerating without much attention to its historical context, cultural significance, or political and economic implications. Very little attention has been devoted to the fact that it is not an autonomous concern specific to welfare but a manifestation of broader cultural trends and a paradigmatic case of what J. M. Balkin calls "cultural proliferation."[9] Cultural proliferation occurs when the culture's dominant interpretive categories, such as independent versus dependent, spread from one area to another. As a result, disparate social practices are deemed to be alike and get treated in similar fashion, as when drug addiction and welfare use are both treated as if they were the result of compulsion rather than choice. The spread of dependency talk, as an instance of the growing cultural power of medicalized discourse, shows that the disease metaphor is itself spreading like a disease in the contemporary period.

In particular, the medicalization of welfare dependency demonstrates that it is associated with cultural anxieties about other forms of dependency, particularly drug dependencies, all of which are being frowned on as a serious impairment to people's ability to function in the world of work.[10] Welfare dependency is now often viewed as a consequence of other forms of dependency. It is for instance increasingly talked about in the parlance of the therapeutic specialties as a "comorbidity factor" associated with passive and dependence-related personality disorders that impair people's ability to be active and self-sufficient.[11] Welfare use itself is increasingly considered as a clinically treatable dependency.[12] The medicalization of welfare use is part of the rise of a larger therapeutic culture. In the process, welfare policy and administration have been transformed to the neglect of more political-economic approaches to combating poverty.

After providing some background on the ascendency of welfare dependency as the focus of recent welfare reform, I use Michel Foucault's idea of genealogy to historicize and outline the cultural context for the growing medicalization of welfare dependency in recent years.[13] I use David Wagner's argument about the resurgence of interest in personal health among the middle class in recent years as a strategy for reinscribing social status distinctions and re-creating the hierarchies of self-worth in the secular meritocracy of late-twentieth-century America.[14] I then examine how medicalizing welfare dependency changes the way welfare programs are administered.[15] I follow this up with an examination of how welfare itself has changed under the influence of a "new paternalism" from an income allocation scheme to a dependency treatment program.[16]

Last, I note how the medicalization of welfare has changed its politics, creating its own specific form of self-defeating resistance where the exception now becomes the rule. In the past efforts aimed at improvements in welfare—viewed as an income allocation scheme—were often founded on the assumption that welfare recipients were just like everyone else except that they lacked money. Logically, then, the solution was to give them more money.[17] However, current attempts to improve welfare—seen now as a form of dependency treatment—are often founded on proving that people are not like everyone else, cannot be expected to work immediately, and should be exempted from the new requirements designed to wean people from their dependency on welfare.[18] Trapped in the discourse of dependency, welfare rights increasingly involves getting special protections for people on the grounds that they are deficient.[19]

With the shift in focus from combating poverty to combating dependency, we have moved from arguments based on equality to those based on inequality.[20] In the late 1990s, good advocacy involves getting as many people as possible exempted from work requirements because they need to be able to depend on welfare to continue to function. The medicalization of welfare dependency therefore creates its own self-fulfilling prophecy in that over time only those people who have severe physical, psychological, and other problems will still be on welfare, and the severity of their problems will justify their exemption from work requirements and time limits. Under these conditions, welfare ultimately reaches the point where it cannot serve as an effective site for the fight against poverty. Once there, welfare's medicalization will have been made complete and the idea that poverty is largely the product of individual deficiency will be very hard to oppose.

The Welfare Dependency Indicator

In recent years the medicalization of welfare has been on a very sharp and steep growth curve. Reflective of this trend, the federal government is investing money in defining welfare dependency, measuring it, identifying its symptomology, and specifying forms of treatment.[21] The rapid increase in the medicalization of welfare dependency is something that many people have helped make happen. A key actor has been U.S. Senator Daniel Patrick Moynihan (D-NY). Although he was the most prominent U.S. Senator to oppose the 1996 welfare reform law, ironically in many ways Moynihan did more than most people to usher in a law that was dedicated to reducing welfare dependency. In 1989, Moynihan wrote that while poverty was the defining social problem of policy in the industrial era, welfare dependency had become the defining social problem of the postindustrial era.[22] Following this pronouncement, Moynihan sponsored the Welfare Indicators Act of 1994 that required the Department of Health and Human Services to send annual reports to Congress on indicators and predictors of welfare dependence. The first *Annual Report on Welfare Indicators,* published in 1997, noted:

> This report is the direct result of the foresight and leadership of Senator Daniel Patrick Moynihan. He sponsored the Welfare Indicators Act of 1994 to make it clear that reduction in welfare dependence is a national goal, and that regular measurement and assessment of progress toward that goal is necessary. The act calls for such measures, just as, for example, the Employment Act of 1946 called for regular measures that led to a better understanding of the critical problem of unemployment in this country. In introducing the bill, Senator Moynihan declared that the policy and responsibility of the Federal Government must be to strengthen families and promote their self-sufficiency. This report is a first step in documenting our progress toward that goal.[23]

The stated purpose of the Welfare Indicators Act is:

to provide the public with generally accepted measures of welfare receipt so that it can track such receipt over time and determine whether progress is being made in reducing the rate at which and, to the extent feasible, the degree to which, families depend on income from welfare programs and the duration of welfare receipt.[24]

Called the Welfare Indicators Act, the law is nonetheless exclusively focused on monitoring welfare dependency. The first annual report noted that the initial step in such monitoring was to define welfare dependency, which it proceeded to define as follows:

> A family is dependent on welfare if more than 50 percent of its total income in a one-year period comes from Temporary Assistance for Needy Families, Food Stamps and/or Supplemental Security Income, and this welfare income is not associated with work activities.[25]

The report also specified risk factors associated with welfare dependency, classifying them into three main types: economic security measures, measures related to employment and barriers to employment, and measures of teen behavior, including nonmarital childbearing. Armed with its first report, the federal government will now sponsor research into risk factors and encourage states to develop systems to monitor them, in the quest to eradicate the newly quantified condition of "welfare dependency."

All this is taking place, I would suggest, in a highly medicalized idiom. The research agenda is framed as if welfare dependency were a public health problem. For instance, the fear of welfare dependency's spreading from one generation to the next or throughout a neighborhood has led to government tracking of intergenerational welfare use and neighborhood effects, as indicated in the task force's first annual report.[26] Although the medicalization of welfare is a cultural process, it has received government backing. It has been canonized as part of the statistical accounting of the state.

Modernity's Medicine

Michel Foucault's writings often focused on the way medicine and related areas developed as disciplines, professions, and practices critically important to the constitution of the modern social order.[27] Like the other disciplines, for Foucault medicine was not so much a distinct body of knowledge as an assemblage which combined places, persons, and practices, and served to create specific localized ways of doing things. These practices could not be understood without reference to the context of social interaction in which they had arisen.[28] For Foucault, understanding how medicine came to be constituted was best done by engaging in what he called "genealogy."[29] Genealogy was therefore as much about the present as the past—it offered what Foucault called a "critical history of the present."[30] And such inverted histories were useful in the study of what Foucault called "eventualization," or how some things became possible and occurred as discrete events while others did not.[31] Therefore, for Foucault genealogy explained how discursive practices as enacted in social relations made some ways of relating possible and others not.

Medicine, and other forms of knowledge critical to the formation of social relations, were therefore not pure in the sense of being autonomous from the exercise of power. Instead, they were forms of "power/knowledge." Rather than discovering the way the world and the people in it really were, they imparted to that world and its people a particular configuration and then worked to ensure that things were arranged in a manner consistent with that understanding.[32] Foucault believed that this was true of *all* social knowledge and that the human sciences owed their formation and elaboration to efforts to organize social affairs in particular ways. Developments in medicine, for instance, often were tied to efforts to promote sanitation and public hygiene.[33]

These practical arts of the human sciences were derived from the desire to make a new man for the emerging social order. At their base is the profound irony that the emerging order enabled people to be free autonomous selves, but that people needed to conform to the self-discipline implied by these forms of knowledge in order to achieve that fulfilled state as full human beings. Enlightenment thinking and humanism—but particularly the human sciences in their most practical forms—were thus wrapped in contradiction: people were naturally free but had to be disciplined in order to achieve that freedom correctly. The human sciences were critical to modernity's preoccupation with what Foucault called "governmentality" or the concern to regulate people by aggregating and individualizing them as members of one or another "population."[34]

Governmentality was concerned with populations so that it could manage them and ensure their participation in the social order as needed and expected. Governmentality involved classifying populations, whether as sick or healthy, normal or deviant, productive or not; however, it also individualized them in the sense that the members of each population internalized their commonality with that population. People were to participate in the populating of the social order by helping to create populations—that is, to identify populations and identify with them. People did this particularly by performing the identifying characteristics associated with the population in which they were placed. For instance, the "sick" of medicine were to be the compliant sick who accepted not only being quarantined when necessary but also doing what medicine expected of the sick in such circumstances if they were to get well. The same applied to the mentally ill, the criminal, the deviant more generally, and especially the impoverished.

Under liberalism in particular, if men were to be considered free, ways had to be devised to ensure that they would use this freedom correctly. How was social order of a predictable sort to be formed and maintained once subjects were no longer dominated by a sovereign but had become sovereign subjects themselves? This became the overriding question of modernity. Governmentality was critical to the success of the emerging modern social order.

For Foucault, medicine was probably one of the most significant of modernity's human sciences because it focused on the human body, the visible and empirically observable site for the human subject.[35] With the growing ascendency of secularism, rationalism, and especially empiricism, medicine's focus on the body made it a central medium for constituting the human subject as its own self-determining self. According to Foucault, medicine came by the eighteenth century to influence not just how that body was to be understood but what that body was, how it operated, what its capacities and deficiencies were, and when it was to be considered normal or abnormal, appropriately formed or deformed, and most especially healthy or ill.

As medicine worked its magic in reconstituting the human body according to its own rationality, these classifications were expanded to include more aspects of the human subject. The "normal person," as we know him or her today (whatever that might be), often implies more than what eighteenth-century medicine meant by the term; however, this expanded understanding of normality has itself been medicalized and studied according to medicine's logic of function and dysfunction. But medicine's expansionary tendencies went beyond the human body and the human subject to include the social body. And once the concept of a "social body" had been created (by the nineteenth century this term had become widely accepted as more than a metaphor), then a "social medicine" of sorts became possible.[36]

In the nineteenth century, medical and political rationality joined forces to regulate the social body via the arts of governmentality, and formulated the idea of "police."[37] The science of policing—from surveillance, to reporting, to administering, to quarantining, to treating and rehabilitating—was in many ways the socialization of the logic of medicine. And as with the sick and the criminal, so with the poor, each had their own demarcated space, their own institutionalized setting, be it the hospital, the prison, or the poorhouse. By the nineteenth century, the warehousing of populations in large confined spaces, each differentiated and individualized in increasingly specialized ways, was upon the Western world, and the modern age of advanced governmentality was in full swing. Freedom was now just another word for discipline—self-discipline, that is.

The medical model is not a hierarchy with the doctor or medical professional on top.[38] Instead, a Foucauldian medical model categorizes people as individuals who have capacities and deficiencies that place them in one or another population, so that they can be treated in particular ways and made to conform to the standards of normalcy and health. According to such a model, each person must be diagnosed for empirical indicators, often referred to as symptoms, and assessed as to his or her capacity to undergo treatment. A person's case history is compared to others and the person is placed in a particular population.

Medicine as a discipline is therefore critical to the modern regime of the self. It was never confined to the hospital or even the clinical setting more broadly construed. Instead, it operated in a variety of venues where it became effective in helping to promote the healthy self. By the nineteenth century this included most especially the private setting of the family and that field of action called the "social." And, social relations have in the twentieth century proven particularly vulnerable to medicalization.

The Medicalization of Dependency

As a generalized discourse, medicalization creates possibilities for the redefinition of terms to designate self-worth well beyond the hospital's walls. Peter Conrad and Joseph Schneider have shown that medicalization reevaluates a person's deficiency from "badness to sickness."[39] But as David Wagner has noted, Foucault's analyses reveal that medicalization was often nothing more than a "fig leaf" for the moralization of a problem in a more secular way.[40] Medicalization does not absolve the patient or client of responsibility so much as redefine how they are personally deficient. Medicalization reinscribes hierarchies of worth while simultaneously changing them.

In fact, Wagner has suggested that there has been a resurgence of interest in personal health among the middle class in recent years as a strategy for reinscribing social status distinctions and re-creating the hierarchies of self-worth in the secular meritocracy of late-twentieth-century America.[41] For Wagner, postindustrial economic reorganization in favor of a more efficient, "lean and mean" political economy has placed a heightened emphasis on the middle-class ethic of self-discipline and delayed personal gratification. Wagner suggests that the middle class has used its emphasis on discipline as a cultural marker to designate its members as meritorious and more deserving of the limited number of better-paying jobs in the reorganized postindustrial economy. This has created, a "new temperance" that takes the form of a "moral panic" about the spread of unhealthy personal practices. This "moral panic" has sought to restigmatize certain behaviors, especially those involving illicit drug use, sex outside marriage, cigarette smoking, and other ostensible signs of lack of self-discipline.

Medicalization, therefore, is a particularly effective way of getting people to embody the kind of person called for by the liberal contractual order—that is, an independent, autonomous, self-sufficient, self-disciplined self who can be counted on to fulfill his or her contractual obligations. Medicalization becomes even more important in the late-twentieth-century postindustrial order where people are transformed into economic actors with less collective security than before from the family, community, firm, and government. In a society of individual entrepreneurs, where people must look to themselves to ensure their economic survival, the need to embody the self-disciplined self is heightened and the failure to do so is seen as an even greater failing than previously. This opprobrium applies equally to a single male without children, a male primary wage earner of a two-parent family with children, and even a single mother with children.

The medicalization of "dependency" in its many forms is therefore quite logical in this context. As Foucault helps us understand, medical and political rationality complement each other in promoting the health of the "social body." Personal health must in good part be understood in terms of that which promotes social health, and vice versa.[42] The healthy person is a self-disciplined citizen, and conversely practicing the self-discipline needed to perform as a public person constitutes a significant part of being healthy. It is at this juncture between the personal and the social body that "dependency" emerges as a medicalized problem. The dependent self is neither personally nor socially healthy. The dependent self fails to measure up to the implied personal and social standards of the liberal contractual order.

Not surprisingly, dependencies of various kinds have been prominent among the moral panics that have periodically wracked Western societies over the last several hundred years, whether they have been concerns about drug use, welfare, or other matters.[43] In the process, the medicalization of dependency has become increasingly associated with the idea of addiction, in ways that suggest the complementarity of medical and social rationality. Addiction implies a debilitating but compulsive behavior over which the addicted person has no control. Wagner suggests that addictions have proliferated in the highly medicalized discourse of the "new temperance," such that a growing number of personal practices are categorized as if people were psychically dependent on them. Today, even what has in the past been considered a "basic drive," such as eating or engaging in sex, is seen as addictive behavior if practiced in excess. And addictive behavior is seen as less socially productive.[44]

This raises the issue of at what level of frequency does a certain behavior get recategorized from use to abuse? And when does a dependency become a debilitating dependency? Not all dependencies are debilitating. Breathing is a sign of dependency on oxygen that all humans have and is fundamental to sustaining life. Eating is as well. At what point does a dependency become a debilitating addiction or compulsion? And when is an addiction a disease? When moral panic or a social movement keen to stigmatize a certain behavior develops, the conditions become ripe for the transformation of a dependency into an addiction and for that medicalized understanding to lead to the idea that the people who suffer from that addiction are diseased and in need of regulation and treatment, whether because they eat too much, have sex too frequently, or use drugs too often. The medicalization of these behaviors tends to gloss over the great variation within and between groups of people practicing any one of these behaviors. Medicalization tends to lump dependents together irrespective of how they are affected by their dependency and whether their dependency really is or is not debilitating. Medicalization also tends to promote the idea that these dependencies are like diseases and can spread. Therefore, irrespective of whether their behavior is self-destructive or not, the dependent need to be quarantined or at least marginalized so that their debilitating compulsive behavior does not become a model for others.

People who practice the stigmatized behavior are marginalized irrespective of whether their behavior is debilitating or not. Dependency discourse "makes itself real" by creating the conditions under which the dependent are reduced to a marginal status regardless of whether or not they can do what "independent" people do.[45] For instance, the drug user who consistently uses an illicit drug, especially one that is habit-forming, may very well find him or herself labeled an addict in need of treatment and no longer a self-disciplined responsible person, even though he or she may remain a productive worker, an active member of his or her community, a responsible parent, and the like. The stigmatized can overcome their marginalization only by changing their behavior. In this sense, medicalization becomes its own self-fulfilling prophecy that makes itself real. As the popularity of the medicalized metaphor of dependency increases, this sort of myopia can spread to other areas far beyond the clinic's walls, beyond medicine proper to allied fields and practices, till even social relationships that are said to have no biological tie are nonetheless labeled as debilitating dependencies in need of treatment and marginalization. After a while, it becomes difficult to see welfare dependency as a metaphorical dependency; instead it comes to be seen as if it were literally like a chemical dependency, in need of the same kind of clinical treatment and social marginalization. In the self-fulfilling world of medicalized welfare dependency, recipients must accept that they need treatment and only then can they get the benefits they need.

Given the liberal contractual culture, behaviors that are labeled as dependencies are particularly vulnerable to political/medical interpretation since the independent self is what the political order seeks to create. To label something a dependency, irrespective of whether it is medicalized as an uncontrollable compulsion or addiction, is to make a political statement. Once the politics of discourse come into play, some dependencies are selected as being antithetical to the type of self called for by the existing political order. Women's dependence on men in the family is not singled out as a dependency; it is not medicalized, termed an addiction, or subject to treatment. In fact, even today it is still quite the reverse, as mental health discourses tend to medicalize women's discontent with such dependency and try to get them to adjust to it. Women's resistance to their subordination in the family has often been categorized as a form of illness by the mental health professions, and generic diagnostic categories such as "border-line personality disorder" have proven useful for the medicalization of discontent as an illness.[46]

However, women's dependence on the state for income assistance is another matter; such a dependence is increasingly considered an illness in need of treatment.[47] This is especially the case in the postindustrial culture's renewed emphasis on personal health as a sign of self-discipline. Welfare dependency is being approached as if it were a clinically treatable disease and welfare recipients are being treated as a separate class of people who need to be marginalized, if not quarantined, because their "underclass" behavior is a threat to the broader culture that valorizes self-discipline in the name of self-sufficiency.[48]

There is, for instance, the growing interest in the idea that welfare dependency is transmittable, like a virus spreading from mother to daughter. Rebecca Blank quotes from a 1995 statement by U.S. Representative John Mica (R-FL) arguing for welfare reform: "I submit to you that with our current handout, non-work welfare system, we've upset the natural order. We've created a system of dependency."[49] Blank argues that this statement reflects a new attitude that sees welfare as an "addiction." She notes, however, that there is little evidence for the idea of "welfare addiction" or that it spreads from mother to daughter:

> [T]here is very little evidence that welfare is "addictive," that is, that women who go on welfare lose all motivation to work. . . . Most daughters of AFDC recipients do not use welfare, but more do become recipients than do daughters whose mothers were never on AFDC [because they are] more likely to be poor adults.[50]

However, the 1996 welfare reform law reflected the "welfare addiction" perspective, stating as undisputed fact that daughters who grow up in families on welfare are three times as likely to receive welfare as adults than women who grew up in families that were not on welfare.[51] Breaking the cycle of poverty has now been replaced by concern over stopping the spread of welfare dependency from one generation to the next, although persistent poverty in families is probably the primary reason why there is such a correlation of welfare use.

Medicalizing the Culture of Welfare Administration

The Personal Responsibility and Work Opportunity Reconciliation Act of 1996 is best known for setting time limits and imposing work requirements on those receiving welfare, abolishing the old Aid to Families with Dependent Children (AFDC) program, and replacing it with the Temporary Assistance for Needy Families (TANF) block grant program. These changes are significant, to be sure. Recipients can only receive federally funded TANF assistance for two years. After that they must be "participating in work-related activities," though states can set stricter requirements. Recipients cannot receive federally funded TANF funds for more than five years in a lifetime. States are required to meet the following work quotas:[52]

	Participation Rates for All Families	Work Hours per Week
1997	25%	20
1998	30%	20
1999	35%	25
2000	40%	30
2001	45%	30
2002	50%	30

Yet these changes should not be evaluated out of context. I want to suggest that they are part of the dramatic change in the culture of welfare administration currently taking place. This cultural shift can be seen at many levels. One significant dimension of this shift is in the emphasis on welfare administration from dispensing checks to families to monitoring the work-related behavior of parents. This monitoring goes beyond checking to see that work requirements are fulfilled and includes a panoply of related behavioral requirements. The changes are rooted in a "new paternalism" that is encouraging a particular type of medicalization of welfare dependency. This "new paternalism" explicitly assumes that welfare recipients are childlike, that they lack basic competence, that they are passive and dependent in medicalized ways, and that welfare policy therefore needs to "tell welfare recipients what to do."[53] Lawrence Mead, the primary theoretician on behalf of the "new paternalism," writes:

> Many welfare recipients seem to need pressure from the outside to achieve their own goals. They seem to be looking for structure. The idea of case managers monitoring people easily strikes the better-off as severe. . . . For the poor, however, supervision is often new and welcome. . . . Thus most recipients respond favorably to oversight. . . . [S]aid one supervisor in Riverside [CA]: "It reminds them that you *care*, and that you're *watching*."[54]

To my mind, the "new paternalism" represents the triumph of a particular medicalized viewpoint.[55] Welfare is still seen as a "moral hazard" that can trap people in a life of dependency; however, this moral hazard is increasingly articulated in medicalized terminology as habit-forming, whereby its addictive qualities strip people of their self-discipline and their ability to act as responsible adults.[56] In response, welfare administration must be changed to instill the needed discipline that recipients lack. Like a new drug, welfare administration *itself* becomes a form of treatment designed to transform recipients and wean them from lives of passive dependency on welfare. Mead writes:

> Traditionally, administration was considered a tool to deliver policies conceived in economic terms. Such are the problems of bureaucracy in America that some economists have advocated that administration be minimized by delivering social benefits through voucher or market mechanisms. Paternalism gives up that strategy, for now not only the delivery of benefits but *policy itself* is administrative. The goal is to supervise behavior, largely outside institutional walls, something that can only be done by routines where staff members check up on clients. . . . [T]he potential for paternalism rests on the progress of public administration.[57]

The "new paternalism" is articulated in what I have previously called the "economistic-therapeutic-managerial" discourse of welfare policy. In that idiom, the problems of welfare dependency are narrowly construed as involving the manipulation of economic incentives so that recipients will modify their behavior, leave the welfare rolls, and reduce the problems associated with managing the welfare population.[58] It represents an intensification of what Nancy Fraser has called the Juridical-Administrative-Therapeutic apparatus (JAT). JAT is a form of bureaucratic "needs talk" that imputes to welfare recipients personal deficiencies that need to be treated if they are to leave welfare for a life of "self-sufficiency."[59] The "new paternalism" starts with a strong commitment to the idea that welfare recipients lack the personal characteristics, habits, and behavior needed to act like the middle class. They need to be disciplined in order to take on those traits and behaviors. The solution to welfare dependency is to articulate the problem in these medicalized terms and closely monitor a course of treatment to its logical conclusion, resulting in people leaving welfare.

The "new paternalism" therefore achieves its medicalization of welfare primarily via changes in the administration of public assistance programs. At its most basic level, the new regime makes people's access to welfare conditional upon their demonstrating that they are making progress toward taking and keeping paid employment instead of welfare as their primary source of income. A recipient's contact with welfare from beginning to end is now funneled through this concern. It begins with assessment, continues with financial and employment planning, intensifies with job search, and culminates in leaving welfare for paid employment outside the home. Recipients are continually being evaluated through all these activities to see whether or not they are, in the new lexicon of welfare reform, "job ready" so that they can make "rapid attachment" to the labor market.

The changes in welfare administration start with the semantic abolition of welfare. In some states, welfare agencies are now called offices of "employment and financial planning."[60] In the process welfare workers are being transformed too. Increasingly they are no longer income maintenance workers but are financial and employment counselors or coaches.[61] The shift also often includes the use of private contractors who frequently staff their agencies with people schooled in job hunting skills rather than social work. Often the first priority of these workers is to find an applicant a job even before he or she begins to receive welfare. The new discourse of welfare administration sometimes refers to these private agencies as "hardshell."[62] Hardshell agencies engage in "diversion," which is to say that their primary responsibility is not to get needed income to qualifying families but to "deflect" them from receiving assistance and send them into the labor market. Should such efforts fail and recipients continue to receive assistance, the monitoring of recipient behavior intensifies. There is a growing use of sanctions penalizing recipients for not taking steps to find, get, and keep paid employment.[63] A new world of welfare administration has sprung up within the last few years which reflects a profound cultural shift in the administration of welfare.

A New Screen

The truth-seeking and inspection practices associated with each stage of the new welfare system illustrate the ways in which the reform of welfare administration itself constitutes an important new form of medicalization. In particular, the assessment of welfare applicants now exhibits an increased medicalized discourse over past techniques to determine the facts of any one applicant's case.[64] From the moment an applicant first walks into a welfare office the emphasis is on assessing her for personal problems that might prevent her from being "job ready." The goal is to get recipients to change their behavior, change their psychological outlook, reduce their personal problems, motivate them to work, and make them more attractive to prospective employers. Physical and mental health screening are critical features of welfare administration in the initial stages.[65] Good welfare intake procedures cannot omit the need to screen and slot welfare recipients as to their need for collateral services that can make them "job ready." Important screening considerations therefore include testing for drug use, mental illness, and other conditions that might indicate that an applicant is not job ready. Several states have taken a more punitive tack and have made drug screening a condition for eligibility.[66] Most other uses of screening involve referring recipients to other services that can help them become "job ready."

There is less emphasis on assessing a recipient's need to enhance her or his employability through education and training. The Personal Responsibility and Work Opportunity Reconciliation Act allows recipients to count only one year of training or education beyond high school as fulfilling the new work requirements. In addition, recipients who do this cannot make up more than 20 percent of the people fulfilling the state's work quota.[67] In other words, welfare reform insists on employment rather than facilitating it and when it facilitates it, it does so only in a highly medicalized way. To the extent that skills are emphasized, they are the "soft skills" of fitting into the social relations of the workplace rather than the "hard skills" of job training. The very term "soft skills" suggests that the administration of welfare is being medicalized as it assesses and monitors the ability of recipients to behaviorally and psychologically integrate themselves into the workplace.

We can see this shift toward a more medicalized form of monitoring in the new forms of case management. For years, caseworkers were assigned to welfare families and made home visits, consulted with the families regarding their needs, and exercised great discretion over the extent to which the family received cash assistance and services.[68] By 1972, partly in response to litigation requiring that procedures be standardized to ensure fairness in the treatment of families, the federal government required states to separate benefits determination from service provision.[69] Welfare families no longer had caseworkers. From the early 1970s until the late 1980s, the welfare administration intake procedures of most states did not involve the assessment of applicant employability to any great extent. However, the Family Support Act of 1988 changed that and reintroduced the role of the caseworker in income maintenance administration.[70]

The 1988 law changed the focus of casework for welfare families. Now casework was referred to as intensive case management and focused on working with recipients to plan their transition from welfare to paid employment.[71] The 1996 law increases this emphasis on intensive case management, and in many states caseworkers, now often employment "counselors" or "coaches," do not offer much social service support for problems unrelated to finding and keeping employment. Often they are not even employees of the welfare agency but work for private contractors instead. Case management does at times involve working with recipients once they take jobs, to help them keep them. This is sometimes referred to as "intensive postemployment case management" and can involve extensive counseling to deal with the emotional stresses associated with the transition to paid employment.[72]

Assessment, diagnosis, and treatment for physical and psychological conditions have become an important part of welfare administration. Helping people change their personal habits and deal with personal problems is central to helping them become "job ready." Counseling now surpasses training as the route to "self-sufficiency." Building self-esteem takes priority over getting an education. Leaving welfare for paid employment is seen in relation to personal attributes rather than job skills. The development of "soft skills" in interpersonal relations is emphasized over the acquisition of "hard skills" in particular trades and professions. Welfare turns to "technologies of the self" and has been medicalized to an unprecedented degree.[73]

Beyond Discipline: Monitoring as Medicine

There are growing reasons to believe that Lawrence Mead is right that the success of the brave new world of welfare reform is contingent upon the progress of public administration. The new case management allows for new information systems to facilitate a system of continuous monitoring of recipients as they make the transition from welfare to work. A June 1998 report from the National Association of State Information Resource Executives (NASIRE) indicates the concern in this area:

> Many states expect that intake and eligibility determination functions will expand to include more complex employment and case management activities. As case managers, human services workers must possess case management skills and have new information technology tools to support activities and provide the information required to move clients from welfare to work.
>
> Case management can encompass the following activities:
>
> • screening of applicants for strengths, job readiness, impediments to self-sufficiency;
> • screening to determine whether additional medical or occupational assessments are required;
> • identifying resources that are available to satisfy unmet needs;

- developing and implementing an individual responsibility plan;
- monitoring and tracking client progress toward achieving the objectives set forth in their plans;
- referring clients to service providers and programs;
- scheduling and coordinating appointments with public and private service providers; and
- tracking clients' progress toward achieving interim goals toward self-sufficiency.

Prior to the advent of welfare reform, information systems were not constructed to administer case management activities. To refocus human services on case management, many states are building systems that allow third parties to conduct transactions with the state, integrate information across agencies, and allow electronic client referral, in addition to existing eligibility determination and benefit disbursement systems.[74]

There is increased concern that while this makes for good theory there are not enough functioning monitoring systems to track welfare recipients. Concerns range from wanting to find out what happens to recipients after they leave welfare to monitoring recipients' behavior while they are on welfare.[75] The Rockefeller Institute's interim report to the Kellogg Foundation on its "State Capacity Study" put the problem quite starkly:

> [N]early all states have not yet developed accountability systems that fit the new welfare. Much of the information passed up to state managers, regional offices, or even local managers is still "thin," often just information on caseloads and work participation rates. There is little information about how people are moving (or not moving) through the work assignment process, nor is it possible to determine whether some people might be held back but for a very specific problem (such as not owning a car), or whether someone is prevented from working because of the lack of child care.[76]

The 1996 law also provides the option to all states to move to some form of Electronic Benefits Transfer system for funding.[77] States insist that they be given the discretion to design these systems themselves to better serve client needs; however, the foregoing suggests that states also want to have discretion so that they can design these systems to better monitor client behavior.

Historically, welfare administration has been based on the medical model's keen interest in documenting the record for each case. Case records have been as central to welfare administration as they have been to medical administration.[78] Welfare case record keeping has been notoriously slow to computerize and the 1996 law has sought to change that, thereby helping to accelerate the medicalization of welfare. In this way, monitoring is the hallmark of the new medicalized welfare administration. Monitoring is welfare's way of showing that by *watching*, it *cares*. I would argue that watching as a form of care is a most telling characterization. In this locution monitoring is explicitly medicalized. To watch is to care, to watch is to provide care, to watch is to create a climate in which the watched feel obliged to modify their behavior. The watched recipient is a clinically treated recipient who can be tracked as to her or his progress in getting off welfare. Welfare reform is first and foremost about a new form of care called watching. And we can see if the caring has the desired effect when the recipient leaves welfare for work.

The new reporting systems are therefore not extraneous gadgetry in the changing culture of welfare administration. On the contrary, they are critical to the cultural shift to move welfare toward a more medicalized practice dedicated to weaning recipients from their dependency on welfare. They are very much tied to the new requirements that recipients sign "individual responsibility plans" (called contracts of mutual responsibility in some states) that bind them to make progress in leaving welfare for employment. For Eugene Bardach, systems of continuous monitoring may be necessary because welfare recipients often do not meet the threshold requirements for personal responsibility expected of people in the liberal contractual order. They cannot be counted on to fulfill their obligations. Bardach writes:

> Behind the "welfare reform" thinking of at least the past decade is an implicit belief that welfare recipients have made a social contract: they get financial assistance while they are down and out; but the taxpaying public requires them, by way of reciprocity, to make various prescribed efforts to get back to work as soon as possible. . . . In practice, however, this was not the idea communicated to clients even in the high-expectations programs I observed. . . . One reason is that some line workers do not believe in the validity of the social contract concept. Conservatives accuse these workers of being bleeding hearts, and the conservatives' skepticism is partly responsible for the emerging consensus on mandatory workfare. But even those line workers who believe in welfare recipients' obligations to society and whose efforts to motivate them are strongly rooted in these beliefs do not usually talk to their clients in terms of a quid pro quo, of welfare exchanged for effort to find a job or otherwise participate in the program. Instead, they emphasize the self-respect to be gained by becoming a fuller member of society. The differences between the emphasis on a social contract and on fuller membership are subtle but important. . . . Viewed in this light, responsibility is not just an obligation, it is also liberation from a life of passivity and disorganization.[79]

Once people have been continuously counseled and coached to meet the threshold requirements of the responsible self, they can be allowed to make contracts on their own beyond the contracts the welfare office requires of them. Therefore, for Bardach medicine precedes politics. But for Gilles Deleuze, medicine may well be all that is left after politics. Deleuze suggests that continuous monitoring is to the postindustrial order what periodic surveillance was to the industrial order.[80] Postindustrial technologies make constant monitoring possible and enable those who seek to install new systems of control to go beyond the industrial preoccupation with discipline. Now the self-disciplined self will be surpassed in a new age of monitoring. With constant monitoring comes a totally administered society and what Paul Virilio calls "totalitarian individualism."[81] Deleuze writes:

> We are in a generalized crisis in relation to all the environments of enclosure—prison, hospital, factory, school, family. . . . The administrations in charge never cease announcing supposedly necessary reforms: to reform schools, to reform industries, hospitals, the armed forces, prisons. But everyone knows that these institutions are finished, whatever the length of their expiration periods. . . . It's only a matter of administering their last rites and of keeping people employed until the installation of the new forces knocking at the door. These are societies of control, which are in the process of replacing the disciplinary society.[82]

Deleuze argues that once constant monitoring is in place the old guarantees, such as signed contracts and case records, will be obsolete. The new information systems hold out the possibility of making even the contractual logic of welfare reform unnecessary. Less emphasis need be given to contracts and promises and more to drug screening and performance evaluations. At that point, medicine will have become the new politics and welfare's new monitoring systems will have replaced the "individual responsibility plans" that recipients currently sign and must fulfill under threat of sanction. Until then, challenging the design of new information systems will continue to be an important form of political resistance in the already highly medicalized world of welfare administration.

Medicalizing Welfare Dependents

The "new paternalism's" medicalization of welfare creates a need for a new kind of information about recipients' every move. It is tied to a fundamental distrust of their ability to act as responsible adults. This distrust has several sources, ranging from the most cynical suspicion that many recipients do not really need assistance to the more sympathetic concern that they are "damaged people" who are unable to live normal lives.[83] For these reasons, it becomes important to identify the incidence rates for these different conditions. High incidence rates would justify a more paternalistic approach to the welfare population on the grounds that they have personal characteristics and suffer from personal problems that make it difficult for them to act responsibly on their own. Given the medicalization associated with the "new paternalism," it is not surprising that this work is in fact now being done. Although much of the work is quite new, estimates are already beginning to appear. For instance, Miles Shore has pointedly written:

> Studies suggest that at least 30 percent of people in poverty have had an identifiable mental disorder within the last twelve months. An unknown additional percentage would rate as pessimistic on Seligman's Attributional Style Questionnaire. Even pessimism is important in view of his findings that a variety of misfortunes accrue to people with a pessimistic style. These considerations suggest that psychological assessment of welfare recipients would be a useful and inexpensive policy. The purpose of the assessment would be twofold: to identify treatable disorder and offer appropriate interventions and to use the information to tailor case management, vocational placement, and other social service interventions to the cognitive and emotional capabilities of the recipients.[84]

It would be hard to ask for a better excuse for paternalism than the portrait of the welfare population as a helpless lot of "damaged people." This is not to say that people who have social and emotional problems ought not to get help. They should; and an important part of social service provision ought to be to help people who suffer from various psychological conditions. But there are real dangers in characterizing the poor as primarily a population of people who are psychologically disabled. First, one must distinguish between cause and effect. Poverty can be an important cause of psychological problems but correcting those psychological conditions will not correct the poverty that produced those conditions in the first place. Second, even if psychological problems were a major reason for people to go on public assistance this does not mean that public assistance ought to be limited to serving the poor who have mental health problems. An alternative point of view would suggest that public assistance is an important antipoverty policy and should serve all poor people, not only those suffering from various psychological conditions.

Medicalization as a Self-Fulfilling Prophecy

Welfare has been made so restrictive and punitive that only people who have absolutely no other options are willing to endure the stigma and the hassle. Welfare is becoming a self-fulfilling prophecy by being so unpalatable and offering such low benefits under highly restrictive conditions that it appears to be designed exclusively for people with personal problems. In fact other people need it as well, but they are increasingly deterred by the program's conditions and requirements.

The sad irony of welfare dependency highlights the importance of inverting the linear, top-down policy paradigm that assumes that problems precede public policies and that policies are fashioned in response to preexisting problems. Deborah Stone, among others, argues that the reverse is a better way to understand the policy process—that is, policies construct public problems in particular ways so as to imply that they are the correct response to those problems.[85] I would go further to emphasize that a public policy not only constructs a self-serving understanding of the problem it attacks.[86] It also operates in a self-legitimating fashion to "make that understanding real," at least in the sense of creating a process of selection whereby only those instances of the problem that are consistent with the policy's construction of it are treated. Therefore, should we choose to limit our focus to the problems treated by the policy, it would appear that the policy is correct in implicitly characterizing the problem the way it has. For instance, in recent years the medicalization of welfare dependency and welfare provision has helped to increase the tendency of the welfare population to consist largely of people who have various personal problems, psychological or otherwise, such that a more medicalized approach to welfare seems appropriate. Thus, the medicalization of welfare dependency is quickly becoming its own self-fulfilling prophecy.

Medicalization's self-legitimation has been helped by the deterioration of welfare as an antipoverty program. For over two decades, welfare has been becoming less attractive as a form of assistance to poor families generally. Kathryn Edin and Laura Lein have effectively documented how most single mothers receiving public assistance have to supplement their welfare checks with income from other sources.[87] This is not surprising since welfare benefits have declined 38 percent in real value over the last twenty years.[88] Not only has the real value of welfare declined but also, with the growing fervor to reform welfare, more restrictions and requirements are associated with receiving it. Finally, with the 1996 reform law, welfare receipt has been time-limited and made contingent on fulfilling work requirements. As a result, welfare has been reduced to being a program that only those people most desperately in need of it will use.

In the process, the welfare population comes to look more and more like the population assumed by the program—that is, a population that is passive, dependent, not likely to take work, and not likely to keep it. This population is more likely to have psychological and other personal problems which make it difficult for its members to provide for themselves. This population makes welfare use look like a product of personal characteristics, habits, and conditions rather than of political and economic structures and processes. Such a population appears to justify a paternalistic approach, although that approach would be inappropriate to a wider population of the poor that could benefit from public assistance.

Welfare's medicalization via the "new paternalism" is therefore ultimately justified by welfare's increasing restrictiveness. Most of the poverty suffered by the poor is due to structural factors that have marginalized them economically. This marginalization has increased, according to evidence of increasing inequality caused by economic change in the postindustrial era.[89] But as welfare becomes increasingly restrictive, many poor families do all they can to avoid it. And as welfare reform moves more people into low-wage jobs, only families that have no choice but to rely on welfare are left. As stated, these families are more likely to have personal problems that appear to justify the emphasis on individualistic causes of poverty, paternalistic forms of programming, and medicalized types of intervention. For instance, like many other states, Oregon reduced its welfare rolls between January 1993 and September 1997 by 33 percent. By early 1998, with the rolls still declining, Oregon estimated that its reduced welfare population was disproportionately composed of people with mental health, drug, and domestic violence problems. About 75 percent of the remaining single mothers on Oregon's welfare rolls had suffered from some form of mental illness or clinically treatable emotional problem in the past year, about half had a problem with drugs, and about half had suffered the effects of spouse battering. In response Oregon devised new procedures to deal with these "hard to place" recipients.[90]

The Exception Proves the Rule: The Medicalization of Resistance

The best evidence of medicalization as self-legitimating lies in the resistance to it. For Foucault, power tends to encode its own resistance, creating the terrain in which opposition must maneuver or specifying the terms in which opposition is articulated.[91] The medicalization of welfare has produced a highly medicalized form of resistance wherein welfare recipients are often left with no other option but to identify themselves as sick and in need of medical treatment in order to get what income support they can from welfare, the only program to offer them such support. Given the medicalization of welfare dependency, poor single mothers who are not in need of medical treatment are encouraged to reconstruct their identities in terms of sickness and health so that they can get the aid they need. While most are reluctant to do so and leave welfare when they can—even taking jobs that leave them with less net income—others might adapt by acting out the implied identity of the new medicalized discourse of welfare administration. For instance, even if your problem is not self-esteem but the lack of employable skills, you may proceed to take classes on building your self-esteem in order to continue to receive aid. You may accept other forms of counseling as well. You may learn new things about the drug addictions you never had, so as to be perceived as a compliant, if now more medicalized, welfare recipient. Therefore, the nonmedicalized may to varying degrees join ranks with the already medicalized on the welfare rolls in order to gain access to the income support that welfare provides. Medicalization is thus used subversively not to so much resist it as to exploit it, given that it is increasingly the only route to assistance.

Resistance is also medicalized in other ways. Most especially, medical status is quickly becoming an important medium through which recipients seek to gain exemptions from time limits and work requirements. The 1996 welfare reform law allows states to exempt up to 20 percent of their caseload under a general "hardship exemption" from having to meet the time limit requirement. In addition, the law specified that states could adopt the so-called "Wellstone-Murray Family Violence Option" named for its sponsors U.S. Senators Paul Wellstone (D-MN) and Patti Murray (D-WA) that temporarily exempts women at risk of domestic violence from having to meet time limits.[92] Subsequent regulations indicated that women exempted for reasons of domestic violence could also be exempted from work requirements.[93] As of March 1999, thirty-one states have adopted procedures related to providing exemptions to victims of domestic violence, and all states have utilized the hardship exemption.[94] There is good reason to believe that more people have requested exemptions than the 20 percent limit can cover.[95] To some extent welfare recipients are in competition with each other over whose hardship will be given priority by the state.

Therefore, a program that sees its recipient population increasingly in medicalized terms is also quickly becoming one that grants exemptions on medicalized grounds. The most damaged will be temporarily exempted from having to meet work and time limit requirements on the grounds that their problems are too severe to allow them to become job ready. Welfare administration thus involves sorting people out in terms of their deficiencies and providing services to help them overcome those problems. Good advocacy increasingly involves ensuring that the special debilitating conditions of particular cases are recognized and that those recipients are able to get the appropriate treatment. Good advocacy involves pointing out which of your clients are not "job ready," cannot make "rapid attachment" to the labor market, and need extra treatment before they are able to get and keep paid employment.

In the same vein, good policy research involves devising new programs to address the high incidence of personal problems in the reduced welfare population still receiving public assistance under the new and highly restrictive policies. Ariel Kalil and her colleagues highlight the complexities involved:

> Welfare-to-work programs may also have to adapt to the needs of clients with more serious barriers to work, such as substance abuse or domestic violence. [There is] a treatment model that would engage families in intensive counseling or therapeutic treatment to address problems such as substance dependency or severe family crises. Models of this type of social service delivery are theoretically based on social work interventions such as Homebuilders family preservation models and other short-term intensive crisis interventions. . . . Although little empirical evidence exists regarding the effects of family preservation interventions on the work effort of welfare recipients, [there is] evidence suggesting that substance abuse-treatment for welfare recipients has had favorable cost-benefit results in a number of sites. . . . Although clients attending mental health or substance abuse counseling sessions will typically not be counted toward a state's work participation rate during this treatment period, [some analysts suggest] that programs may want to consider using such services, for a limited time, as a precursor to moving the harder-to-serve into employment or a "back-end outlet" for those who are identified as having a significant barrier to employment.[96]

Yet the shift to a medicalized advocacy has its risks. For too long, domestic violence in particular was neglected as a major reason for the need to rely on public assistance.[97] But now that it is being recognized, it may become part of a movement that shifts attention away from the economic bases of poverty. The same could be said of other conditions.

The medicalization of welfare dependency is vulnerable to being used for conservative critiques of unmotivated recipients as well as for liberal advocacy to exempt single mothers from work requirements. For instance, upon hearing that many participants in Project New Hope in Milwaukee suffered depression and chose not to work full-time even though their wages would be subsidized, Lawrence Mead stated that welfare dependency is "rooted in an underlying culture of self-defeat."[98] While a life of deprivation may have induced depression in many instances, Mead chose to read the facts the other way around as suggesting that depression caused economic deprivation. Mead's equating depression with culture illustrates starkly how medicalization is one way of locating the problem primarily in the individual and how that too often encourages seeing welfare use as if it were more a product of outlook, habit, and lifestyle as opposed to being something primarily instigated be economic conditions.

Generalizing Trauma

So where does this take us? The logical conclusion of the new form of advocacy is to medicalize poverty completely and suggest that people with low incomes are suffering from a sickness. In fact for years there has been a rich literature that takes a clinical approach to poverty.[99] One prominent perspective in this literature is that poverty is a public health problem; here poverty is sometimes theorized as both a cause and a consequence of mental health problems.[100] In particular, the social and economic marginalization of poor neighborhoods is believed to generate high levels of emotional and psychological distress among residents. From this perspective, people living in poor neighborhoods—the "underclass," as they are now called—are a traumatized lot, suffering from the emotional and psychological burdens of living in such neighborhoods.[101] Problems such as high crime, high turnover of residents, lack of trust among neighbors, a paucity of community resources, and lack of economic opportunities, among other things contribute to the emotional burden of living in such an environment. Residents are likely to have higher levels of anxiety, depression, post-traumatic stress disorder, and other clinically identifiable conditions just from living where they do. The stresses of poverty make poverty itself a major public health problem.[102]

There is much to commend in this clinical perspective. Excellent groundbreaking research is being done to identify the covariates of mental illness and poverty.[103] On the basis of this research, there is good reason to think that living in persistent poverty can itself be traumatizing, over and above the trauma associated with problems that occur with high frequency in poor neighborhoods, such as being the victim of a criminal assault, sexual or otherwise. Thus, the processes of cultural proliferation that are extending the categories of public health to include poverty can lead to recognition of the emotional burdens of living in poor neighborhoods and being poor.

But here too medicalization continues to create its own double binds. While it absolves people in poverty of blame for their lack of income, it reaffirms the idea that they are different and deficient, this time as a traumatized population. Medicalization has its own form of otherness. Here whole neighborhoods of people are seen as other, that is, as sick and in need of treatment. From this perspective, medicalization can even be said to suggest that the neighborhood itself—above and beyond its residents—is in need of clinical treatment. Medicalizing poverty becomes just another way of suggesting that there is a "culture of poverty" keeping "the underclass" down. Rather than political and economic reform, mental health services become the key to attacking the poverty of poor neighborhoods. In addition, there is the risk that solutions articulated in medicalized parlance will emphasize preventing the spread of the underclass rather than in trying to revitalize these marginalized communities.

Thus, although it may be sympathetic and thoughtful in particular instances, the medicalization of poor neighborhoods can undermine community development and the ability of neighborhoods to become self-determining. By emphasizing underclass containment over community development, this approach risks reinscribing the subordination of those neighborhoods and their residents in a clinical relationship. As John McKnight writes:

> Potentially powerful communities can be disabled by alien systems that sponsor and propagate a culture of need and deficiency. If this culture of deficiency comes to dominate a local community, it will lose the power of wise citizenship and succumb to the maladies of clienthood and medical consumption. The essence of the medical mentality is diagnosis—the ability to name and describe the emptiness of your neighbor. As a technique, this skill can be valuable. However, as a pervasive cultural value, it will inevitably blind communities to the capacities, assets, skills, and gifts that are essential to their power, wisdom, and health. The diagnostic culture is a disease infecting many low-income communities. . . . While this emptiness, deficiency, malady, and disease is needed by growing medical systems, it is useless to those who grow healthful communities. The raw material of community is capacity. The raw

material of medicine is deficiency. In this harsh reality is a competition for resources based upon an ideological struggle. The community-building interest is an antidiagnostic ethos focused on gifts to be manifested. . . . [W]e should be guided by the critical honesty of Hippocrates, the founder of medicine as a profession. His oath concludes with a mandate to recognize that "above all," medicine's highest value is to "do no harm."[104]

For McKnight, as for Ivan Illich, the medicalization of poverty is more often than not disabling, positioning those in poverty in a subordinate relationship as the passive, dependent, helpless, and deficient patient or client. Medicalization is also often individualizing, reinforcing the idea that the problem to be attacked is specific to the individual person. This feeds into the tendency to emphasize "allopathic" approaches that try to isolate the disease rather than treating it in terms of the broader context. In the end, medicalization is at risk of "iatrogenesis"—a medically induced malady, where the treatment creates the problem. Allopathic, individualized, medicalized approaches to poverty reinforce the isolation, marginalization and pacification of low-income persons—ironically re-creating the dependency that was ostensibly one of the main symptoms of poverty that welfare reform was so keen to erase.

Poor communities can be depressing places to live in; residing there can be a traumatizing experience; life in an impoverished neighborhood can be very hard.[105] Such communities may very well need the assistance of outsiders, even professionals and experts who can supply the necessary know-how and resources to bring about change in such communities. These interventions may even require helping people deal with the emotional burdens associated with living in such communities. But such efforts need to be undertaken in ways that are not disabling and do not re-create the psychological conditions that undermine change and improvement. Medicalizing poor neighborhoods can reinforce the very problems community assistance is designed to attack. It can reinforce their subordinate, marginalized, and dependent status by making them dependent on the helping professions which have diagnosed them as deficient in medicalized terms.

Medicalization is like any other discourse—it creates its own resistance. However, that resistance is often forced to operate within that discourse, taking its terms of distinction as given and trying to work with them. Even when advocates are careful, they may reinscribe the invidious distinctions the discourse creates and proliferates. The solutions to medicalizing welfare are not to be found in medicalizing poverty. Medicalization tends to reinforce the marginal status of low-income persons and communities as not capable of providing for themselves.

The medicalization of poverty is potentially even more dangerous than the medicalization of welfare dependency. It creates the prospect that all low-income people will be subordinated to the terms of expert discourses designed to diagnose their conditions as allopathically treatable. As a result, the broader political and economic forces that marginalize poor neighborhoods are left to work their will while low-income residents are called upon to change their behavior, raise their self-esteem, acquire a more positive outlook, get more motivated, and the like. While both rich and poor alike can benefit from mental health services, the problems of poverty will not go away no matter how good people feel about themselves. Under these conditions, mental health professionals face the never-ending task of generating hope and optimism despite the grim realities of persistent economic neglect. The virus of medicalization spreads its own traumatic results. Inoculating ourselves against the ability of this virus to subvert the best forms of advocacy is now a major priority of social welfare policy. In the late 1990s, finding ways to confine medicine may be more important than developing new ways to contain the social diseases of poverty and welfare dependency. Once medicine's imperialistic discourse has been vanquished, the critical business of confronting the inequities of the existing political economy can begin again.

Given who is medicalizing whom, there is reason to suspect that David Wagner is right that the middle class is keen to relegitimate its status by emphasizing its capacity for self-discipline.[106] The medicalization of welfare dependency is arguably a related development, for both demonstrate that the lower classes continue to be used to enforce a particular standard of the self. Welfare therefore continues to be about what Frances Fox Piven and Richard A. Cloward have called "regulating the poor"—wherein the poor are regulated not for their benefit but for the benefit of protecting work and family values and the corresponding modes of economic allocation and political entitlement. The regulation of the poor now means encouraging poor people to see themselves as sick and in need of treatment for the illness of welfare dependency. Once they redefine themselves this way, the normality of all other self-regulating and/or self-medicating selves in the "work-first" economy is reaffirmed.

Conclusion

The culture of welfare administration is being transformed as part of a postindustrial social policy that denies that economic change is making it increasingly difficult for low-wage workers to support their families. In the process, welfare administration is being transformed into the critical ingredient of a "new paternalism" that intensively monitors recipient behavior to ensure that recipients make the transition from welfare to work regardless of whether they really can, and regardless of whether there really are jobs for them to take. Lawrence Mead, the leading theoretician of this "new paternalism," puts it succinctly: the success of welfare reform is contingent upon the progress of public administration. But what Mead calls public administration others would call a dystopian nightmare of behavior modification.

Administrative reform is part of the ongoing medicalization of welfare dependency that treats the reliance on public assistance like an addiction from which people need to be weaned. And as welfare becomes a less meaningful form of income support for the poor, those recipients who can leave do so to avoid the punitive treatment, the constant monitoring, the battery of assessments, and the barrage of clinical treatments. If your problem is poverty, the last thing you want are these hassles. Others remain and find themselves forced off nonetheless as states move to meet their work quotas and comply with their new time limits. Increasingly, the only people left are those who in fact need both medicalized assistance and income support. The medicalization of welfare ironically becomes its own self-fulfilling prophecy.

Welfare was once an important site for antipoverty struggles. Theoretically it held out the potential to be a redistribution program that could provide the poor with an income and help reduce poverty. From the later 1960s until the mid-1970s, advocates even got Congress and several presidents to consider a series of guaranteed income proposals. Those days are gone. Welfare is no longer an antipoverty program. Its benefit levels have been sinking in real value for almost three decades, and it does not lift families out of poverty. Welfare has been reduced to being a program for only the most vulnerable families, headed by single mothers whose personal problems prevent them from working. Welfare is no longer about economics; it is no longer about redistribution. It is now about eliminating itself by treating poor single mothers for personal problems and thereby reducing their need for public assistance. Unfortunately, poverty is as persistent in the 1990s as it was three decades ago, and all those poor families who do not need a medicalized regimen still need economic redistribution.

4

Deconstructing Devolution

Racing to the Bottom and Other Ironies
of Welfare Reform

Welfare reform is important on several levels. It is, for instance, arguably the most significant manifestation of the much heralded "devolution revolution" promised by the 1994 Contract with America.[1] After years of complaining that the federal government had become too powerful, and after perennial calls for a "new federalism," the Contract proclaimed that Congress was going to take real action and hand power down to the states.[2] The result was the Personal Responsibility and Work Opportunity Reconciliation Act of 1996 (PRWORA).[3] States were to be given the discretion to become the "laboratories of democracy" that they were often said to be.[4] Skeptics cautioned that the states might well use their new-found discretion to intensify an ongoing "race to the bottom," competing to see who could outdo the others in cutting back on welfare benefits so as to avoid becoming a "welfare magnet" that would attract low-income persons from other states.[5]

In the following chapter I argue that neither the concept of "laboratories of democracy" nor that of a "race to the bottom" does justice to the ironies of welfare reform. Instead, *welfare reform deconstructs itself.* First, I examine the issue of devolution to suggest that welfare reform does not provide as much state discretion as is often assumed. Also, I criticize the "race to the bottom" argument on the grounds that there is very little evidence for welfare migration because the real value of welfare benefits does not vary as much as is commonly believed. However, while welfare migration and the variation in benefits on which it is premised are not substantial, I do accept that state policy makers act as if they were. They are still wary of revising welfare in ways that might make their states welfare magnets. This wariness will intensify under welfare reform, especially since the devolution created by the 1996 legislation is questionable.

Devolution is therefore suspect. States are not as free as they appear to be. Given new federal mandates in the law, they are under substantial pressure to move recipients off welfare and into paid employment as quickly as possible even as they are leery the federal government may change the rules. And the collective actions of the states tend to undercut the freedom of each state to act individually. Consequently, states will also not be "laboratories of democracy." Welfare reform ironically creates a new system of decentralization that discourages state experimentation in pursuit of other approaches to fighting poverty. Welfare reform promotes an environment in which states feel the need to emulate each other. The restrictions initiated by one tend to be adopted by others.[6] In the process, states may force recipients to move to other states where they can still get benefits. As devolution deconstructs itself, they may actually end up making the myth of migration still another self-fulfilling prophecy of welfare reform.

The Undecidability of Federalism in Welfare Reform

Welfare reform demonstrates just how hard it is for federalism, that is, the relationship between the national government and the states, to reform itself. As Kala Ladenheim suggests, there is a "Zen-like" paradox to devolution.[7] Federal policy makers have to exercise national power in order to enable power to devolve to the states. In the process, they are tempted to hang onto national power. The ironies of devolution suggest that as we remake federalism we reinscribe it; federalism cannot help recreating itself even as it changes. The dilemmas of devolution today show that the politics of federalism continues to be about refashioning the system—not to replace it but to reform it. In the process, the core stays intact while changes are made around the margins. The "devolution revolution" in welfare reform may result in limited, but nonetheless real, grants of discretion that get squandered in the attempt to be like everyone else. As a result, federalism changes but stays the same. States exercise discretion but mimic each other. A national pattern of welfare reform settles into state administration.

Part of the reason for the ironies of devolution derives from the undecidability of federalism. Federalism's undecidability is a sign of its textuality. The "federal" metaphor conflates the allocation of power between the national and state governments as much as it clarifies. In fact, like so much else in politics, federalism is a field of ambiguous metaphors. The literary tropes which adorn our analyses of federal issues serve to mobilize support or opposition to shifts in governmental authority between the national government and the states. These linguistic devices can be overused and can often dangerously oversimplify; however, often they also effectively encapsulate the implications of changes in the federal system. A "race to the bottom" has for some time served as an important metaphor to illustrate that the United States federal system—and every federal system for that matter—is vulnerable to interstate competition.[8] The "race to the bottom" implies that the states compete with each other as each tries to underbid the others in lowering its taxes, spending, regulation, and the like, so as to make itself more attractive to outside financial interests or unattractive to unwanted outsiders. It can be opposed to the alternative metaphor of "laboratories of democracy."[9] The laboratory metaphor implies a more sanguine federalism in which subnationals use their authority and discretion to develop innovative and creative solutions to common problems which can then be adopted by other states.[10]

The contrast between a debilitating "race to the bottom" and the constructive social learning of "laboratories of democracy" has a symmetry all its own. John D. Donahue has recently noted in *Disunited States* that in a 1933 U.S. Supreme Court case Associate Justice Louis Brandeis wrote a dissenting opinion that later came to serve as the basis for the popular phrase "race to the bottom" (*Liggett Co. v. Lee*, 288 U.S. 517, 558–59, 1933).[11] Just a year earlier, in another dissenting opinion (*New State Ice Company v. Liebmann*, 285 U.S. 262, 311, 1932), he had suggested that the federal system allowed each state to serve as a "laboratory" for democracy.[12] With these two opinions, Brandeis helped develop what were to become the controlling metaphors for thinking about the potential and pitfalls of contemporary federalism. In the United States today, the major issue of federalism across a variety of public policy arenas can be phrased without abuse of literary license in terms of a choice between these two metaphors: Will devolving authority to the states lead to "laboratories of democracy" or a "race to the bottom"? Or will there be a race to the bottom and laboratories of democracy simultaneously—since states may innovatively develop ways to outrace their competition in cutting back.

Welfare reform is a primary case in point. The Personal Responsibility and Work Opportunity Reconciliation Act of 1996 has been touted as producing a "devolution revolution."[13] This legislation dramatically ended the sixty-one-year-old federal cash assistance program for low-income families initiated under the Social Security Act of 1935—Aid to Families with Dependent Children (AFDC)—and replaced it with a fixed block-grant program called Temporary Assistance for Needy Families (TANF). Some have suggested that the law did not represent a significant change since AFDC had already given states significant discretion in setting benefit levels and eligibility requirements.[14] Others have emphasized that the shift from AFDC to TANF was a major move that gave states greater latitude and in the process also ended what had become a federal entitlement guarantee for low-income families with children.[15]

But in fact the 1996 legislation was not the dramatic act of devolution that it has frequently been made out to be.[16] It did impose strict quotas on the percentage of adult recipients who had to participate in "work-related activities," starting at 25 percent of the targeted caseload working twenty hours a week and rising to 50 percent of the caseload working thirty hours a week by the year 2002. The law's definition of "work-related activities" was also quite narrow, limiting education and training to no more than one year, after which time only taking a job or doing community service would count. In addition, as amended, the law has limited the number of recipients in education and training programs to no more than 30 percent of those counted as fulfilling the work quota. This includes recipients in high school. The 1996 law also prohibited states from spending TANF funds on recipients who had received assistance for more than two years and were not working. Perhaps most controversially, the law "time limited" welfare, not only by prohibiting recipients from receiving welfare for more than two years if they were not working but also by prohibiting them from receiving assistance for more than five years in a lifetime. The law changed welfare policy in the United States in a variety of other ways as well, including limiting the access of legal immigrants to public assistance and of the unemployed to food stamps.

Nonetheless, it could be argued that these restrictions were not that onerous for states, as many of them were already experimenting with these and other limitations in order to move recipients from welfare to work. The law allowed states to set even stricter limitations and to impose tougher sanctions on recipients, including termination for failure to comply. In addition, the 1996 law required each state only to appropriate for TANF as little as 75 percent of what it did for AFDC in 1994 (80 percent if they failed to meet their work quotas). It also allowed states to divert up to 30 percent of the federal block-grant funding to related areas of spending; and they were not required to spend the block grant on cash assistance.

All the while, welfare rolls have been plummeting, falling faster and further than expected by most observers. The rolls had started falling in March

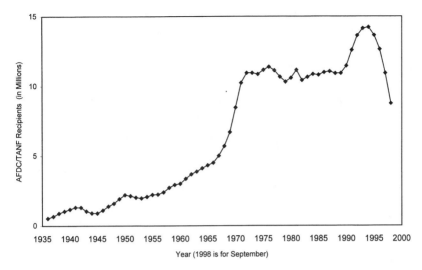

Figure 2: U.S. Welfare Recipients, 1936–1998. *(United States Department of Health and Human Services, May 1998)*

1993 after peaking at slightly over 14 million recipients nationwide. The welfare rolls have declined 44 percent nationwide from 14.12 million in January 1994 to 7.96 million in September 1998. In some states the declines have been much higher, exceeding 60 percent in Alabama, Colorado, Florida, Kansas, Mississippi, Oklahoma, Oregon, South Carolina, and West Virginia, while surpassing 80 percent in Wyoming, Wisconsin, and Idaho.[17] In most states these declines began in 1993, before the legislation was enacted, and can be attributed in part to improvement in the economy and experimentation by the states authorized through waivers they had received under the old AFDC program. Much was made, initially particularly by the Clinton administration, of the importance of welfare reform in accelerating this development, which first started under federal waivers.[18] Other studies countered that the decline in the rolls was due largely to the economy.[19] More recent reports suggest that states have played a role in the reforms, albeit a negative one. These reports indicate that states have indeed been using their new found discretion in a variety of ways, from instituting procedures to divert people away from welfare to imposing sanctions on families that fail to fulfill the new requirements.[20] As a result, even as the welfare population is shrinking, it is increasingly concentrated in the central cities and is increasingly comprised of single mothers of color who have found it more difficult to leave assistance for work.[21] These changes have once again raised the question: Is there a race to the bottom?

With declines in the rolls, most states have found that the initial funding levels of the TANF block grant afford them greater flexibility than was perhaps first anticipated.[22] TANF block grants are fixed for each state at an annual appropriation for any year between 1992 and 1995 that the state chooses. As a result, all states have experienced declines in the number of welfare recipients from 1996 to 1999, but have received the same amount of money.[23] Many states are using their windfall to do a variety of things from saving for future expenditures to investing in more education and training, from raising the salaries of child care providers to diverting the money to highway programs. By March 1997, forty states had also applied for food stamp waivers to continue food stamps for the unemployed living in areas of concentrated unemployment.[24]

Perhaps more significantly, states are also given the flexibility to segregate state funds for TANF and the families that receive state-only support. With the option of establishing a segregated state-only funded TANF program, states could move some recipients out of "welfare as we know it" into an alternative welfare program, such as one that combines welfare and child-support enforcement where welfare benefits are a supplement to families receiving low levels of child support. Segregating state-only TANF funds may be the one feature that makes welfare reform a significant part of any alleged the "devolution revolution." States will hopefully explore this idea further over time.[25]

States also have the discretion to protect those who cannot meet the work requirements even if jobs are available. States can exempt up to 20 percent of the caseload from having to meet the time limit. Whether all states will use this option effectively remains unclear, and which groups will be exempted is even murkier.[26] The 1996 law also contains a provision entitled the Family Violence Option, which gives states significant latitude to exempt any recipient from work and time limits if there is reason to believe that enforcing such requirements will put the applicant at risk of being a victim of domestic violence.[27]

Not all states have found the block-grant funding advantageous. Should the block grants remain fixed but the welfare rolls rise, more states will confront difficulties in the future. Until 1999 only one state (Hawai'i) had not had a decline in recipients since 1996 and was being forced to cut benefits under TANF.[28] A more widespread and immediate problem for many states, even those with growing economies, is the shortage of entry-level positions for low-income workers. In states like Wisconsin where the economy is growing in ways that has actually created a labor shortage, this is less of a problem.[29] Yet, even in Wisconsin, there is evidence that though recipients can find work, they often are worse off financially.[30] Elsewhere there are signs that providing jobs for welfare recipients in already overcrowded job markets may only increase unemployment for other low-income workers.[31] This can also lead to increased ethnic tensions; in some states, welfare recipients are often citizens who are white or black, while other low-wage workers are disproportionately noncitizens who are Latino and Asian.

In response to pressures from trade unions and others, in May 1997 President Bill Clinton announced that he would act to ensure that the federal government used its authority under the new law to require states to pay welfare recipients at least the minimum wage for their jobs.[32] Several governors immediately denounced this move, saying it would make it impossible for them to use their discretion under the law to affect real welfare reform. By then Clinton had also made another decision to use federal authority under PRWORA to prevent states from contracting out with private corporations for the overall administration of their welfare programs. Governors were quick to respond that this would limit their ability to "reinvent" welfare and produce real reform.[33] The resistance to both proposals underscored the possibility that the work requirements were designed more to get people to leave welfare rather than to ensure that they got work that could support their families.

However, it is important not to lose sight of the big picture. Welfare reform is undoubtedly the most visible example of the recent push for "devolution" of power to the states. States do have some discretion, to be sure. The 1996 law does provide that no federal official "may regulate the conduct of States under this part or enforce any provision of this part, except to the extent expressly provided in this part."[34] However, the discretion granted by the 1996 law is to be used largely for a specific purpose. States are to use their funding in order to move families from welfare to work. This, the law says, is essential to protect family values. From the first sentence of this legislation and its pronouncement that "marriage is the foundation of society," we sense that whatever devolution there is to be, it will be for this specific federally pronounced purpose.[35] This legislation represents an effort not simply to devolve more power to the states but to do so in a way that involves both the states and the federal government in promoting family values through the enforcement of the work ethic.

While the windfall created by the decline in the rolls creates real opportunities for states to exercise their new found discretion, states are still under pressure to meet federal work quotas and to impose the mandated time limits. As a result, the 1996 legislation is turning out to be less than a "devolution revolution" even under the best of circumstances. Even state discretion to reduce funding is now caught up in fulfilling the welfare-to-work mission. There is evidence that as the welfare rolls have declined, states have indeed cut their spending; however, they have not cut it as much as they could, choosing in many cases to spend more for each person still left on the rolls but only on more services to help them get off welfare, not on increases in cash assistance.[36] But while states can cut back or set aside money, whatever they do they must be focused on moving recipients into paid employment as quickly as possible, with less emphasis on education and training than previously. This is the federal framework and states must fit into it or face the consequences. Devolution in this much heralded case is therefore at best ambiguous and the allocation of power in the federal system remains undecidable.

Welfare Reform and the Specter of Welfare Migration

For now most states seem to be willing to fit into the new federal framework that emphasizes the rapid movement of recipients off welfare and into paid employment. However there are increasing signs that federal mandates are not the only source of constraint on states. In addition, states are collectively taking actions that work against individual states being able to exercise discretion on their own. While it is to be hoped that states will use their new found discretion to come up with better ways to provide public assistance to poor families, whatever innovation does take place will probably be conservative in nature, as states fear that by being liberal in their approach they will become "welfare magnets" that attract the poor from other states.[37]

Welfare reform is doomed in good part because it is haunted by the specter of "welfare migration." While evidence for such migration is increasingly suspect, its presence as a preoccupation among state policy makers is very real. It casts a long shadow over states' postreform deliberations and threatens to make sure that welfare reform deconstructs itself.

Like the impoverished families they purport to describe, tales of welfare migration have traveled from one state to another over the past two decades, gravitating especially toward states offering higher benefits.[38] In light of these tales, state policy makers worry that they will not be able to protect their own borders from out-of-state recipients who might be attracted by generous benefits. Such fears have become so widespread that some observers now suggest that we have already had an ongoing "race to the bottom," as states have for years been cutting their benefits in order to avoid becoming more attractive than other states.[39] Not surprisingly, these anxieties have prompted demands for even greater discretion to deter welfare recipients from other jurisdictions.[40] One might even argue that the perceived need for greater flexibility to combat the migrant poor played a role in the campaign that produced the 1996 law.

As a central motive for this transfer of authority, concerns over welfare migration figured prominently in the act's passage. Indeed, these concerns were explicitly addressed in several provisions of the act itself. In a move that undercut the U.S. Supreme Court's landmark 1969 decision striking down residency requirements for welfare (*Shapiro v. Thompson* 394 U.S. 618, 1969), the law allowed states to set different eligibility standards for people who had lived in the state for less than one year, so they could pay them at the benefits levels of their previous state of residence.[41] Title 42 of the U.S. code was amended to allow states to provide welfare to recent migrants in accordance with rules and benefit levels existing in their states of origin.[42] Other amendments gave states the option of treating "families moving into the state from another state differently than other families" for the first twelve months of residence (Section 404[c]).[43] These provisions, and the state-level demands that produced them, testify to the power that welfare migration claims have come to exert in policy-making circles.

One particularly troubling claim was that welfare reform itself would increase welfare migration as recipients cut off in one state would move to other states to continue to receive assistance. Therefore, it was argued, states needed the ability to discourage migration.[44] This argument became the basis for the provisions allowing states to treat newcomers differently and to require persons who had lived in a state for less than twelve months to receive the benefit of their prior state of residence. By mid-1997, fifteen states had adopted two-tier benefit schedules.[45] By mid-1998 the concern that reform may push recipients from one state to another had already intensified in states adjacent to those where people had been cut from the rolls.[46] In May 1999, the option that states could establish two-tier benefit schedules was however rejected by the U.S. Supreme Court in the case of *Saenz v. Roe*, 119 S. Ct. 1518 (1999), with the likely effect that states would become even more concerned about welfare migration.

Yet, the problem of welfare migration is not just a derivative issue arising in the aftermath of the "devolution revolution." It is an old problem with deep historical roots in the local control of public assistance.[47] In the United States the tradition of treating poor relief as a local matter has reflected a variety of political forces. It has served business interests who benefit from the regulation of local labor markets through the expansion and contraction of relief.[48] It has allowed white residents in southern states to maintain greater control over the social and economic dimensions of local race relations.[49] The separation of public assistance from federal social insurance programs has also kept control over incendiary moral issues at the local level, where they are felt most keenly, and away from the federal level where they might prove to be politically volatile for elected officials. More generally, jurisdiction over social provisions in the United States has reflected deep-seated moral distinctions between the undeserving and deserving poor: "This has been the historic pattern. The more ambiguous or more deviant the perceived moral character of the poor, the more local the control of relief."[50]

Alongside these various political forces, however, local control of public assistance has also flowed from a long-standing cultural commitment to the idea that helping the poor is a local obligation. This belief has a double-edged meaning that can be crudely summed up as "our poor are our responsibility, and your poor are your responsibility."[51] The moral obligation to assist one's neighbors has traditionally been followed closely by the fear that someone else might be less generous, and hence "their" poor might become the burden of one's own jurisdiction. In addition, unfamiliar poor people have typically been viewed with a stronger degree of moral suspicion.[52] The basic tenets of these beliefs were incorporated in the Elizabethan Poor Law of 1601 and the English Act of Settlement and Removal of 1662.[53] These laws established a tradition of organizing poor relief at the local level, and affirmed that poor people were the independent responsibility of each home parish. They were part of policies adopted by the earliest colonial settlements in America where strangers were "warned out" under suspicion of not being able to support themselves.[54] Similar beliefs motivated local attempts to exclude poor "strangers" in the U.S. colonies during the seventeenth and eighteenth centuries.[55]

Over time, the "newcomer" became a subject position in the law, marking the moral significance of community boundaries. In the nineteenth century, poor outsiders continued to be viewed with suspicion; and local communities continued to take legal action to bar them from receiving assistance. In *The Mayor of the City of New York v. Miln*, 11 Pet. 102 (1837), for example, the U.S. Supreme Court upheld the constitutionality of a state law prohibiting poor people from entering New York City, declaring it a reasonable measure to guard against "the moral pestilence of paupers."[56] Following the Civil War, pensions for northern (but not for southern) veterans once again grounded the moral standing for public assistance in the litmus test of residence.[57]

During the Great Depression, widespread poverty prompted a renewed interest in stemming the migration of poor people. In 1931, the California legislature instituted a three-year residency requirement for "pauper aid." In February 1936, the City of Los Angeles "became sufficiently desperate to send 150 police officers to state border crossings to turn back indigents."[58] This so-called "bum blockade" was politically popular but clearly illegal, as the American Civil Liberties Union effectively demonstrated in short order.

When the Social Security Act created a new set of federally administered social insurance programs in 1935, it left poor relief to the states. The lower tier of public assistance programs established in 1935 varied from state to state, encompassing a diversity of means tests, benefit levels, forms of surveillance, and disciplinary procedures. By contrast, the nationalization of social insurance provisions made local residence virtually irrelevant for a privileged class of beneficiaries (primarily white males with proven work histories), and thereby protected them from local efforts to limit relief and deter outsiders. As Linda Gordon notes, poverty programs administered at the state and local levels have remained "far more vulnerable to political attacks, declining tax bases and interstate competition. Imagine states trying to rid themselves of elderly residents by lowering Social Security old-age-pension benefits."[59]

Under the system created in 1935, poor people confronted a patchwork quilt of public assistance programs characterized by "length-of-residence requirements, pervasive invasion of privacy, and unregulated state discretion over eligibility conditions and the amounts of grants."[60] In the 1960s, however, the wide latitude afforded to the states under this system (and the resulting efforts to deter and discipline welfare recipients) became a target for "welfare rights" activists. Legal advocates won a series of landmark decisions that strengthened national standards for welfare provision. In *King v. Smith*, 392 U.S. 309 (1968), the Court struck down substitute father rules on the grounds that states could not establish their own criteria for making people ineligible unless authorized to do so by federal law. In *Shapiro v. Thompson*, 394 U.S. 618 (1969), the Court ruled that state durational residency requirements for the receipt of aid undermined the fundamental constitutional right to travel and in *Goldberg v. Kelly*, 397 U.S. 254 (1970), the justices ruled that welfare benefits could not be denied without first ensuring due process. The *Shapiro* decision is particularly noteworthy because it directly addressed the question of local obligations to poor outsiders. In its decision, the Supreme Court struck down forty state residency-requirement laws, ruling that states that imposed a one-year waiting period before allowing new residents to claim benefits penalized the constitutional right to interstate travel and thereby denied them equal protection under the law.[61]

In the wake of these legal decisions, until the mid-1970s U.S. welfare history was characterized by an ever-expanding trend toward national control: from local charity early in the country's history, to the federal provision of Civil War pensions to northern soldiers, to a national system of social insurance benefits, to the stronger enforcement of equal protection and national standards for public assistance. However, in the aftermath of the "new federalism" of the 1980s and the "devolution revolution" of the 1990s, such an account would seem naive and teleological. Indeed, in emphasizing the continuity of local control over poor relief in the U.S., it is important that we not lose sight of the fact that the 1996 legislation marked a critical reversal of the trend toward national standards for local administration.[62]

The 1996 legislation therefore institutionalized a two decade-long movement toward enhanced experimentation at the state and local levels—a movement that has been rationalized in part by the claims of some states that they need to discourage "newcomers" from receiving higher benefits.[63] Ironically, the desire to combat welfare migration now threatens to squander any potential for creativity promised by the new system, as states cut budgets to repel would-be migrants rather than serving as constructive "laboratories of democracy." Indeed, greater discretion has not only given states more latitude to act on their fears of poor migrants, but it has also made them more susceptible to demands to cut program budgets and related taxes.

Relative to the national government, states have traditionally been more vulnerable to economic pressures exerted by business mobility; and state policy makers are well aware of this.[64] As Frances Fox Piven and Richard Cloward have argued, "[I]n the twentieth century, it is the state governments that are more sensitive to business political pressures, simply because states (and localities) are far more vulnerable to the threat of disinvestment. This has been true for a long time."[65] Thus, even if the 1996 reforms have done nothing to reverse the potential for poor people to migrate in and businesses to migrate out, they seem likely to exacerbate policy makers' fears of falling out of line with other states. Instead of creative experimentation, such fears seem likely to encourage packlike behavior. In this manner, anxieties over migration that go back at least as far as the seventeenth century English poor laws continue to haunt American welfare reform at the end of the twentieth century, casting a pall over the prospect that states may serve as "laboratories of democracy" as they "race to the bottom" to cut back and avoid becoming "welfare magnets."

Without Cause or Effect

There is much irony in the prospect of states' using their new discretion to engage in packlike behavior. A good part of the irony stems from the fact that the variation between states in the real value of welfare benefits is not as great as it is believed to be, thus eliminating the primary rationale for welfare migration. Furthermore, given the lack of variation in the real value of welfare benefits, there is not much welfare migration to be found. Yet both benefit variation and welfare migration are treated as truisms in welfare policy circles, which allows the myth of welfare migration to cast a real pall over welfare reform.[66]

Empirical research on the question of whether welfare recipients migrate to states with higher benefits has provoked much debate. The earliest studies based on aggregate data suggested that welfare migration did not exist to any great degree.[67] A second wave of studies offered evidence that welfare migration might exist after all.[68] Writing in 1992 at the tail end of this wave, Robert Moffitt concluded a review of the welfare incentive literature by stating that the research on migration was "suggestive but inconclusive."[69] During the 1990s, however, a third wave of studies has provided a number of important critiques of earlier measurement techniques, and has consistently concluded that welfare migration is largely nonexistent.[70]

Welfare migration is not significant in part because the variation in benefit levels is overrated. Despite the discretion states always had to set AFDC benefits, it is simply not clear that the benefits offered under the old system varied enough to matter to recipients. Moreover, there is little evidence so far to suggest that states have responded to the new TANF block-grant system by dramatically revising their benefit schedules. In 1997, as in past years, most states left their benefit levels unchanged: three states raised benefits while six lowered them.[71] Thus, the structure of incentives assumed to bring about welfare migration has remained substantially the same in recent periods. Has this structure included enough benefit variation to motivate migration? The critical assumption underlying the powerful "welfare magnet" metaphor is that it has.

Analysts who study this problem tend to assume that there is wide variation in benefit levels across states because they generally assess benefits from what I have called a "top-down" managerial point of view that emphasizes the value of benefits in terms of their cost to government.[72] At most, benefits are adjusted for the variations in the cost of living index across states.[73] However, benefits should be assessed in terms of the real buying power they provide recipients, that is, in terms of the uses to which recipients put them, not some generic cost of living index that includes many things recipients cannot afford.

Food and housing expenses take up the bulk of the typical welfare family's budget.[74] After food stamps and some of the cash grant go toward food expenses, almost all the rest goes to pay for housing. If we adjust benefit levels for the variation in the cost of housing, we find that there is very little variation across states, thus making welfare migration economically irrational in most instances.[75] About two-thirds of each additional dollar the average recipient gets by moving to a higher benefit state is taken up in higher housing costs. In 1993 a family of three moving to a state one standard deviation higher in combined benefits would have received an average of $95.64 per month in additional income.[76] Additional housing costs would have eaten up an average of $66.18 of this income, leaving a net gain of $29.46 per month. In 1996, the average net gain produced by a similar move would have been only a little higher, at $42.24 per month.

To place even this small net gain in perspective, we must also consider research demonstrating that welfare checks rarely cover the cost of necessities, and that recipients must look to close kin, off-the-books employment, and elsewhere to cover additional expenses.[77] The reality is that recipients go broke everywhere; and the odds are slim that a recipient can change this outcome by moving to a state with higher benefits, given that such a move is likely to entail higher housing costs and the loss of informal kin support. Therefore, there is reason to doubt that there is much welfare migration and that benefit variation is the primary reason for it.

There are other reasons why benefits may not induce migration. Due to declines in the real-dollar value of cash benefits, the basic welfare package of cash assistance and food stamps now covers less than two-thirds of the average recipient family's expenditures.[78] As the gap between what recipients spend each month and what they get from government grows, so too does the amount of "slippage" in studies that measure the economic allure of a state by its welfare benefits. To the extent that welfare migration forces recipients to give up the informal networks of support they enjoy in their home communities,[79] higher benefits in a neighboring state may represent a lower overall income. Insofar as recipients cannot be sure what types of informal support might lie across the state border, welfare benefits are not likely to be a clear signal to a better standard of living. From a bottom-up perspective, welfare benefits are only part of the income mix, and they must be evaluated in that broader context.

Even if we focus only on those recipients who have decided they must leave their current locations, we must still ask whether recipients consider moving out of state in order to claim higher welfare benefits. It is astounding that in spite of all the research on this issue, very little of it addresses this specific question. Perhaps there is not much interstate migration for a very simple reason: it is not a salient option for recipients.[80] This possibility is strengthened by evidence that welfare recipients tend to identify strongly with their parental roles, and to base their welfare claiming decisions on the way these will affect their children.[81] In many cases, the life improvements that might accrue from interstate moves (such as living in a safer neighborhood or near better schools) can also be brought about by moving within a given state. Indeed, while welfare recipients do sometimes move from one community to another, more than 90 percent of their moves are within-state.[82]

The Uncertainty of State Rules

Given that interstate variation in the real value of benefits is small and that benefits constitute a declining proportion of the recipient family's budget, there are good reasons to believe that the relevant incentives for welfare recipients are *not* limited to benefits. Ironically, with all the discussion of state experimentation under the new TANF system, the possibility that variation in other features of state programs might negatively influence the likelihood of welfare migration has been virtually ignored. In sum, while welfare benefits may vary too little to induce migration, welfare administration may vary too much to present clear incentives to recipients.

While benefits do not vary sufficiently in real terms to encourage welfare migration, eligibility requirements have become so complex and can vary so widely that they create massive uncertainties, which discourage migration. Many a recipient who might want to move does not do so out of fear of the unknown and the prospect of poor treatment in the new state. The loss of exemptions from various requirements and access to additional benefits like housing vouchers in one's home state are the primary forms of variable treatment that recipients take into account when deciding not to move.

States must also confront this predicament now. Each state is at risk of being left behind in the race to use its new found discretion to tighten up; however, states cannot be too sure what the others are doing. Just tracking each other has become a full-time activity.[83] This increased discretion has been building for some time. Its origins predate the 1996 law. Since 1962, Section 1115 of the Social Security Act had authorized the Secretary of Health and Human Services to waive parts of the law in order to enable a state to initiate an experimental, pilot, or demonstration project that could help better realize the objectives of AFDC.[84] The Reagan and Bush administrations had liberal policies for granting waivers but continued the past practice of requiring cost neutrality, meaning a project could not lead to higher expenditures in any one year. The Clinton administration accelerated the waiver process and relaxed the cost neutrality rule by applying it over the life of the demonstration project instead of each year. Between January 1, 1992 and August 15, 1995, thirty-five states received fifty-three waivers to test AFDC changes. By May 1996, the Clinton administration had approved sixty-one waivers in thirty-eight states. Most waiver requests reflected one or more of the following assumptions about current AFDC rules: that they discourage work and encourage long-term enrollment; that they discourage marriage and encourage out-of-wedlock births; and that they fail to promote personal responsibility.

By mid-February 1996, all but ten states (Alaska, Idaho, Kansas, Kentucky, Maine, Nevada, New Hampshire, New Mexico, Rhode Island, and Tennessee) and the District of Columbia had federal approval to test departures from specified provisions of AFDC.[85] Many projects have required multiple waivers. Some states had received approval to operate some or all demonstration components statewide; but many waivers are limited to selected areas. AFDC waiver projects can be classified broadly as restricting or liberalizing some elements of the program.[86] Restrictive ones include:

- time limits on benefit duration (twenty-four states);
- stricter work requirements (thirty-one states);
- linking benefits to school attendance and/or performance (twenty-six states);
- limiting benefits for additional children (fourteen states);

- reducing benefits based on relocation (two states);
- requiring fingerprinting as a condition of eligibility (one state).

Liberalizing projects include:

- treating earnings more generously (thirty states);
- expanding eligibility for unemployed two-parent families (twenty-five states);
- increasing the resource limit (twenty-eight states);
- increasing the vehicle asset limit (twenty-five states);
- expanding transitional medical and child care benefits (twenty-one states).

States can continue to operate programs established by waivers under the 1996 law though they must meet its work quotas. Of the forty-three states with waivers in place when the new law was signed, thirty continued them in 1997, nineteen on a statewide basis.[87] These waivers undoubtedly complicate the picture of state variation, making it harder for recipients to know how their situation would change should they move to another state. Even without waivers, the list of eligibility standards has been long and growing, making welfare migration less likely and interstate competition more uncertain.

Devolution Deconstructs: The Irony of Welfare Reform

There may be no real welfare migration because there is not enough benefit variation and too much rule variation. Yet states still act as if welfare migration were real. Fifteen states had used their discretion under welfare reform to enact laws to set up different eligibility standards for welfare applicants who have lived in their current state of residence for less than twelve months.[88] This could be a sign that states had engaged in misguided policy making based on bad information. Or perhaps states were beginning to appreciate how ironic welfare reform really is.

With the Supreme Court invalidating lower benefits for newcomers, states may now have even greater incentives to tighten up and make welfare less attractive. With a block grant, they receive funding at set levels and can ill afford to take on additional recipients above previous levels. States are already required to tighten up in order to create incentives for people to move from welfare to work so that federal work quotas will be met. And now, states may feel additional competitive pressures to follow the others in cutting back to avoid the prospect of becoming a welfare magnet that picks up those denied welfare in other states. Welfare reform therefore can be said to deconstruct itself, stifling the state innovation it calls for.

Even without the Court's decision, the 1996 law adds many important opportunities for states to use their discretion in ways that ironically engender more fear of welfare migration. As states put themselves under more pressure to use their discretion only to tighten up and make their programs less attractive, they may force other states to do the same. At that point they enter into a vicious cycle. Reform sets a downward spiral in motion, whereby state discretion to restrict access to welfare exerts pressure on other states to do the same, each use of discretion making welfare reform less discretionary as states feel they cannot act in ways contrary to what the others are doing without the risk of becoming a welfare magnet.

Several progressive features of existing welfare systems are particularly vulnerable. The length of state assistance to two-parent families who are needy because of the unemployment of the principal wage earner continues to vary. Since September 30, 1998, states have been freed to stop such aid altogether if they so chose, thereby returning to the flexibility they had before the Family Support Act of 1998 required them to offer assistance to two-parent families for at least six months in a year.[89]

Other categories of eligibility have also been affected. States must deny aid to parents under eighteen unless they live in an "adult supervised setting" with their parents, guardian, or adult relative, or in a "supportive living arrangement" such as a "maternity home" or "second chance home." But, states have some latitude in determining exemptions.[90] States have been free to deny aid to persons who had been convicted of drug felonies after August 22, 1996. In 1997, thirty-three states said they would do so. Only eight states chose to require drug testing, but one of them was New York, which has a large share of the country's welfare population.[91] It is likely that these various eligibility standards will face competitive pressures.

States also have greater latitude now than previously in setting conditions for the redetermination of eligibility for the continued receipt of aid. In the past states could set conditions such as work requirements. In addition to workfare requirements, in the 1990s states added conditions such as learnfare which requires children to remain in school, as well as other "fares." Now they can specify all those conditions and more. States can choose to require recipients to sign "Individual Responsibility Plans" describing how they will make the transition from welfare to work. Recipients can be penalized for not fulfilling the provisions of their plans. Twenty-one states have added the "family cap" which does not condition aid but does deny additional aid to a child born while the mother is on public assistance.[92] Again, discretion will arguably be squandered in a competition of restrictiveness.

The federal government will not allow the use of federal TANF funds for any recipient who has received assistance beyond two years without participation in "work-related activities"; however, states can set stricter limits. Twenty-six have, with thirteen requiring work immediately as a condition of receiving aid. The federal government will not allow the use of federal TANF funds to provide aid to a family that has a recipient that has already received aid for five years in his or her lifetime. New York and California have decided to provide limited aid beyond five years, but states can specify stricter time limits and twenty-one have, with twelve specifying a two-year lifetime limit. Fifteen of the states with shorter lifetime limits than the federal limit also have stricter work requirements.[93]

States have also differed from one another regarding the fulfillment of work requirements, with some states emphasizing education and others immediate placement in paid employment with little opportunity for education and training.[94] Under the 1996 law, only one year of education or training can count as fulfilling the requirement regarding participation in work-related activities. States can choose to finance benefits for recipients who do not meet these requirements, such as students in their second year of post-secondary education. Yet by 1997 only Maine had chosen to do so, and by early 1999 only a few other states were making similar efforts.[95]

On the issue of work requirements, it is important to add that child care provisions for recipients who are required to work have always varied across states.[96] This variation is likely to increase further now that child care is no longer guaranteed. While states must exempt recipients who cannot find child care from participation in work-related activities, recipients are not exempted from the five-year ban, regardless of the availability of child care. Given that many welfare recipients combine welfare and work for part of their time on public assistance and that approximately 60 percent of those on the rolls have worked at some point in time in the past two years, the availability of quality child care has always been an important consideration for many welfare recipients.[97] Now its importance will augment even further as recipients plan to leave welfare within five years and need access to child care along the way as they prepare for paid employment.

The issue of exemption from various requirements is important and is likely to continue to be. States can exempt up to 20 percent of their caseloads from time limits and can vary the way they allocate these exemptions. For instance, states can exempt parents whose children are below a certain age. States can implement the Domestic Violence Option as part of this and exempt women at risk of battering and abuse. In 1999 thirty-one states adopted this exemption. Medical disability is a work exemption in thirty-three states; mental health problems in thirty states; and AIDS in twenty-six states.[98]

It seems likely that this new intergovernmental system of welfare provision will continue to foster some of the conditions that undercut welfare migration. The greater latitude given to states in deciding how to provide welfare seems likely to leave clients feeling even more uncertain regarding their eligibility for benefits in a new state. At the same time, however, people eliminated from the rolls or "diverted" from receiving assistance in the first place will have an increased incentive to migrate. Therefore states now confront competitive pressures that make them unlikely to offer more generous amounts of assistance. Benefit levels are likely to vary even less in the future than they do now. In fact, under the new system of block grants, states have stronger incentives not to raise benefits and instead to "race to the bottom," settling in alongside one another at progressively lower benefit levels.

Conclusion

There is an ironic twist to the alleged "devolution revolution." Welfare reform has granted states an ambivalent discretion, one that suggests that devolution deconstructs itself. In the context of fears of welfare migration, the greater latitude given to states may actually discourage experimentation. With a bold stroke, devolution was supposed to create fifty laboratories of democracy in which state policy makers acted independently and innovatively to devise their own programs to meet the needs of public assistance recipients. Instead, devolution may have sown the seeds of conformism. All across the country, welfare reform has led to massive purges of recipients. State policy makers have made it clear that they want to avoid becoming "welfare magnets." As a result, they seem most likely to follow the pack—to use their new found discretion defensively to avoid becoming more liberal than other states. Unsure of the new federal regime, states find emulation, not innovation, is the name of the new game.

Yet the race to the bottom may no longer be about benefit levels, as previously assumed. Now it very well may be over who can impose the greatest number of restrictions and sanctions.[99] Under the new mandates, each state is keen to impose restrictions on access to assistance; this in turn may spur other states to respond in kind. For instance, the federal government will not finance benefits for a recipient if she is not working after two years. Similarly, the federal government will not finance welfare benefits if a person has received benefits for a day over five years in her lifetime. These mandates obviously make it costly for any state to exhibit "too much" generosity in providing benefits. The ironies of devolution not only double back on themselves—not only does devolution get squandered in a preoccupation with federal restrictions. By allowing states to impose even stricter requirements of their own, these mandates also push states toward an even faster, more defensive race to the bottom. State policy makers may now perceive themselves as being at risk if they do not follow other states either in adhering to federal standards or in creating tougher ones. In this manner, the new state-level discretion over time limits and work requirements encourages a spiral of escalating restrictions.

In particular, with the court once again striking down residency requirements, states need to guard against recipients who have exhausted their benefits in one state moving to another less restrictive state where they can still get benefits under the national five-year lifetime limit. This is no nightmare of some imagined dystopian future. Under the conditions created by welfare reform this is a real fear in the here and now. Already in 1997, twenty-seven states required work before twenty-four months were out; and twenty-one states limited the receipt of welfare to four years or less.[100]

While evidence for welfare migration is scarce, states continue to fear it. And they now have a welfare system that, like water, can seek its lowest level. Although one can never make predictions with certainty, the incentives of the new system and fears of welfare migration combine to make it highly likely that the states will drift toward lower benefits, shorter time limits, and stricter work requirements. The net result may be analogous to a cat chasing its tail.

But as states reshuffle themselves to the bottom, they may actually create the very welfare migration they fear. While recipients confronting benefit differences might not have had sufficiently strong incentives to migrate in the past, the case will be different for those who are barred from welfare participation in their current state of residence. Thus, states that move expeditiously to tighten time limits and work requirements may force poor people to flee to other states out of sheer necessity.[101] This may actually increase now that the U.S. Supreme Court has invalidated the option to require newcomers to receive the benefit of their prior state of residence. Without the two-tier benefit schedules in place, states may feel compelled to cut back further in order to keep the dreaded welfare migrants away. Such actions may amount to taking a myth so seriously that it becomes real. Welfare migration has probably been no more than a ghost haunting welfare reform in the past. But if that ghost succeeds in generating a race to the bottom, it may create a class of impoverished welfare migrants that is very real.

5

Redefining the Family, Redefining the State

The Politics of Incorporation and the Case of Same-Sex Marriage

The Personal Responsibility and Work Opportunity Reconciliation Act of 1996 is not the only example of the way the conservatives' "devolution revolution" in social policy deconstructs itself. The homophobic Defense of Marriage Act of 1996 (DOMA) was another. It was an ironic assertion of national power allegedly designed to protect states' rights. Proponents of the law claimed that Congress was acting to preserve each state's autonomy to decide which marriages it would recognize. Yet in the process Congress undermined the authority of states in the intergovernmental system. While disallowing same-sex marriages, Congress made the intergovernmental system a little less collaborative. Proponents claimed that DOMA was protecting state autonomy by allowing states not to have to recognize same-sex marriages from other states; however, the law did this in a way that simultaneously weakened the role of states in matters of social policy that have traditionally been reserved to them.

The sad and short history of DOMA underscores how otherness can be a critical issue in the intergovernmental system of social policy. In the following chapter, I examine how the homophobia of DOMA was facilitated by the xenophobia of federalism. DOMA was originally prompted by the possibility that the Supreme Court of the State of Hawai'i was about to legalize same-sex marriages. Same-sex marriage may have started as a local issue in faraway Hawai'i but it ended up with Congress and the president saying they were against it. As a result, federal legislation has defined marriage for purposes of federal law as limited to unions between a man and a woman, preempted state powers to define marriages for purposes of federal law, and interfered with the process by which one state recognizes the marriages of another. In the end, after intense political debate and extensive campaigning by fundamentalist groups from outside the state, the voters of the state of Hawai'i passed a constitutional amendment limiting marriage to a man and a woman and the state legislature enacted a limited domestic partnership law.[1]

In this chapter, I argue that in addition to the rights of gays and lesbians, DOMA raises the issue of how the family is the assumed basis for social policy. In the process, the question of same sex marriage has highlighted the problem of federalism. The analysis below details how in both cases a politics of metaphors is at work to decide the terms of effective participation in the public sphere. I suggest that this use of metaphors reflects a "politics of incorporation" whereby marginalized persons or places are shown to be not really different from those that are legitimated. This politics of incorporation uses what J. M. Balkin calls "cultural software."[2] Cultural software refers to the way ideology articulates affinities between the familiar and the unknown by using existing metaphors and models available in society. This ideological process makes ostensibly different things alike. In fact classic civil rights strategy has been to use the available "cultural software" so that the marginalized are incorporated into the public sphere by showing how they are not really different from those who have already been included. In what follows, I consider the advantages and disadvantages for using the available "cultural software" to play with the existing categories of marriage and state in order to execute a "politics of incorporation" on behalf of gay rights.

The Family Hour

Welfare is not the only social policy that reflects anxiety about the family as a fundamental site for reproducing the orders of entitlement and the terms of inclusion in the existing political economy. Case in point: in the summer of 1996, while welfare reform was being debated, the national government enacted the Defense of Marriage Act of 1996 (DOMA). Before he joined the leadership of the House in insisting on the impeachment of President Clinton, representative Bob Barr (R-GA) sponsored the Defense of Marriage Act, he said, because it represented a historic attempt to protect "the very foundation of society—the family unit."[3] For the first time in the history of the federal government, DOMA provides a national definition of marriage for purposes of federal law and limits marriage to a heterosexual union between a man and a woman. This national definition at least partially preempts state governments' authority to specify which marriages ought to be recognized. Further, while DOMA also allows state governments the option of not recognizing same-sex marriages solemnized in other states, it does this in a way that inappropriately interferes with the process by which one state recognizes the marriages of another state. Therefore, DOMA is about states' rights as well as family values.

In fact, DOMA protects conservative family values at the expense of conservative states' rights. The federal legislation arose in response to the possibility that the Supreme Court of the State of Hawai'i was about to legalize same-sex marriage on the grounds that the equal protection clause of the state's Constitution prohibited discrimination based on sex and the state therefore could not deny marriage licenses to same-sex couples.[4] While this ruling pertains strictly to the offshore State of Hawai'i and its Constitution, undoubtedly this case did and still does have legal implications for the entire country regarding the extent to which the federal government can intervene in a state's power to license marriages. Alternatively, the case also raises the possibility that the U.S. Constitution's own equal protection clause may imply that people have the right to enter into a same-sex marriage irrespective of state constitutions and laws.[5]

Therefore, while DOMA may have sacrificed states' rights for family values, it also demonstrates that the struggles over one are bound to affect those over the other. The metaphors at work in the politics over DOMA have yet to establish that a gay marriage is like any other marriage. They may also be undermining the effectiveness of states in the intergovernmental system. However, as the following analysis suggests, the metaphors of politics are never final and their fluidity can help promote the classic, if risky, civil rights strategy of incorporation whereby the marginal can be incorporated as legitimate members of the public sphere by showing that they are not really different from what has already been included.

Why Same-Sex Marriage Is Like Any Other Marriage: An Issue of Federalism

The politics of metaphorics starts when one thing stands in for another.[6] We may ask: when is same-sex marriage not a marriage? When is it a partnership? When it is a partnership, it seems it is always, in heterosexual terms, a limited partnership. It is a limited partnership whose exclusivity is not prized for it is a barren, childless, nonfunctioning procreative partnership. Therefore, according to heterosexist discourse, it cannot be a nurturing family entitled to be solemnized as a real marriage, enfranchised as an agent of the state, and entitled to its benefits by virtue of fulfilling the obligations of families that the state expects to be fulfilled.[7]

The Defense of Marriage Act not only announces the national political leadership's willingness to accept this cramped understanding of marriage and to support discrimination against gays and lesbians, but it also represents the government's desire to preserve the hegemony of the traditional family. To be sure, DOMA reflects the state's growing need to resuscitate its origins in the traditional heterosexual family in order to legitimate itself and its social policies even as the traditional family is fading fast. The welfare state—including most especially the largest part, namely, Social Security pensions, as well as the wage structure and so much else in the existing political economy—is still premised on the never realizable and now thoroughly anachronistic system that assumes that the modal family had a homemaker who was supported by a breadwinner who earned a wage sufficient to support a family.[8] Social welfare entitlements, wages, and other material benefits in the existing political economy only make sense if the traditional two-parent family is assumed to be normative. And just as the welfare state and the political economy more generally are premised on the traditional family, the traditional family is dependent for its well-being on the wage structure and the benefits systems, both public and private, social welfare and other. Gay marriage threatens not only heterosexual hegemony; it also threatens the underlying, if increasingly unsustainable, ideal that the state should help structure the economy to be consistent with this family-wage/breadwinner system. The strains intensify as traditional families function less and less effectively and as alternative family arrangements proliferate in response to changing social mores and increased economic pressures.

DOMA protects the family-wage/breadwinner system by excluding same-sex marriage from its definition of marriage for the purpose of securing federal benefits. Heterosexual hegemony and the family-wage system are sustained in law even as they become decreasingly sustainable in practice. In law, same-sex marriage is not like any other marriage; it is denied its metaphorical performance and as such excluded from the realm of entitled marriages. Such symbolic enactments have real material consequences— only certain marriages are deemed to be real and consequently only some partners qualify for benefits, social welfare or fringe, public or private. The politics of metaphorics informs critical practices of the contemporary welfare state.

Apart from disentitling same-sex couples, by defining marriage for federal law DOMA also deprives states of a role they previously had, which was to determine which marriages got to count as real marriages not just for their state laws but for federal ones as well.[9] However, DOMA goes further in taking power from the states. It also paradoxically affirms state power in a way that undermines it by specifying that state governments are not required to extend "full faith and credit" as specified by Article IV of the United States Constitution to other states' laws if those laws legalize gay marriages.

In fact DOMA has a complicated relationship to the "Full Faith and Credit Clause" (Article IV of the Constitution). As Hawai'i had moved closer to legalizing same-sex marriages, a rapidly growing number of states used what case law calls the "public policy exemption" regarding Article IV to pass legislation stating that they will not recognize gay marriages solemnized in Hawai'i or any other state. The "public policy exemption" implies that the receiving state does not have to extend "full faith and credit" to the laws of the sending state if the sending state's laws violate good public policy in the receiving state. Whether the receiving state can use the "public policy exemption" and not accord full faith and credit to the laws of the sending state cannot really be known in advance for an issue like same-sex marriage and must ultimately be decided in federal court.[10]

On one level, DOMA embraces the "public policy exemption" for it seemingly supports the idea that states should decide whether they want to extend full faith and credit to the same-sex marriages of other states. On another level, DOMA does not leave the issue of interstate recognition of same-sex marriages to be arbitrated between states in federal court. Instead, DOMA uses another part of the Full Faith and Credit Clause to assert a role for Congress to free states from having to accept the same-sex marriages of other states even before court arbitration has determined whether this is an appropriate use of the public policy exemption. The Clinton administration's Justice Department issued an advisory opinion during the debates over the legislation indicating that DOMA was consistent with the Full Faith and Credit Clause where it states that "Congress may by general Laws prescribe the Manner in which such Acts shall be proved, and the Effect thereof."[11] But it remains to be seen whether the United States Supreme Court in the future will agree that DOMA does not exceed such prescribing power, especially since DOMA has decided ahead of time (before court arbitration) that states can use the public policy exemption if they want not to recognize the same-sex marriages solemnized in other states.

The Defense of Marriage Act therefore represents a centralization of power in the United States Congress. Ironically it was passed at a time when Congress had pushed for a "devolution revolution" in welfare.[12] But the politics of this reverse action can be understood from a variety of perspectives. Beyond facile election-year posturing or more genuine commitment to family values, there is the use of federalism to win on an issue like same-sex marriage. E. E. Schattschneider once pointed out that some issues, such as civil rights, were moved from the state to the national level by expanding political conflict, a process he called "the socialization of conflict," to give them the appearance of relevance to additional groups of potential supporters. Alternatively, the "privatization of conflict" was pursued by states' rightists when they tried to move issues from national to state levels and reduce the relevance of an issue, such as voting rights, to these additional groups. Schattschneider wrote:

> The attempt to control the scope of the conflict has a bearing on federal-state-local relations, for one way to restrict the scope of conflict is to localize it, while one way to expand it is to nationalize it. One of the most remarkable developments in recent American politics is the extent to which the federal, state and local governments have become involved in doing the same kinds of things in large areas of public policy, so that it is possible for contestants to move freely from one level of government to another in an attempt to find the level at which they might try most advantageously to get what they want. This development has opened up vast new areas of the politics of scope. It follows that debates about federalism, local self-government, centralization and decentralization are actually controversies about the scale of conflict.[13]

For Schattschneider, federalism is about regulating conflict, framing issues, aligning coalitions, and winning power to decide public policy. Moving issues up or down the intergovernmental system can shift the advantage from one side to the other. There is reason to believe that moving the same-sex marriage issue to the national level in the 1990s has made it harder for advocates for gay marriage to win their cause. In this regard the gay and lesbian rights movements are currently different from the civil rights movement of the 1960s. The former have been successful at the state level, which success is being overturned at the national level. In the 1960s, the civil rights movement's major successes came from the national government overturning the resistance to it at the state level. But just as Congress was beginning to move to a vote on DOMA, the United States Supreme Court overturned Colorado's state ban on local civil rights legislation for gays, making the shift in levels more complicated.[14] The more critical shift therefore may be from the courts to Congress. In this regard the gay and lesbian rights movements have a parallel in the civil rights movement. Both initially had greater success in the courts than in Congress. For now, in the 1990s Congress remains more hostile to gay and lesbian rights than it was toward civil rights in the 1960s.

The Defense of Marriage Act was drafted in response to a Hawai'i State Supreme Court case, *Baehr v. Meike*. The Hawai'i Supreme Court had remanded this case to a lower court to decide, in the face of inaction by the Hawai'i State Legislature, why a state statute prohibiting same-sex marriages was not in violation of the Hawaiian State Constitution's equal protection clause.[15] With three same-sex marriages about to be solemnized in Hawaiian state law, Congress, with the backing of President Clinton, moved to define marriage as a heterosexual union for the purposes of federal law and allowed state governments not to recognize the gay and lesbian marriages of other states.[16] In the process, not only has same-sex marriage been undermined nationwide, but so has Hawaii's effectiveness in having its laws recognized by other states.

Therefore, apart from same-sex marriage, the distinctive indigenous Hawaiian sense of *'ohana* (community as family) and the Hawaiian state's otherness more generally become an issue for the entire nation.[17] Throughout the congressional debates over DOMA, representatives from mainland states repeatedly asked in effect why unelected judges from a far away island state should be allowed to decide what is a marriage for the American people.[18]

Why Hawai'i Is a State Like Any Other State: An Issue of Marriage

Even before it acquired statehood, Hawai'i was a potential source of alternatives to mainland social practices and policies.[19] With statehood, however, its differences—its social welfare liberalism, its nonwhite majority population, its multiculturalism, its miscegenation, its postcolonial status, its isolation, and other features—have made it suspect as a credible actor within the constitutional system.[20]

The suspicion has a variety of sources. First, Hawai'i has its own unique history of racism as a U.S. territory violently taken from the nonwhite indigenous population in 1893 and annexed in 1898 after President Cleveland, who opposed these developments, left office.[21] Second, almost two centuries of rampant economic imperialism and unabashed racism by mainlanders and other *haoles* (whites or foreigners) eventually generated relatively successful resistance in an ethnically diverse but united working class.[22] Third, there are its still remembered, if long subordinated Polynesian, Micronesian, and Asian subcultures with different social practices from those that dominate the mainland states,[23] including most especially the indigenous Hawaiian idea of *pono* (implying a collective well-being that comes from everything being as it should be).[24] Fourth, the Japanese had for a time made extremely high levels of capital investment in Hawaiian tourism, banking, and other commercial fields.[25] Fifth, the continuing and pervasive presence of the U.S. military makes for a subeconomy that is distinctively tied to the military-industrial complex.[26] Sixth, relatively liberal welfare and health policies add further to the othering of Hawai'i as a suspect state.[27] Seventh, a revitalized sovereignty movement of indigenous Hawaiians that is not entirely without state government support is making calls for a variety of actions ranging from the settling of claims to expropriated lands to some form of sovereignty association (or a "nation-within-a-nation") to the outright ending of statehood.[28] And last, there is the gnawing fear of an "other" culture that might infect the mainland with its alternative values and social practices.[29]

For these reasons and others, Hawai'i is a potentially suspect actor in the intergovernmental sphere, representing a people of different identities and circumstances, "other" than those prized by the people in power in the other forty-nine states. Legally, it is a state government but politically it may not always be entirely so in terms of its laws receiving the "full faith and credit" of other state governments. Hawaii's status as a state government has been challenged in the process of challenging gay marriage. At risk is Hawaii's statehood in the realm of the interstate. Hawaii's most populous island, Oahu, incongruously has an "interstate" highway (H-1) that stops at the water's edge. Hawaii's interstate relations regarding marriages are similarly suspect.

However, as the preceding narrative implicitly suggests, Hawaii's potentially suspect status applies to all state governments whose effectiveness in the intergovernmental system is determined by politics as much as it is by law. The political viability of states is contingent upon how they negotiate the ineliminable paradoxes of intergovernmental discourse. I say "negotiate" rather than "resolve" because in intergovernmental discourse, the status of states, like the status of anything in any discourse, is ultimately undecidable. The effectiveness of all state governments in the intergovernmental system is enhanced by living with, rather than resisting, what Homi Bhabha has called "the anxiety of signification,"[30] that is, the tension of being in between competing representations. For Bhabha, the anxiety of signification is an unavoidable feature of all discourse because every discourse relies on competing representations to categorize its subject, though these representations inevitably do an injustice to its complexities.

In intergovernmental discourse, the relevant competing representations are: (1) state governments as autonomous state governments with "states' rights" to do things, such as solemnizing marriages or administering welfare programs, in their own way; and (2) state governments as "state partners in a broader federal system" in which they accept devolved responsibilities, function as experimental laboratories for the entire system, and delimit their autonomy in order to perform their role as part of the federal-state relationship. This metaphoric anxiety suggests that each state must continually traverse the relay between autonomous-state government with states' rights and partner-state government with responsibilities for federal collaboration.

Slavoj Žižek might say that this is the uncertainty principle of interstate government.[31] According to the Heisenberg uncertainty principle, in the rarefied world of quantum mechanics we cannot simultaneously establish the velocity and location of a particle wave. It is as if its "identity" must remain undecidable. The same could be said of all identities, including states as actors within the system of intergovernmental relations. We can never know anything as a thing-in-itself except through our own interventions, which artificially impose a stabilized identity on what is in flux. For Žižek, this is not just a problem of epistemology but also a problem of ontology. Not only may things as such be knowable only in terms of some artificially imposed identity, but things in discrete form may not exist except in the inverted form of their opposite—that is, the duality marks their undecidability.

The stabilized state that gives any "thing" its identity is a place holder, a cutout, a cipher that marks the real absence of the thing to which is referred. Rather than a real identifiable thing out there, there is a stabilized identification that points to a process of becoming. Particles, people, states, whatever, are stabilized identities that point to processes at work, performances that are enacted. The work of these processes is to achieve an effect by oscillating between contrasting poles so that a principle of "complementarity" is initiated. However, complementarity here is not so much the place where the poles reinforce each other as it is the place where their mutual exclusivity requires continual work to be one and then the other—that is, to oscillate between them. Ironically, a "thing" therefore gets to be a thing only by resisting stabilization in one or other artificially imposed identity and by oscillating between the mutually exclusive poles that are used to identify it. Effective statehood, for instance, is achieved by resisting total adherence to either pole—both autonomy and partnership. Relative to the way intergovernmental discourse allocates the proportions at any one point in time, too much emphasis on either states' rights or federal partnership causes a state government's effectiveness in the intergovernmental system to be diminished.

Negotiating the paradoxes also implies accepting irony. Autonomous state governments get to exercise states' rights by being partners in a federal system, and state governments fulfill their role as partners in the federal system by exercising their capacity for independent action. All state governments must constantly reconstruct their statehood in intergovernmental discourse by practicing the quantum mechanics of interstate relations and living in the in between, thereby accepting the anxiety of signification that statehood implies. And to be constructed in discourse is to be actualized in practice, for discourse implies more here than a language or system of representation. Rather, it is a way in which practice is constituted.[32] Any state government can be a state government in name or theory; however, to be a state government effectually in practice or discourse, it has to do the iterative work necessary to legitimate itself.[33]

Therefore, Hawai'i is a state like any other and it gets to be so both by reiterating its partnership in the federal system and by claiming its autonomy. Hawai'i can propose a welfare reform program of its own to the federal government, it can even call it PONO, as in fact it has. Yet PONO here, in another act of misappropriation of this key Hawaiian term, means Pursuit of New Opportunities, and the program has nothing to do with the distinctive Hawaiian tradition of *pono* and its implied sense of collective well-being. Indeed, the PONO program is no different from other recent welfare reform initiatives, with its emphasis on cutbacks and time limits.[34] And given intergovernmental discourse, this is to be expected. If there is too much Hawaiian distinctiveness, whether it stems from indigenous traditions or not, Hawaii's welfare program will be rejected by the federal government and not all Hawaiian marriages will receive full faith and credit from other states.[35]

In fact, DOMA underscores the codependency between federal and state governments in the intergovernmental system. With DOMA, the federal government intervenes to usurp some state power in order to preserve other state powers, most prominently the right of states not to have to extend full faith and credit to other states and recognize their gay marriages. Of course, the federal government itself has been a vexed entity historically in intergovernmental discourse and its powers have been hotly contested in constitutional law. For some, as most famously proclaimed by Ronald Reagan at his 1981 presidential inauguration, it is a creature of the states created for the purpose of fulfilling their compact as a union. But for others, such as Abraham Lincoln, it was created by "We the People" before states even existed and therefore it is above them.[36] The federal government's identity needs to be constantly recreated first as federal, then as national. It is both representative of the federal system and a supreme partner within it. Thus the federal government as a national government or the national government as a federal one has historically been profoundly ambiguous in intergovernmental discourse and subject to continual reassessment in constitutional law. Yet, contrary to popular protests by southern politicians in the 1950s or even numerous political leaders and scholars in the 1990s, federal (that is, national) power is often used to sustain states' rights in the federal-state system.[37] That system has always been one where the exercise of national power can both supplement and delimit state power.[38]

Therefore, while DOMA is primarily about same-sex marriage, it is also about the power of states in the intergovernmental system. The act requires opponents of same-sex marriage to articulate the silent implicit biases which provided a basis for their ability to use federal power to deny gays and lesbians the rights that others gain from marriage. In the process, the liberal contractual order must put its secrets at risk, as its contrivances about family, state, and their relationships are made explicit. Despite desperate attempts to maintain the existing system, its biases in favor of the state and heterosexual family become more visible and more clearly vulnerable to contestation.

At this point, we have the opportunity to reconsider both the powers of states and the rights of marriage by being attentive to their contingent character. Under such scrutiny, state governments can explicitly recognize their own contingent character—culturally, socially, politically, and legally. All state governments, for instance, can begin to face up to their colonization of indigenous peoples. State governments can examine their own violent origins, legitimated by constitutional foundations operating as post hoc rationalizations, and see that these rationalizations are constantly in need of reiteration and even revision to counter the claims to legitimacy made by excluded groups. Then all state governments will be able to see that their sovereignty is contingent upon denying the sovereignty of others, and can decide how to address these counterclaims to sovereignty (see Figure 3).[39] From this perspective, we can see how state sovereignty is constantly in need of re-creation in the face of the legacy of the appropriation of tribal land. As Frank Pommersheim, the noted Indian Law scholar, has put it: "[Tribes and states] stand as mutual sovereigns which share contiguous physical areas and some common citizens—tribal members who reside on the reservation are both tribal members and state citizens, while non-Indian residents of the reservation are state citizens but not tribal citizens."[40] And with similar questioning about its authorizing foundations, marriage might be legitimated on grounds other than procreation. Over the long haul, therefore, all marriages face the prospect of being freed from the confines of family discourse, just as all states can be legitimated on grounds other than the contrivances of contractual and federal discourses.

The Politics of Incorporation

Every hegemonic order incorporates marginal groups by making concessions which convey the message that the dominant order serves their interests.[41] Both the "core" and the "periphery" (to borrow some metaphors) are therefore at risk of being changed by such a politics of incorporation. Marginal elements are at risk of being co-opted. Hawai'i may be permitted to be an effective participant in the intergovernmental system, but then it must, as it already does, work within the limitations of that system. Same-sex marriages may win recognition as valid marriages but they must work within the confines of the family-wage/breadwinner system. Nonetheless, this process suggests that both intergovernmental and family relations may also be changed in response.

As an act of verisimilitude, as a metaphorics of politics, same-sex marriage reflects the classic civil rights strategy of saying that someone's marginal identity is like an established one. The gay marriage strategy therefore employs a metaphorics that has been known for a long time, if by more "agentistic" names, as a classic civil rights strategy of incorporation. Incorporation resonates with the use of the Fifth and Fourteenth Amendments to incorporate the protections against national power in the former into the equal protection clause of the latter, and thereby extend civil rights protections to counter state-government sanctioned discrimination. How-

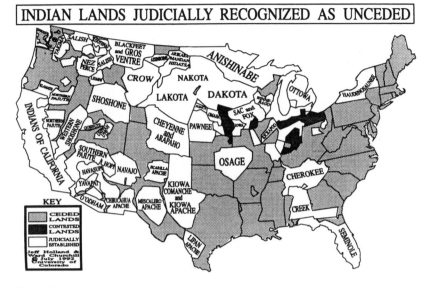

INDIAN LANDS JUDICIALLY RECOGNIZED AS UNCEDED

Figure 3.

ever, in political rather than legal terminology incorporation means that gay and lesbian partnerships must be constructed as a family in order to be legitimated as deserving of the same rights as other families. Incorporation implies both intergovernmental and intermarriage equivalencies.

While the entitlements of marriage may eventually flow to gay partners, this may be at the expense of the possibility of grounding entitlements outside the family. Perhaps it ought not to be tied to a particular social formation with its own selective reading of who we are and how we form families in order to prove our self-worth in the eyes of the welfare state. However, gay and lesbian rights for now will in all likelihood be extended in accordance with the incorporation strategy articulated in the idiom of the family. If this is the case, we need to be alert to how "family" has justified many exclusions and legitimated a variety of forms of violence.[42]

Such are the risks of the "politics of incorporation" and its uses of metaphor. The "politics of incorporation" uses the "cultural software" of available models and metaphors to show that the different is very much like the familiar.[43] Difference is respected but similarity is recognized. Similarity is appreciated but difference is not denied. The "politics of incorporation" allows for a balancing of sameness and difference. This balancing of sameness and difference serves as the ground for a contractual morality in which mutual obligation is founded on an implied identity of people who have the particular attributes, capacities, and needs associated with the modal type of the promising sovereign self who makes the liberal order possible. Gays and lesbians cannot have rights as gays, or as others, or as just plain people. Gays and lesbians have rights to the extent that they conform to the implied identity of contractual society. The politics of incorporation, balancing sameness and difference, evaluates gay partners as married couples. These would be the terms under which same-sex couples would be legitimated as entitled beneficiaries deserving of the same rights as other couples. Some conservative gays in particular and others as well have championed this strategy as a way "that has been able to show straight America that 'we're just like you.'"[44]

These are terms of incorporation which make for inclusion in the public sphere. The public sphere itself is an imagined space in which we place those things that might be the focus of political action and public policy making. It is an imagined contractual realm where we think about our public commitments as if they were contracts. In their own way both John Rawls and Jürgen Habermas have called for some regulative function that structures our participation in these matters as if it were "an original position" or "an ideal speech act."[45] Here politics is not even possible until we equate our quotidian practices with some other idealized activity. Inevitably, political participation is grounded in reenacting likeness. Nothing is possible—not even politics—until we accept the metaphorics of practice. A same-sex partnership must be shown to be like something else. Nothing can be given an entrée in to the public sphere on its own terms alone. It must be translatable. Thus, politics begins when we seek to defend or resist this practice of iterability, when we affirm or deny which families are really families.

In fact, the politics of incorporation may not be as conservative as is assumed. Slavoj Žižek suggests that the advocates for traditional family values stand to lose the argument that gays are irredeemably promiscuous if same-sex marriage is approved. Žižek argues that this is yet another way in which the dominant discourse can be "undermined from within":

> Strictly analogous is the relationship between the horrible content (wild promiscuity) behind the sublime mask of marriage and *same-sex marriage,* this traumatic point, the ultimate *bête noire,* of the Moral Majority. That is to say, why is same-sex marriage so traumatic for the Moral Majority attitude?

Because it disturbs the premise according to which homosexuals, seeking only quick promiscuous pleasures, are unable to engage in a profound personal relationship—the uncanny proximity of same-sex marriage to "straight" marriage thus undermines the latter's uniqueness. The paradox is thus that the Moral Majority attitude secretly *wants* homosexuals to remain promiscuous pleasure-seekers: when they "want more," marriage as the symbolic ritual asserting their deep personal commitment, the Moral Majority necessarily perceives this as an obscene travesty of the true marriage bond.[46]

Feminism provides a basis for both supporting and questioning the ethic of sameness that informs the idea of same-sex marriage. At base is the central issue under discussion here: what are the consequences of grounding state entitlements in family relationships? Feminists such as Nancy Fraser have long noted that women have often been given rights and entitlements only as wives and mothers, not as citizens or human beings.[47] Consequently their subordination to men is reaffirmed. Katha Pollitt and others have raised this concern in relationship to gay marriage. Even as a supporter of same-sex marriage, Pollitt asks:

> But even as we support legalizing same-sex unions, we might ask whether we want to distribute these rights and privileges according to marital status. . . . The truth is, we are moving toward a society in which the old forms of human relationships are being disrupted and reshaped, and sooner or later the law must accommodate that reality. Legalizing gay marriage is part of the process, but so is diminishing the increasingly outmoded privileged status of marriage and sharing out its benefits along different, more egalitarian lines.[48]

Likewise, Wendy Brown is concerned about the politics of protection and regulation.[49] Gay and lesbian freedom, like women's freedom, may lie beyond the terms of incorporation into the discourse of rights and entitlements. Pursuing freedoms as if they were reducible to the rights and entitlements guaranteed by the liberal state only ensures that whatever freedom is gained will be at risk of becoming what Rousseau called "civil slavery." Civil slavery comes about when political or "natural" liberties, including collective power for self-legislation, are surrendered in exchange for securities guaranteed by the state.[50]

Gay and lesbian rights, like the rights of indigenous peoples, may lie beyond the terms of incorporation into a contractual order that assumes the rights bearer has a particular identity with attendant needs and wants. Indigenous peoples' claims to land are often translated into commodifiable property rights that entitle the claimants to reimbursements they may not want, while denying them the relationship to the land they seek outside the liberal contractual order.[51] If gay and lesbian rights are defined as rights to marriage within the liberal contractual order, gay sexuality is reduced to a domesticated traditional family-centered form. Furthermore, gay and lesbian rights are also reduced to a legalistic form that allows the exercise of such rights to be delimited to what the state considers appropriate. Although such rights will be protected they will also be regulated, which opens up the possibility that more expansive and more self-determining versions of gay or lesbian identity could be delegitimated, perhaps even criminalized in the future.

These concerns animate Shane Phelan's particularly noteworthy critique of same-sex marriage.[52] Her concerns arise from the troubling relationship between kinship and citizenship under U.S. liberalism. To her mind, same-sex marriage would reinscribe the biases of heteronormativity that follow from reliance on the traditional family ideal as the basis for structuring the political and economic order and the entitlement rights that full citizens derive from that system. With other feminists, she emphasizes that under liberalism, citizen rights accessed in the public realm are founded in part on one's kinship relationship in the private realm. Same-sex marriage would continue to tie public citizen rights to private kinship relationships and would reinforce the family as the foundation for the political and economic order and the basis for full citizenship. Same-sex marriage would perpetuate the implicit bias that individuals must go through the family in order to establish full rights as citizens. Same-sex marriage would continue to reinforce the notion that the heterosexual, procreative family is superior to other forms.

Phelan fears that same-sex marriage is therefore too co-optive, reinforcing the prevailing family biases in the public realm and continuing to encourage the marginalization of nonfamilial citizens, such as gays and lesbians who are not in established or formally recognized relationships. Until family and marriage are sufficiently pluralized to guard against such marginalization, Phelan believes that it is a better strategy to push for domestic partnership, which will give gays and lesbians access to rights without relying on the family.

Phelan's analysis has great merit; however, domestic partnership is perhaps not a separate strategy as much as another variation. As Phelan herself accepts, for the present (and for some time to come) the family is an unavoidable element in considering issues of social inclusion, especially access to social policy entitlements. While domestic partnership can be said to be a way of accessing rights as an individual independent of the family, it is designed to accord benefits to partners as if they were family. Domestic partnership allows gays and lesbians to be covered for health insurance and other benefits along with their partners. In a sense it is unavoidably a family policy as was emphasized in Hawai'i.

While Phelan is right that the family has biased citizenship rights, both domestic partnership and same-sex marriage are ways of pluralizing family as the basis for rights. It could well be that the decision to emphasize the one over the other is a pragmatic and strategic one. Same-sex marriage may be less likely to be successful if the opposition interprets it as a threat to the traditional meanings of marriage and family. But it may be the preferred strategy if by getting married gay and lesbian couples help diminish fears of gays and lesbians as different.

The politics of incorporation is therefore not invariant in its consequences, nor is it linear in the kinds of development it engenders.[53] For instance, Lisa Duggan makes this concrete in the case of gay rights. As with other oppressed groups, the push for civil rights protections by gays and lesbians had provoked a backlash in the form of "No Promo Homo" initiatives in Oregon, Colorado, and elsewhere. In response, Duggan questions whether such civil rights strategies need to be reconsidered. Ironically, Duggan suggests that gays and lesbians pursue the classic civil rights strategy of insisting on strict neutrality by the state. She calls this "queering the state."[54] Duggan's idea of "queering the state" is a form of dissent that attacks the way the state currently uses its power to accord special privileges to heterosexuals. Rather than enforcing heteronormativity, the state should be pushed to more strictly uphold classic liberal commitments to neutrality. For instance, the state should not discriminate against same-sex couples in recognizing marriages and it should not privilege heterosexual families when it comes to determining eligibility for Social Security and other benefits. Such a politics of incorporation would remake the state to be more consistent with the idea of neutrality even as it recognizes the need to account for lesbian and gay identity. Identity politics that emphasizes difference is first supplemented and then supplanted by a politics that emphasizes dissent. Rather than holding out for special recognition of difference, dissent is voiced until the state ceases to accord special recognition to heterosexuals.

Like Michel Foucault's conception of power, incorporation can potentially engender its own resistance, but also enlist that resistance as an allied practice.[55] The politics of incorporation thus creates opportunities as well as dangers for changing the way things are. Marriage will change if it includes gays, just as the intergovernmental system of relations between state and federal governments changes whenever distant annexed territories like Hawai'i are treated as effective participants in that system.

Both states and marriages can experience what we can call "chiasmatic encounters," as in the literary sign of the chiasmus that indicates the reversibility of terms. The chiasmus was Theodor Adorno's preferred aesthetic for highlighting the reversibility of logical hierarchies sedimented in discourse.[56] Adorno's interest in the chiasmus anticipates Jacques Derrida's interest in the "fabulous retroactivity" of discourse whereby a preferred presence (for example, heterosexual marriage or mainland state) cannot be shown to be deserving of its preferred status by independent criteria, but only by distinguishing itself from some denigrated other (for example, gay marriage or off shore state).[57]

Once this codependency of presence and absence is demonstrated, we can begin to question the contingencies that cause one to be preferred over the other and to see their similarities as well as their differences. To be sure, incorporation has its dangers, for it can forestall political change, but the "chiasmatic encounters" it engenders—whereby family and state relations are revised and even made reversible—also hold out the possibility of realizing those changes. Judith Stacey goes as far as to suggest that gay and lesbian families are paradigmatic of the family's postmodern condition.[58] Families today are all "queer" for they are of necessity, in these changing times, forced to deal with the multivalences associated with change. They need to allow for new and different arrangements that combine old practices with new ones in order to cope more effectively. Under these conditions, once gay marriages are seen as real marriages, all marriages will become more open to change in ways that enable them to adjust to the new social realities. And the queering of intergovernmental relations is no less necessary in an era when an alleged "devolution revolution" has heightened federal regulation of the family. Once all states are seen as the contingent entities they are, we can begin to renegotiate which governments get to act for whom.

Conclusion

The Defense of Marriage Act (DOMA) illustrates the insistence of contemporary social policy on traditional family values that have never been the reality of real families and that are becoming even less sustainable today, given the social changes occurring at the century's end. Yet DOMA also highlights the contradictions of the intergovernmental system for making social policy. With DOMA, the contradictions of social policy and federalism deconstruct themselves and the federal government expands its authority in the name of protecting state autonomy. It does so to deny real families legal recognition in the name of protecting "the family." Family values and states' rights conspire to undermine each other.

In this deconstructive context, DOMA illustrates how important "cultural software" is for contemporary public policy. Not only are family and state made ambivalent here; the fixing of metaphors on their behalf is not sustainable either. The mobility of metaphor cannot be denied, nor can its relevance to social policy. Policy makers repeatedly turn to the "cultural software" of existing models to make sense of a changing world. The politics of incorporation, whereby those on the outside are identified as being like those on the inside, continues to create the possibilities for inclusion. Difference is respected in part by appreciating similarity. Similarity is recognized but difference is not rejected. While a politics of incorporation has its risks, they may be worth taking. With such a politics in place, we may come to accept that a same-sex marriage is like any other marriage and that Hawai'i is a state like any other state. Perhaps we might even go further and rebuild the family, the state, and their relationship to each other.

6

A New Space for Welfare
Policy Research
Benefit Decline on the Internet

At the end of the twentieth century, social welfare policy discourse is being transformed by the Internet. This is an important development, given that the Internet is being heralded as the new "public sphere."[1]
The "contracting of America" is taking place in a new space where it turns
out social science and politics easily comingle. But how do we begin to
practice social science and politics in this brave new world of the information superhighway? In this chapter, I examine how social welfare policy research is affected by the extension of the metaphor of the public sphere to
cyberspace. In particular, I suggest how this example of metaphorical extension exemplifies what J. M. Balkin calls "cultural software"[2] raises important
issues regarding the relationship of social science to social policy.

One established response to this issue follows Max Weber's suggestion
that science and politics are best kept separate to ensure a credible, impartial, and scientifically authoritative social science that can, in the popular
phrase, "speak truth to power."[3] Another equally established position, ani-
mated by Karl Marx, has been that science should be a motor engine for political change. To paraphrase Marx's well-worn cliché, the point of social science is not to understand society but to change it.[4] However, neither response is sufficient for the virtual realities of social science and politics
today.[5]

The following analysis takes the side of Marx but by way of a negative example. It accepts as inadequate Weber's plea for an apolitical social science
as the road to political legitimacy. But politicizing social science or even just
allowing for recognition of the politics already present in social science is
fraught with its own dangers. The much discussed Cato Institute study of
1995 demonstrating "why welfare pays" provides a cautionary tale in this
regard.[6] Widely publicized via the Internet and by other means outside aca-

demic journals,[7] the study highlights the unavoidable dangers of a politicized social science. In the following chapter, I consider the role social science plays in social policy politics today,[8] particularly with regard to its enhanced role in social policy via the emerging public space of the Internet. I raise concerns about how, contrary to the claims of its proponents,[9] the emerging public sphere of the Internet is at least as exclusionary as the public spheres it is quickly replacing.[10]

The Cato study is a negative example that demonstrates that while social science may best be seen as part of politics, the political use of social science information can certainly be troubling. Erasing the false boundary between social science and social policy politics, or between science and politics more generally, can lead to more self-reflective and critical investigations that offer, if not a more robust objectivity, then a critical perspective that interrogates its own value positions.[11] However, the blurring of the distinctions between science and politics, objectivity and subjectivity, fact and value, calls for more rather than less attention to the scientific quality of politicized research.[12] A political social science must be particularly alert to the pitfalls associated with making scientific claims in the current highly charged environment where think tanks on the Internet increasingly outflank more established academic means of disseminating information. This is even more a concern given the high thresholds for who can participate in the newer forms of information exchange.

Rewriting Boundaries

The uses and abuses of social science in politics and the politicization of social research highlight the porousness of boundaries between the practices of knowledge and power. Under such conditions, the symbols of knowledge and the force of power are tightly entwined.[13] This underscores the importance of considering how boundaries are drawn, by whom, and to what effect.[14]

For instance, once national boundaries are seen as something other than geographic,[15] the question is not whether symbolic representation misrepresents some obdurate material reality but whether the symbolic/material divide is itself a critically constitutive and self-legitimating discursive practice central to the making of boundaries generally.[16] To draw boundaries is to reinscribe the artificial distinction between the symbolic and the material with a materiality it creates for itself. Whether drawing national or other boundaries, such a mapping creates a politically represented space that is a space for political representation.[17] The boundary materializes distinctions in space just as it spatializes distinctions in discourse. This suggests that space itself can be dematerialized and recognized for the mappable representation that it is.[18] A space is therefore a symbolic practice that has its own political economy of value, a lingua franca of distinction including and therefore privileging some representations and excluding and banishing others, or even calibrating distinctions of value among those that are included. A space alternatively becomes a cartography of representation, a mapping of boundaries of inclusion and exclusion.

Boundaries are therefore symbolic practices that have material consequences. There are more boundaries than material ones or who is to say what is so material about any boundary? Nor should the allegedly metaphorical "boundaries" of the mind or of discourse, of our consciousness or the medium of communication, be considered any less real. These boundaries may be the most consequential of all the limits we confront.

Cyberspace and Public Sphere

Neil Postman, interviewed in 1995 on the McNeil-Lehrer NewsHour aired by the Public Broadcasting System, defined cyberspace as the place our minds go to when we are on the Internet.[19] I would argue that attempting to legislate what can or cannot be represented on the Internet is primarily about what it is possible to imagine in cyberspace, that mappable, if ethereal, reality of the imagination.[20] The symbolic/material practice of electronic communication called the Internet or cyberspace is a "frontier" at least as protean as that frontier called the American West.[21] Frontiers in the postmodern world collide as inner space expands and outer space contracts. And all frontiers immediately invoke regulation, just as all "wilderness" implies "civilization." As a mappable discursive space, cyberspace becomes a frontier to be regulated. Cyberspace becomes a definable reality given the extent to which we can bring its boundaries into focus. As a brave new frontier, it becomes an untamed arena of practice in need of domestication.

As a new electronic, virtual sphere of communicational exchange, cyberspace highlights the symbolic character of the supposedly more established political sphere of ideational exchange.[22] The virtualness of cyberspace suggests the simulated character of all spheres of exchange. Real exchange is not necessarily confined to face-to-face conversation or the monetarized system of passing money around. Nor are monetary terms the only terms of allocating value.[23] All systems of exchange are simultaneously doubled, for symbolic value implies material value and material value is forever only comprehensible symbolically. It therefore becomes possible to imagine the political sphere itself as a virtual space for rehearsing public action. It is the counterfeit, imperfect version of the idealized public sphere of open democratic deliberation.[24]

But countering the cyber sphere with the political sphere does not mean that one is more virtual and the other more real. Anonymity haunts each and performativity is valorized in both.[25] An "acting" president like Ronald Reagan is sometimes the more effective president in the political public sphere, just as the androgynous and nameless is often more genuinely open and honest in the communicational electronic sphere.[26] Both spheres prize virtual reality for its reliability and dependability. Both are self-reflective arenas that encourage the remaking of their rules and the redrawing of their boundaries even as participants learn to play by the rules and to follow them.[27]

In particular, the idea of the public sphere is an important piece of "cultural software," as Balkin calls it, that spreads from one area to another, making disparate practices conform to similar standards.[28] Cyberspace gets evaluated by the same standards as that other space, the public sphere. In trying to suggest that cyberspace—like the political sphere that is often misleadingly represented as already being an open democratic public sphere—has a virtualness that makes its regulation both a problem and a prospect of political potential. David Post thoughtfully, if too enthusiastically, writes:

What is happening here? Surely the center of gravity of our law-making and law-enforcement apparatus is shifting away from the familiar rules and instruments that have served us, whether for good or ill, in the world of atoms. That's the polite version. Less politely, cyberspace looks a lot like Hobbes's quasi-mythical construct, the state of nature, where the inhabitants have "no common Power to feare" and where there is "no government at all." Of course, law and an ordered society will emerge from out of the state of nature—or at least so Hobbes (and Locke, and most of the other Enlightenment philosophers) believed—by means of a "social contract" voluntarily entered into by the inhabitants. Indeed, only law that emerges from something resembling this process—only law as to which the "consent of the governed" has been obtained, in Jefferson's phrase—is a truly legitimate exercise of state power.

There has always been a strong fictional element to using this notion of a social contract as a rationale for a sovereign's legitimacy. When exactly did you
or I consent to be bound by the U.S. Constitution? At best, that consent can
only be inferred indirectly, from our continued presence within the U.S. borders—the love-it-or-leave it, vote-with-your-feet theory of political legitimacy. . . . But in cyberspace, there is an infinite amount of space, and movement between online communities is entirely frictionless. Here, there really is
the opportunity to obtain consent to a social contract. Virtual communities
can be established with their own particular rule sets. . . . That potential—
not the availability of video on demand, or interactive games, or any of the
other technological wonders—is what makes the emergence of cyberspace a
truly extraordinary political event. . . . Existing sovereigns must defer to the
inhabitants of this new place regarding those matters in which the legitimate
and unique interests of those inhabitants are paramount. . . . But the inhabitants of cyberspace, too, must develop mechanisms to recognize and respect
the legitimate interest of individuals outside their borders.[29]

Post's celebration of the consensual nature of cyber sphere communities
needs to be questioned, if for no other reason than that he overlooks the
high thresholds people must pass in order even just to get on the information superhighway and enter cyberspace. But, his contrast of the cyber
sphere and the political sphere offers the possibility of seeing both as virtual
spaces constructed out of the questionable status of the social contract as an
originating and authorizing basis for the cyber/public spheres. They are
both metaphorical. Most importantly perhaps, his contrast between the
cyber sphere and the public sphere highlights the discontinuous, overlapping, and open textured nature of all spheres as the unfinished virtual realities they are. The political sphere is therefore open to integration into the
cyber sphere and vice versa. Both can rely on the other to supplement them
to make themselves complete.

Social contract discourse colonizes the cyber sphere, and the domesticated and regulated cyber sphere becomes a legitimate site for the public
sphere. As that happens, both are transformed. Yet their ineliminable virtualness as symbolically constructed spaces is what initially enables this transformation to take place. Now it becomes possible to read the *New York
Times* (http://www.nytimes.com) and e-mail the President of the United
States (president@whitehouse.gov) without getting offline. And it becomes
possible for the president's staff to e-mail form-letter responses that enable
people to feel included in the public sphere even when they are not. To be
sure, the critical ingredient necessary to make this transformation possible is

the spatialization of these spheres according to some sort of cartographic practice, that is, according to some logic of boundary maintenance.

Significantly, however, Post fails to consider that this logic of boundary maintenance involves identifying who and what is to be included in a virtual space.[30] The terms of inclusion and exclusion for identities, ideas, and interests as represented symbolically must be specified for a space to be made real, even if a good part of exchange in it is over the rewriting of these terms of inclusion.[31] Therefore, for the integration of the overlapping spheres of cyber and public space to take place, their rules of inclusion must be articulated in the sense of being made translatable, one to the other.

In particular, in order for the domesticated political exchanges allowed in the public sphere to be expressed, the unregulated frontier of cyberspace must be stabilized. Surely this is one reason why the decency requirements of the Telecommunications Act of 1996, which included the constitutionally invalid Communications Decency Act, passed without much public debate and almost no opposition in Congress.[32] While there were legitimate concerns about the ready access of children to sexually explicit images and texts in cyberspace, the unconstitutional prohibitions in the law went beyond such concerns, to the domestication of cyber exchanges about political matters such as and including abortion.[33] Cyber fear generated an excess of regulation.

This is why even the practice of some users of assuming multiple and anonymous identities in cyberspace becomes a problem that must be addressed before cyberspace can be safely integrated into the broader public sphere.[34] The conventional public sphere, as constructed in newspapers, magazines, books, radio, television, and other media calls for identifiable self-regulating selves prepared to accept personal responsibility for their discourse and to be sanctioned when they break the law.[35] As authors, commentators, critics, analysts, or even writers of letters to the editor, participants in the conventional public sphere are usually denied the opportunity to assume multiple or anonymous identities.

The Telecommunications Act also suggests that the public sphere of policy making is critical to the construction and reconstruction of the cyber sphere and that the cyber sphere of communication and the exchange of ideas has already become a potential source for influencing public discourse. This is why regulating it is so salient an issue. The Internet has its origins in the United States Department of Defense's desire to link separate computers for purposes of national security.[36] Therefore, from its inception the Internet was a conglomeration of computing systems tied together through the actions of the political sphere. While today's Internet entrepreneurs may be loath to admit that their private constructions had such a public basis, the needs of one sphere helped articulate the rationale for the other. So it was with the earlier highway system, namely, the interstate, as opposed to the Internet, highway system. The interstate highway system was also originally justified on the grounds of national security, serving to create a means for the rapid evacuation of people from urban centers should a nuclear attack occur. And as with the Internet, the interstate wound up serving quite different purposes, not of national security but again of privatization, in that case not of informational exchange but of living arrangements. Ultimately, it gave rise to the suburbanization of the United States.[37]

The cyber and political spheres are interdependent, although this interdependence is unevenly articulated. Nor are they readily distinguishable, as information passes from one in order to influence the other and as legislation discussed in one restructures the other. At some point the distinction breaks down and the political sphere exhibits cyber qualities, with government agencies distributing information over the Internet and citizens debating the terms of free speech.

This blurring of boundaries is indicative of the multiplicity and indeterminacy of both spheres. While the blurring of distinctions between the cyber and public spheres invalidate the autonomy of such realms of exchange, their coherence as identifiable unities also evaporates. The Internet becomes a series of overlapping, discontinuous exchanges most of which are oblivious of the others. Discrete newsgroups proliferate as customized fanzines on preciously specific topics. Virtual rooms, called MOOs (MUD-Object-Oriented, wherein MUD is the acronym for Multi-User-Dimension), grow exponentially, creating virtual spaces for a variety of exchanges. Visual, audio, and textual spaces combine and interact.[38] New domesticated sites connect more directly to the public policy processes of the conventional public sphere. Some even emphasize the exchange of social scientific information. Some mirror what is provided in the print medium or is available on television and radio. Magazines like *Slate* and *salon.com* are available only on the Internet, along with electronic versions of printed journals of policy-oriented magazines such as *The American Prospect*. Chat groups grow alongside the virtual version of the *New York Times* which includes its own audio and video supplements with speeches by President Clinton and other key policy actors. The world becomes a set of discontinuous, overlapping spaces of virtual exchange.

One major lesson learned from the merging of the cyber and public spheres in recent times is the artificiality of mutually exclusive realms of social action.[39] These spheres are symbolically constructed spaces of representation subject to struggle over their practices of boundary maintenance which are constantly subject to renegotiation. In fact, such negotiation is often the primary purpose of what is called politics among the participants of such spheres. Participants hope through such a practice of politics to enhance the performance in these spheres by trying to change or maintain the terms of exclusion and inclusion.

Rewriting the terms of inclusion and exclusion affects which identities, ideas, and interests can be acted out within these spheres. To rewrite the rules to allow for new identities, ideas, and interests is to reconfigure who can participate, what concerns are expressed, and what responses are possible. Post celebrates the fact that cyberspace creates an opportunity for a "real" social contract; however, William Reddy and others have emphasized that the contractual order calls for a particular type of embodied identity— one that provides the predictability and reliability needed for contractual exchanges.[40]

The forms of anonymity and performativity possible in cyberspace may undercut the stability of an embodied identity as needed by contractual society. Therefore, either cyberspace will be cordoned off from the public sphere or it will be reorganized to be consonant with it. Struggles over boundary maintenance are not just struggles over who sets the agenda. Rather, these struggles illustrate that all spheres of exchange are virtual realities that allow for symbolic practices with material consequences. Such fragile realities are not easily kept mutually exclusive, discrete, and distinguishable. Being malleable, they are prone to becoming overlapping discontinuities—never fully autonomous, always incomplete, usually vulnerable to influences from practices in other spheres, and often busy articulating their interrelationships.

All this is to say that the Internet today is an important site for policy politics as well as commerce.[41] Furthermore, the Internet is a place where the power to influence both consumption choices and policy preferences is exercised by those who can meet the threshold requirements for having their information included while others' is excluded. Consequently, it is an arena for social science, for that academic matrix itself has historically been constructed for the purpose of promoting politics.[42] Social science and politics, like the Internet and the public sphere, are virtual spaces whose supposed mutual exclusivity and alleged autonomy have always been undercut by struggles over boundary maintenance. And on the Internet, social science, like everything else, is subject to the potentially politicizing practices of those who want their information disseminated and that of others excluded.

Social Science and Politics

Modern social science was founded on an explicit, if paradoxical, commitment to both the separateness and the relatedness of social science and politics. At one level, Max Weber's famous companion essays, "The Vocation of Science" and "The Vocation of Politics," argue for the need to separate politics from science; however, at another level they suggest that social science and politics need to be related.[43] Weber was deeply concerned that politics was devoid of a moral compass and in need of the tutelage that only social science could provide. The job of social science was, as later commentators put it, to speak "truth to power." To be able to do so, Weber believed that social science must achieve legitimacy by virtue of its reputation as an authoritatively reliable source of nonpartisan and scientific knowledge.[44] Ironically, therefore, for Weber social science's political influence depended on its remaining apolitical.

This paradox has played out in the twentieth century and, not surprisingly, it has remained unresolvable. Social science has tended to align itself with the power structure rather than to challenge it. Evidence for this can be found in Dietrich Reuschemeyer and Theda Skocpol's 1996 edited volume of well-documented if insufficiently critical essays on the role of social science in the formative stages of the modern welfare state across a variety of countries during the catalytic years of the late nineteenth and early twentieth centuries.[45] According to several of the contributors to this volume, liberal reform-minded social scientists, including professional academics and amateur practitioners inside and outside government promoted policies that helped rationalize a social order disrupted by a changing economy.[46]

Likewise, Stanley Aronowitz has suggested that modern science, especially social science, has been at its most powerful when aligned with the dominant structures of power.[47] In other words, social science's quest for political influence via political impartiality has often resulted in its political co-optation, subjecting its empirical studies to political appropriation by the powers that be. Furthermore, objectivistic social science has not always been prepared to respond to bad social scientific information, which it has allowed to circulate in policy circles in relatively uncontested fashion.[48]

This is not to deny that numerous persons, practices, and publications represent the merging of social science and politics.[49] United States Senator Daniel Patrick Moynihan from New York represents a forceful example, perhaps even more so than former Secretary of State Henry Kissinger. Moynihan achieved tremendous influence in the Senate, and earlier in the executive branch, as an academic expert on welfare, although his scholarly writings were largely stories about his attempts to influence social policy rather than systematic studies of poverty and welfare. Moynihan has successfully played both ends against the middle. He used his academic credentials to gain political influence and his political influence to serve as the basis for his scholarly writings.[50]

The Public Interest, a popular neoconservative policy journal with which Moynihan is closely associated, provides an excellent outlet for such "armchair" scholarship. It often reports stories about research. Such second-hand reporting makes it difficult to seriously assess the studies under discussion. While such writing makes social science more accessible to the broader policy-interested community, it has obvious defects that proponents of the "public scholar" overlook. Left-wing scholars such as the late Christopher Lasch have been outspoken advocates of the "public scholar" as a paradigm for how academics ought to write in order to produce "common knowledge" for the general public.[51] Yet their pleas for relevance via simple prose have their own dangers, perhaps as great as right-wing calls to scholars to remain disconnected from political life in the ivory tower. Dilution to the point were the methodological fine points of research are obscured is one of the glaring deficiencies associated with such second-hand reporting. The devil is indeed in the details.

"Orphanages: The Real Story," a short article in *The Public Interest* by the economist, Richard B. McKenzie, illustrates my point.[52] The article reports the results of a survey of alumni from three orphans' homes. The author finds that "the results do seriously undermine some of the critics' most sweeping, if not reckless, negative assessments applied to all orphanages." McKenzie does note that the survey has some limitations, including the fact that respondents were not drawn randomly but from alumni mailing lists which might be biased in favor of those who had favorable experiences at the orphanage. This caveat is probably an understatement, given the richly detailed histories of abuse at orphanages.[53] By the time such second-hand reporting lands on the desk of talk show policy-fabler Rush Limbaugh, the conversion of social science to politically tendentious rumor is complete. While social scientists often resist recognizing the political character of their scholarship even when it addresses policy problems, others are now increasingly outflanking academia and are willing to deploy allegedly scientifically derived facts for political effect.[54] The Cato Institute is just one noteworthy example, situated somewhere between *The Public Interest* and Rush Limbaugh.

Cato's Political Science

The Cato Institute in Washington, D.C., is a privately financed research and advocacy organization, heavily dependent on a variety of corporate sponsors and dedicated to promoting a conservative-libertarian line on public policy. It does not just do research; it also actively raises money for and organizes lobbying campaigns to influence policy. In late 1995, it started a multimillion dollar fund-raising campaign among private corporations, foundations, and individual donors to push for the privatization of social security. Its research is tied directly or indirectly to its political efforts. Its resources make it a ready player in the Internet field.

Not to be left out in the rush to use cyberspace to disseminate its politicized research,[55] the Cato Institute has been at the forefront of Washington think-tank efforts to post its research on the Internet. With extensive background information and graphics, biographies, and pictures of its staff, as well as information bulletins, reprints, on its home page at its address on the World Wide Web (http://www.cato.org/hom.html), the resources of the Cato Institute are available to Internet users.

As might be expected of the libertarian Cato Institute, it has consistently taken a critical line on public assistance. It has been at the forefront of those who point out that during the last three decades federal noncash benefits have grown, disproving liberal arguments that welfare benefits have been cut. One of the Cato Institute's studies posted on the Internet attracted substantial attention during the debates about the 1996 welfare reform legislation.[56] This study caused a major firestorm among welfare policy analysts. Never adjudicated by academic reviewers, this unpublished but widely available study was popularized through an op-ed piece in the *Wall Street Journal*.[57] For months, its credibility was largely unquestioned and its influence grew in Congress and in statehouses around the country. California Governor Pete Wilson cited it in support of his 1996 attempt to overhaul that state's welfare system and slash public assistance benefits.[58] The details of the Cato study illustrate the strange and dangerous brew that gets concocted when social science and politics are mixed indiscriminately and when the cyber sphere and the public sphere begin to work hand in glove. The Cato study shows that incompetent and tendentious, "top-down" managerially oriented, and allegedly objective research, devoid of any attempt to understand social life from the situated subjectivities of those who experience it, circulates quickly to influence public policy makers in convenient if troubling ways.[59]

The authors of the much publicized Cato study suggest that the "welfare package" of combined benefits pays too much, with that popular "other" state, Hawai'i, leading the way. In Hawai'i, they say, a family of three on public assistance takes in the equivalent in earnings of a $17.50 an hour job—an annual income of $36,400 (in 1995 dollars). This finding received tremendous play on radio and television talk shows, prompting legislators in the allegedly traditionally liberal state to join others around the country in calling for cuts in public assistance and new rules to discourage welfare dependency.

Like so much else in U.S. politics, this renewed interest in welfare benefits is best seen as a debate among conservatives over what conservative (not liberal) policies have wrought.[60] Conservative suspicions about giving cash benefits to the needy have led to a proliferation of noncash benefits such as food stamps. Reluctant to provide cash assistance, conservative policy makers have supported the provision of services and benefits in kind instead of cash assistance. Over time, there has been a proliferation of benefits and services. Adding all these programs up, the Cato study suggests that the combined benefit package is large. Yet recipients rarely if ever qualify for all these services at the same time, often languishing on waiting lists for years in order to get benefits such as housing assistance.

Therefore, as we might suspect, there are also several methodological flaws in the Cato Institute's estimates. First, it makes problematic assumptions about access to benefits. It calculates the real value of the "typical welfare package" by adding the estimated cash value of what it calls the "six most common types of welfare assistance—AFDC [Aid to Families with Dependent Children], food stamps, Medicaid, housing, nutrition assistance and energy assistance." But, how typical is this package? In 1990, less than half of all poor families even in supposedly liberal Hawai'i received AFDC. Although some people may be getting too much, others are not getting enough or even any welfare benefits at all.[61]

But even if we focus on AFDC families, very few of them ever simultaneously receive all six of the benefits listed. Even fewer get benefits in the amounts suggested by the Cato study. To be sure, lack of access to all the benefits is a real problem. For instance, most people studying this issue consider AFDC and food stamps to be the two most basic programs, and most AFDC recipients do indeed also receive food stamps. But not always. In 1992, 13 percent of AFDC recipients in the United States. did not receive food stamps. It is much worse for other programs.[62]

The Cato methodology assumes that if a large unspecified fraction of public assistance recipients receive a benefit, it should be considered part of everyone's package. However this approach is seriously flawed. The AFDC recipients who get energy assistance are probably not the same people who receive housing assistance, for instance. The Cato study does nothing to address this problem.

The greatest flaw in assuming access to benefits in fact concerns housing subsidies. These subsidies can be large, amounting to as much as $850 a month in 1995 for a family of three on public assistance in Hawai'i, for instance.[63] Yet, in 1997 only about 25 to 30 percent of all poor families in the United States receive housing subsidies of any kind.[64] An even smaller proportion of public assistance recipients received the high benefit subsidies estimated by the Cato Institute. Housing subsidies are social policy's equivalent of winning the lottery.

Not only is access a problem, but so is assuming that benefits are like wages. Comparing welfare benefits to wages overlooks the fact that workers get benefits too. In addition, they receive some of the benefits welfare recipients get, such as housing assistance, though their source is often tax credits and deductions. They receive subsidies from their employers in the form of health insurance premiums, clothing allowances, and the like.

Yet even if wages were adjusted, cashing out welfare benefits in kind has its own problems. Benefits, such as housing assistance and health insurance cannot be converted into the equivalent of cash to buy what the market has to offer. In addition, often these benefits can only be used in selected places. Not all rental units, for instance—even if offered at the right price for cash-paying tenants—are available to people who pay their rent with housing vouchers. Like Medicaid's health insurance, housing subsidies can only be used if providers are willing to accept them as payment. This selectivity can lead to highly contrived markets that are subject to price inflation. Housing vouchers and health insurance for the poor in particular may result in paying the poor more for less. Assuming that noncash benefits work like money can easily lead one to overestimate the cash value of such benefits.[65]

Ignoring this critical methodological question, the Cato Institute study estimates the cash value of Medicaid by estimating the total per capita expenditures paid to hospitals, clinics, providers, doctors, and the like, and capping these estimates at the average price for a health insurance premium in those states where the estimates go over that amount. But Medicaid is hardly a handout of money to the poor, who increasingly have trouble finding medical care at prices Medicaid will pay. The poor often go without the care they need when they most need it. Recipients often end up in emergency rooms getting more costly care and requiring Medicaid to pay for services at higher emergency room rates. These inflated costs give the illusion that Medicaid is contributing more to recipients' incomes and well-being than it really is.

A third problem with the Cato study (especially for high-cost states like Hawai'i) is that it fails to account for interstate variation in the cost of living. It does not compare benefits to costs, such as the high cost of renting in many urban areas. Honolulu, for instance, has a high cost of living relative to all other states except Alaska. Its welfare package is therefore not as out of line as the Cato Institute study suggests, when compared to benefits in other states. Welfare recipients in Hawai'i, in fact, may have just as hard a time as welfare recipients in other states.

One easy but credible way to get a handle on this cost of living issue is to compare the basic welfare package of most recipients with the average cost of housing. For those without housing subsidies, over half of a welfare family's budget goes to housing over half the time.[66] The basic AFDC-food stamp package in Hawai'i in 1994 for a family of three with no other income was $712 a month in AFDC and $354 a month in food stamps, for a total of $1066.[67] The basic needs standard that the state had set for what such a family needed to live on was $74 a month more at $1140. Compare this $1066 AFDC-food stamp monthly benefit to the monthly "fair market rent" for a two-bedroom unit (as estimated by the U.S. Department of Housing and Urban Development) for metro Honolulu in 1994—$1069.

In other words, the cost of housing in Hawai'i is so high that a recipient family of three would have to sell all their food stamps at face value and then combine that cash with its AFDC grant, just to come up $3 short for the average rent. The only way this family can scrape by is by looking for the least expensive housing. Even then, their benefits would not allow them much of an existence. Most studies indicate that food stamps only finance about three weeks of the monthly food budget for families living in poverty.[68] Even if food stamps and other nutrition programs at school and elsewhere could cover the entire monthly food budget, that leaves no more than $712 a month for rent and all other expenses other than the major health care costs covered by Medicaid. That can hardly begin to pay for housing and other major expenses, given Hawai'i's high cost of living.

Nonetheless, Hawai'i may actually be doing a better job than most states in providing benefits relative to the cost of living. Yet, whether Hawai'i, let alone any other state, is doing enough is subject to tremendous debate. Kathryn Edin and Laura Lein have demonstrated that low-income single mothers with children who rely on public assistance increasingly need to supplement welfare with income from other sources.[69] They make it very clear that neither Hawai'i nor any of the other states provides the average recipient with the generous benefits suggested by the Cato Institute. Most recipients do not get anywhere near the benefits listed by the Cato Institute study. Simply put, this study is highly misleading. And no one is helped when such misleading data starts shaping the public dialogue.

"Idea Central" as a New Public Sphere

The Cato study has proved to be extremely influential in the policy-making process, as the case of Pete Wilson suggests. This is true even though it is profoundly misleading and factually dubious. It has influenced public policy—perhaps it has even played a role in the passage of the draconian Personal Responsibility and Work Opportunity Reconciliation Act of 1996.[70] All this has happened despite a 1996 study by Public Agenda, the polling organization founded by Daniel Yankelovich and Cyrus Vance, which indicated that most people living in the United States do not think benefits are too high and that in their view the problems with welfare lie elsewhere.[71]

Nevertheless, the influential, if counterintuitive, Cato study has had what can only be called a postmodern lineage, not easily addressed by the conventional means of either scholarly or political rebuttal. The Cato study was not disseminated via conventional academic journals in the print media. An op-ed piece by its authors appeared in the *Wall Street Journal* referencing the study, which had been made available via the Cato Institute's home page on the Internet.[72] While the op-ed piece popularized the study, its availability was most easily accessed via the Internet. And it has been via the Internet that the most detailed responses to it have been broadcast. A new home page has been created for policy wonks at the Internet address for "Idea Central," the "virtual magazine of the Electronic Policy Network" (http://epn.org/idea.html), which was established by the public policy journal *The American Prospect.* A subset of "Idea Central" is the policy page entitled "Welfare and Families" (http://epn.org/idea/welfare.html). There are links to studies by the liberal-leaning alternative Washington think tank, the Center on Budget and Policy Priorities (http://epn.org/cbpp.html). And a thorough social science-based critique of the methodology of the Cato study as it applies to California is listed there.[73] This is the most significant response to the Cato study. It has served as the basis for the most trenchant criticism in the conventional political sphere: an op-ed piece by Bob Herbert that ran in the *New York Times* in late April 1996.[74]

However, in the exclusive setting of the Internet, the Cato Institute with its greater resources has dominated the discussion. In its most recent foray, it has sent a written response by first-class mail to its critics, a response it had earlier posted on its home page allegedly rebutting arguments such as those detailed in the foregoing analysis.[75] How the Cato study fares in the future raises another question, namely, how we might conduct a politically efficacious and scientifically ethical social science both in the rarefied space of the Internet and elsewhere.

While the dissemination of information via other means is not without its risks, the Internet poses its own unique great dangers. Users can wander in and out of information sources, often without the aid of background information. "Surfing" and "browsing" have become popular pastimes, laudably allowing them to gain access to information they might not even know existed but also enabling them to acquire information without knowing who created it or how. A simple search on the Internet will present the Cato study for ready reading to anyone who wishes to read it. The Cato Institute no longer has to mail its reports to designated lists of potential readers. Now it need only post its report on the Internet to allow whoever stumbles on it to make of it what they will. On the whole, the easy access afforded by the new technology probably does more good than bad. You would think, however, easy access to information was contingent upon access to the technology, which is not readily available to everyone, especially not to those most affected by welfare policy. Therefore, the access issue has at least two sides— greater access to information, but only for those privileged to have access to the technology.

What is potentially a greater source of danger is that the Internet allows for far more rapid dissemination than does the traditional print media.[76] Numbers are repeated so rapidly that they get reported as fact before people even have a chance to check them. The sheer weight of the repetition of the "facts" is enough to legitimate them. The Internet makes rumormongering a worldwide sport. Old habits are rehearsed in a brand-new setting and the foibles of humans live on in the impersonal technology. A prime example of this was the TWA 800 story that Pierre Salinger championed in 1997. This story suggested that the U.S. government had inadvertently shot down TWA flight 800 over Long Island. First mentioned on the Internet, the story rapidly spread to the point where it was seriously presented by high government officials *before* the appearance of supporting evidence. Unfortunately, the evidence was not forthcoming even months after the allegations caused widespread concern.

To return to the Cato report, the casual policy browser can come across it, download it, reproduce the numbers on his or her own website, and forward the report to others. These other users forward it back and forth to each other, legitimizing it further, circulating bad statistics, and helping promote support for welfare policy retrenchment. All this is done before the end of the work day and before anyone has had a chance to seriously examine the research. While it might not always happen this quickly, the saga of the Cato study gives rise to real concern about the speed with which information is disseminated via the Internet.

Yet, this is still the lesser evil. Perhaps we should not be worrying about how cyberspace poses problems for the old public sphere so much as how it creates a new one. As Slavoj Žižek has recently written:

In the social conditions of late capitalism, the very materiality of cyberspace automatically generates the illusory abstract space of "friction-free" exchange in which the particularity of the participants' social position is obliterated. . . . The predominant "spontaneous ideology of cyberspace" is so-called "cyber-revolutionism" which relies on the notion of cyberspace—or the World Wide Web—as a self-evolving "natural" organism. . . . The idea of the World Wide Web as a living organism is often evoked in contexts which may seem liberating—say, against state censorship of the Internet. However, this demonization of the state is thoroughly ambiguous, since it is predominately appropriated by right-wing populist discourse and/or market liberalism. . . . In other words, far more interesting than bemoaning the disintegration of community life through the impact of new technologies is to analyze how technological progress itself gives rise to new communities which gradually "naturalize" themselves—like virtual communities.[77]

And Paul Virilio reminds us that cyberspace is not only a place for reporting on social welfare issues, but is itself quickly becoming a social welfare issue. It cannot be dismissed as a factor in changing social relations, given the growing number of ways in which people can interact over the Internet. Virilio writes:

> As we have seen, the "information revolution" that has today superseded the revolution in industrial manufacturing is not without danger, for the damage done by progress in *interactivity* may well be as harmful in the future as that done by *radioactivity*. The "computer bomb" previously denounced by Einstein will shortly necessitate a new type of *deterrence:* no longer military and nuclear, as it had to be when the major danger was the "atomic bomb," but this time political and societal. Unless social disintegration has already entered an irreversible phase, with the decline in the nuclear family and the boom in the population unit of the *single-parent.*[78]

But concerns about the personal and political consequences of the new virtual public sphere are not yet on the agenda for most social welfare scholars, who still live in constructed worlds that fail to recognize the integration of the cyber and public spheres and deny the ways in which social science and politics are entwined.[79] They view the one as the real public sphere and the other as not. And they distinguish between real social science and fake social science and believe that one need only attend to the former and can neglect the latter. It is therefore distinctly possible that the Cato study is subclinical for social welfare scholars. Not published in an academically reviewed journal, it is not legitimate and does not merit the attention of scholars. It is both too political and too cyber. The policy advocates are left to fight over it via the Internet. Be that as it may, for better or for worse the Cato study raises the issue of social science and politics in the information age. If social scientists want to be politically effective, they need to do more than simply reconsider Weber's edict to separate politics and science. They need to be willing to enter the fray wherever it may be, both in cyberspace and in the public sphere more generally.

While social scientists still harbor the myth of autonomy, others are importing social science into politics in less than responsible ways. Helen Longino has effectively argued that scientific work has never been autonomous from the social context in which has been conducted.[80] While many social scientists continue to deny this context-dependent relationship, others already positioned in the world of political struggle are free to invoke the methods of social science without fear of being accused of transgressing an imagined but powerful boundary separating science and politics. Cloaking their studies in the mantle of scientific factuality, their creative fictions enter the highly exclusionary policy arena basically unchecked. They do so more and more rapidly via the Internet and with with little opposition, given the greater restrictions on access and participation by possible opponents.

The solution to the problem lies not in buttressing the quickly collapsing boundaries of the cyber sphere and the public sphere. Nor does it lie in trying to shore up the walls erected to separate social science and politics. Instead, a constructive response must recognize the political significance of creating democratic access to the cyber sphere and of disseminating social science research through this medium. Constructive engagement begins with the recognition that social science and politics have always been entwined, especially with regard to the welfare state.[81] Once social scientists realize that they have always lived in a politically constructed house whose walls are artificial, they too can leave home and practice their social science in the broader world of politics. Once social scientists accept that their authority ultimately should derive not from their station in society but from the quality of their arguments and facts, they can do political work with their social scientific research.

There might still be good reason to fear that others—often on the other side politically—inside and outside the academy will seek to discredit them for politicizing their research. But such attacks will be premised on outmoded and invalid arguments concerning the need to separate politics and science. Such contests will highlight the need to question the boundaries of social science and politics, a much needed exchange in the information age when the rapid dissemination of bad research can have substantial influence on the political sphere. And when social scientists are willing to cross these artificial boundaries and become public actors willing to question what gets said in the new metaphorical public sphere, both social science and politics will be the better for it.

7

After Social Security

Searching for a Postindustrial Ethic

The power of cultural categories is never univocal.[1] However, in some cultures social policy categories are more inclusive and tolerant than in others. How can the power of cultural categorization be tapped so that social policy in the United States becomes less divisive and exclusionary? How do we undermine the persistent distinctions of deserving and undeserving and the economic inequalities these distinctions engender? How can we rework the existing categories of work and care, self-sufficiency and dependence, charity and contract, and in particular those of insurance and compensation in order to reduce the poverty and marginalization that afflict the poorest one-fifth of the families with children in the United States today? These are theoretical questions of practical significance for the current postindustrial period. They raise issues regarding the ethical grounds for social policy. In the following chapter I address these issues by focusing on the idea of a universalistic welfare state and its role in constituting a postindustrial social policy.

A Postindustrial Ethic

The national, industrial, political economy is a thing of the past. While changes associated with the shift to a more global postindustrial system are neither inevitable nor unalterable, those in power have succeeded in claiming that they are. Ironically, often their primary response is not to fashion a new ethic for organizing social provision but instead it is to argue that the old standards of work and family are even more important than ever and that social welfare entitlements need to be scaled back in order to be in consonance with the old verities.[2] As a result, postindustrialism has given rise to the "contracting of America" and the welfare state has been retrenched in the interests of adherence to traditional standards of work and family in a changing world.

However, the old norms are decreasingly sustainable, given the social and economic changes taking place. In 1960 5 percent of children were born to single mothers, while in 1994 slightly more than 30 percent were.[3] Single-parenthood has increased; and the wages necessary to support a family have stagnated for over two decades, declining for low-skilled workers.[4] The persistently negative trends in work and family associated with the changing postindustrial economy have been particularly difficult to absorb for those in the bottom fifth of the income distribution. Declining job security, limited benefits, stagnating wages, and other threats to the ability of the family to function as an economic unit ensure that for the bottom fifth the traditional family is increasingly unsustainable even as an ideal.[5] It is also in jeopardy with the other four-fifths, though not always with the same economic consequences. In the face of such tumultuous economic and social changes, the work and family ideals of the industrial order may well be in need of revision if they are to guide us in a changing world.

In fact, traditional work and family norms were never all that sensitive to the necessities of life for most families. For that reason alone, throughout its history the dominant norms of the industrial order were periodically seen as being under assault.[6] Never the prevailing reality—though once the reigning ideal—the traditional two-parent family, with its male "breadwinner" and female "homemaker," was the assumed basis for the system of social provision that emerged in modern industrializing America.[7] This "family-wage breadwinning system" assumed that it was the responsibility of the male head of the traditional family to earn a "family wage" to support that family. To the extent that that family could not support itself through no fault of its own—as when the wage-earning spouse died, became disabled, unemployed, or retired—it would receive assistance.

The Social Security Act of 1935 and the system of welfare provision it codified were based on the foundation of the traditional family.[8] But, this was a mythical foundation. It was an idealized standard that most families could never meet in practice, given the refusal of most employers to pay a family wage, the need for multiple wage earners in a family, and the frequency with which male heads did not support families by virtue of desertion and divorce rather than disability and death. The increases in underemployment and nonmarital births in recent years did not present a fresh challenge to the traditional family model so much as intensify its preexisting unrealizability to the point where it could no longer even serve as a credible ideal.

The push to roll back hard-won social welfare entitlements reflects a desperate attempt to save traditional social norms at the expense of undermining support for real families. For instance, initial evidence since the welfare reforms enacted through the Personal Responsibility and Work Opportunity Reconciliation Act of 1996 started to take effect indicates that after one year anywhere from a quarter to a third of the people leaving welfare do not have jobs and have also seen their incomes fall when leaving welfare.[9] Welfare can be changed by insisting on work; but ensuring that people are able to find work and keep it is another matter. Rather than desperately clinging to the industrial family breadwinner model as a founding ethic for social provision, an alternative postindustrial ethic needs to be formulated. Rather than trying to end welfare at the century's end, we should be trying to articulate ways of adapting social provision to better address the changing realities of families.

Yet, what if the problem is not deciding what the new norms ought to be so much as whether we ought to have norms at all? This is not meant to invite the charge of immorality, but it is to suggest that the question of a postindustrial ethic presumes the issue of ethics. Social policy analysts usually endorse this presumption and see social philosophy as the foundation for social policy.[10] But I want to challenge the assumption that this is how we should see our task. In fact, it is questionable whether social policy has historically been grounded more in social philosophy than in politics. What is to be done is more a political than a philosophical question. In addition, a norm-based social policy I argue will inevitably be exclusionary because it always sets a standard to which people must measure up. Welfare programs that privilege the "deserving" over the "undeserving" poor—that is, poor families based on the traditional two-parent model versus poor single-parent ones—may be an extreme case of prejudice; however, any social policy has standards to measure whether one is deserving, be it welfare, unemployment compensation, retirement insurance, or disability. I agree with Etienne Balibar, that universalism is a false god that allows invidious distinctions to be made by stealth under the cloak of alleged neutrality.[11] Universal standards are never fully and absolutely universal. Instead, a universal standard imposes a distinction comprehensively across an entire population. Ironically, therefore, the more universal the standard the more discriminatory it is. Balibar critiques the idea of universal human rights (referred to in the French revolutionary document as the "rights of man"[*sic*]). However, the same critique applies to universal social policies that claim to treat everyone according to some allegedly neutral standard of deservingness. Therefore, seeking a new norm to replace the old one may only result in our replacing the old discrimination with newer forms. While a new norm might say that all citizens are universally guaranteed the right to food or shelter or even a minimum income, the definition of a citizen is likely to be tightened as it has in European countries with more developed welfare states.[12]

What, then, is the alternative? What alternative would be best for us today? I want to pursue the idea that a postindustrial ethic should be a non-foundational one, in the sense that it would resist grounding social policy in normative standards regarding privilege and entitlement. It would not reject norms so much as oscillate back and forth between norms and contingencies.[13] It would engage in such cross-referencing in order to rework the categories of privilege and entitlement so as to compensate people for being left behind. Such chiasmatic encounters, such textual wordplay, I suggest, would translate into the serious work of undermining the exclusionary practices that arise from normative standards.

In what follows, I pursue this postindustrial ethic by examining a debate between two noteworthy scholars, Nancy Fraser and Iris Marion Young.[14] I take their arguments in a different direction than their initial concerns. Their debate is ostensibly about whether a political economy of material redistribution ought to take precedence over a cultural project focused on symbolic recognition. However, it has also helped to highlight the related issue of whether a new social ethic ought to be grounded in a normative base or whether it should be a more contingent, situational practice that responds to problems as they arise. Fraser has thoughtfully proposed a new normative foundation that is more attentive to the needs and circumstances of women and she builds those considerations up into universal standards. Young has proposed a more contingent practice that recognizes that all universal standards are forms of self-regulating power that inevitably maintain their hegemony by marginalizing some identities and practices at the expense of others.

In this chapter, I apply these two positions to the real world of social welfare policy. I contrast universal insurance policies with targeted compensatory programs. The former is an example of a policy based on a foundational approach while the latter is based on a contingent approach. I demonstrate in particular the difficulties of making either alternative workable in practice, by employing a textual strategy that helps expose the implied subtext of social policy in either case. I conclude that we need to learn from both approaches, in that social policy must establish standards and then compensate people for being disadvantaged by them.

This sort of hybrid approach oscillates between fixing norms a priori in theory and responding to contingencies in practice.[15] Such an approach is much needed in no small part because the real world of the social welfare state is a world of politics and power. The social welfare state itself is a hybrid that fits neither the pure model of capitalism or nor that of socialism. The social welfare state is not resolvable by recourse to the formula of theoretical models. Instead, it is destined to be forever a political object, not entirely resolvable in theory and in need of constant readjustment in light of the contingencies that arise. Therefore I examine the contingencies associated with social welfare entitlements as insurance and as compensation in the system of social provision in the 1990s to suggest how this hybrid social welfare state can continue to be made relevant to the postindustrial dangers confronting all families, but especially single mothers with children.

Norm-Based Social Welfare

Today's rearguard action of insisting on rewarding those families that are said to conform to the myth of the "traditional family" while punishing those that do not is a cruel and vindictive manifestation of the refusal to confront the way postindustrial change is making the traditional values of family and work unsustainable even as ideals. This punitive insistence on enforcement of traditional values which the changing economy makes increasingly unrealizable therefore represents a postindustrial ethic only in the most unreflective sense. It is in fact the opposite of a postindustrial ethic. It is an insensitive and futile denial, seeking to re-create the old world in the face of the new. It is an ethic that seeks to address the realities of postindustrialism by wishing them away. It is an ethic that insists that regardless of circumstances families must conform to traditional standards in order to qualify for assistance and must accept surveillance and the possibility of punishment if they fail to do so. Rather than help families be effective, families must first be so in order to gain access to needed assistance. This of course overlooks the painfully explicit contradiction that such denial contains: if families could prove their effectiveness first, they would not need the assistance they are seeking. If women always married first before having children and fathers always worked at decently paying jobs, far fewer families would need assistance. The question is not how families can be made to fit into existing policies, but how can we change our policies to support families, given the changes they have had to endure?

The prevailing anxious ethic is a patriarchal one. We could counter it with a feminist one. This is what Nancy Fraser does in an important article entitled "After the Family Wage."[16] Her writings on the normative foundations of the welfare state are significant attempts to reveal the implicit biases built into the norms which inform existing social welfare entitlements and to develop alternative normative foundations that can make for a more just system of social protections. In my mind, no work in this vein today is as important as Fraser's. Fraser also thoughtfully makes the case for the need for a normative theory as the foundation for a social welfare state.[17] She is increasingly impatient with writing that eschews normative theorizing and focuses on deconstructing the normative foundations of the social order.

Fraser's normative theorizing highlights the patriarchal biases of the existing "family-wage" system. She shows that the system privileges male-identified productive work as the basis for social entitlements to more generous social insurance. It does so at the expense of female-identified reproductive work that is limited to receiving inferior benefits from public assistance. Fraser demonstrates convincingly that the welfare state has profound male biases that do real violence to women in need of assistance.

Much of this has already been articulated by others. Fraser's analysis revisits the well-developed distinction between a male-identified "work" ethic and a female-identified "care" ethic. She shows that the family-wage system is based on a work ethic that privileges the male-identified subject position of the worker over that of the female-identified caregiver. Yet Fraser goes further in demonstrating that the family-wage system is no longer sustainable in light of the socioeconomic changes occurring in the postindustrial era. While others have also demonstrated this, few have done this as well as Fraser. She argues effectively that the family-wage system is passing away and in particular that an alternative ethic needs to be developed for postindustrial social provision.

It is here that Fraser's work is most distinctive. She explicitly develops normative models for social provision that would be an improvement on the existing patriarchal system. Under one model—that of the "Universal Breadwinner"—women and men would be treated more equally and the social protection provided would be consistent with that ethic of social provision. However, Fraser emphasizes that women's particular circumstances, especially as they continue to be the primary caregivers, will often leave them behind in spite of equal treatment. On the one hand, women would gain equal treatment but at the risk of having to adapt themselves to the male-identified order. On the other hand, women who still chose to be caregivers would likely be disadvantaged under a system where women were given an equal opportunity to be like men and where productive work was still privileged over reproductive work. For instance, antidiscrimination laws or even affirmative action laws in hiring would not help women who remained at home with the children, and should they be divorced, social welfare entitlements would not help single mothers as much as unemployed women.

Under a second model—that of "Caregiver Parity"—women's role as the primary nurturer and caregiver would be valued as much as men's role as the primary breadwinner. Yet while this model avoids the androcentrism of the breadwinner model, it risks marginalizing women in the ghetto of reproductive labor once again. Fraser therefore finally turns to a third model for creating the normative basis for a postindustrial social welfare state.[18] This model would reflect an ethic of care as normative and men and women alike would be protected in terms of their ability to fulfill their reproductive roles. It would be more aggressive in explicitly stating that in order to achieve social justice for women we have to do more than treat them as equal to men. Instead, we need to consider women's subject position as normative to the point where we expect both men and women to be in similar circumstances as women, with similar needs as women. Then we must organize social protections in terms of those needs rather than the needs traditionally associated with someone fulfilling the responsibilities of male-identified productive work. While Fraser recognizes the difficulties in achieving this model, she regards it as superior to the others:

> Much more work needs to be done to develop this third—Universal Caregiver—vision of a postindustrial welfare state. A key is to develop policies that discourage free-riding. *Contra* conservatives, the real free-riders in the current system are not the poor solo mothers who shirk employment. Instead, they are men of all classes who shirk carework and domestic labor, as well as corporations who free-ride on the labor of working people, both underpaid and paid. . . . The trick is to imagine a social world in which citizens' lives integrate wage earning, caregiving, community activism, political participation, and involvement in the associational life of civil society—leaving time for some fun. This is a world not likely to come into being in the immediate future, but it is the only imaginable postindustrial world that promises true gender equity. And unless we are guided by this vision now, we will never get any closer to achieving it.[19]

Fraser is probably trying to underscore how difficult it will be to achieve a gender-just social order when she ends that agonizingly long list of citizen responsibilities with "time for some fun." But her point is deadly serious: men need to add many more responsibilities to their day if gender equity is to happen. Given all that, gender equity is not going to occur overnight.

However, that is really the least of the problems with the Universal Caregiver model. While Fraser's specific alternatives to the patriarchal welfare state are politically progressive and would make for a much less painful world for many women, her whole cloth normative approach has two major deficiencies. First, she remains committed to the idea that normative theory in and of itself can specify the basis for social provision. Second, she refuses to accept the possibility that the contradictory and contingent character of actually existing social welfare policies may require a more flexible ethic of social provision. In the end, she does not accept the possibility that social provision might have to be developed even when we are unable to specify the grounds for doing so.

Fraser comes close, however. For instance, she does at least implicitly address the fact that the subject positions she interrogates are as much a product of the state as they are of civil society. Her analysis opens the door to considering how social policy has been complicit in reinscribing women's reproductive work as subordinate and how new policies could be complicit in creating new forms of subordination. Thus, male workers could be disadvantaged by a political economy premised on privileging caregiving. One might argue, though, that such a privileging of one subject position over another would be in the service of rectifying inequities in society. But other more troubling examples come to mind as we think about the model. What about couples without children? What about unattached individuals? After a certain point, we come full circle and ask why we can't have a universal welfare state founded on a nondiscriminatory norm that treated all individuals alike irrespective of their family ties, whether they were married or not, and so on? Now, further on the horizon arises the question: Can we have a universal welfare state founded on a nondiscriminatory norm? Or is all norm-based social policy in the real world of social welfare doomed to having to attend to compensating people who are disadvantaged because they do not measure up to the standards implied by that norm?

Norm-Based Universalism

The search for a postindustrial ethic of social provision can benefit from parallels in other areas of social thought. Unfortunately, social welfare theorists seldom make these connections. For instance, the search for a foundational norm for organizing social provision usually leads to a proposal for a universalistic social welfare state that will not make discriminatory distinctions but will protect all citizens, couples, and families from social and economic insecurity. However, theories of a universalistic social welfare state have largely ignored the fact that the idea of universalism has been subject to much more contention in other areas of thought. Taking those debates into account raises the possibility that a universalistic welfare state is not only politically impossible at this juncture but politically questionable as well.

Although Fraser's foundationalism does account for critiques of universalism, the writings of many others do not.[20] Instead, Fraser's theorizing raises an issue in another direction. While her writing is well informed about a variety of theoretical debates, it is less attentive to the specifics of social policy. It is here that her attempt to articulate a normative foundation for the social welfare state run into its greatest difficulties. Despite Fraser's sensitivity to the biases of various universalisms, her lack of attention to the specifics of social provision allows her to insist on the need for a foundational ethic for social policy. Fraser herself recognizes that the allegedly universalistic standards currently in place need to overcome their existing male bias by switching to a foundational norm based on women's needs and responsibilities. Fraser's models are quite explicit in this regard and she is sensitive to the exclusionary nature of these norms. She is, however, less helpful in specifying how we would deal with the dilemmas these exclusions pose. Her foundational approach does not equip us to address these.

It is in the specifics of the real world of the welfare state that the goal of universalism flounders. In theory, a universalistic welfare state would be a just and fair way to ensure social security. Universal standards imply impartial treatment. Liberal society's commitment to a neutral state logically encourages the idea of universalism as the way to structure whatever social welfare protections are deemed necessary for people to participate effectively in the social order. In addition, universalistic social policies are often seen as one way to minimize the marginalization of groups least consistent with the dominant social norms, such as nonworking single mothers. Universalistic programs are also often preferred on the grounds that targeted "programs for poor people make poor programs." Universalistic programs are not only more inclusive but more likely to garner broad public support, whereas programs targeted at the poor or minorities are likely to become associated with those groups, thereby ensuring their marginalization.[21]

But in practice universalism is always relative to some implied norm or context. The implied context of social policies is evident in the way people are rewarded if they are considered to have earned their benefits, are seen to have legitimate needs, or have met other criteria which make them consistent with the policy's implied modal recipient or beneficiary. And applying for benefits inevitably involves a performance that the applicants enact to demonstrate that they are like the assumed worthy recipient. Universalistic social policies are inevitably always based on some norm of social provision that determines who is eligible for what aid, under what conditions. In this sense no policy is ever entirely universalistic since its normative foundation privileges some identities and practices over others.

Once we confront the issue of a normative foundation for the universalistic welfare state, we have to ask whether we can identify such a nondiscriminatory norm or whether such a norm is always at risk of being discriminatory. There are a variety of obstacles to realizing the universalistic ideal of norm-based social policy. First, social welfare provision does not take place in the abstract, but is always embedded in a historical and institutional context.[22] In other words, universalism in social welfare provision would be more feasible if the messiness of the real world did not intrude. Historically, "actually existing welfare states" are hybrid political economies that fall between capitalism and socialism. Real welfare states socialize consumption to varying degrees, while existing within systems of private production. Each has a logic of its own that will inevitably make for its own version of universalism.

"Historical institutionalism" and other attempts to account for the real-world context, however, often overstate the distinctiveness of the variety of forms of "welfare capitalism" and as a result tend to trivialize the systematic contradictions built into the welfare state.[23] Yet as an idea welfare capitalism is itself a hybrid that universalism will find quite contradictory. In practice an "actually existing" universalistic welfare state must almost always serve the contradictory goals of promoting individualism and collectivism. Under these circumstances, universalism will vary across systems in creating standards that balance state and market, work and care, right and need.

If attained, a universalistic welfare state would in any one instance be where the state prevents markets from infringing on the basic needs of citizens. Such a comprehensive welfare state would involve the total "decommodification" of labor, where workers' basic needs were guaranteed through social welfare entitlements. By definition the total decommodification of labor is not capitalism—in which labor is a commodity bought and sold in market transactions. As long as welfare is part of capitalism, however, such a mixed system will have contradictions which are not easily resolved. Getting from individualism to collectivism is not easy and is subject to numerous political conflicts.

If "historical institutional" approaches minimize by historicizing the contradictions built into all welfare states, "social democratic" theories of the development of the welfare state may be too optimistic in suggesting that an increasingly inclusive universalistic state is the logical outcome of the developmental process. These theories correctly emphasize the role of political conflict in creating the contingencies of welfare state development.[24] At any one point in time the welfare state will reflect the compromises made between the forces of individualism and those of collectivism. But those agreements are not irreversible and have proven subject to renegotiation. For instance, many other industrialized societies have made greater progress in achieving the universal entitlement ideal than the United States; however, the United States is not alone in being under intense pressure to roll back its welfare entitlements. All welfare states are confronting demands for disentitlement as a necessary response to the pressures of globalizing markets. In other words, the social welfare state is under assault everywhere as pressure grows to realign it with the changing capitalist economies in which it is housed.[25] But the compromised nature of the welfare state reflects agreements between real actors who resist simply rewriting the social contract. For instance, even in today's era of rollbacks the stronger the labor movement is politically, the greater is the balance between classes, the greater the social welfare entitlements, the more universalistic the coverage, and the more resistant those entitlements have been to repeal.[26]

Therefore, "actually existing welfare states" have their own historical and institutional context within which they work out a compromise between the forces of individualism and those of collectivism. They are hybrids that reflect compromises between ethics, systems, and classes. They are the residue of the conflicts over the relations of production that are built into the state. The "relations of politics" in the social welfare state thus replace the "relations of production" in the economy as the major fulcrum of political-economic conflict.[27] To varying degrees the social welfare state always reflects the compromises of what is called the "social contract." These compromises inevitably make for contradictions in social welfare policy. As products of compromise, social welfare entitlements are of necessity contradictory, reflecting the competing interests embedded in each compromise. Unavoidably, therefore, they are always forms of assistance that enable people to meet their needs to some extent while simultaneously being forms of regulation that constrain people's ability to act, by making the receipt of aid conditional on their conformity to standards as to who is deserving of assistance.

Social welfare entitlements are also regulatory in another sense. They do not just regulate recipients; they also regulate themselves. Therefore they must be self-regulating, as all products of power relations are, to ensure that they remain consistent with the terms of agreement defining who is entitled to what, under which conditions. A noteworthy way of being self-regulating is by not being universalistic. Social welfare entitlements legitimate themselves by distinguishing themselves from alternative, more questionable, forms of assistance. As Frances Fox Piven and Richard A. Cloward write:

> By segregating the poor into different programs, American welfare policy reinforces the separation of the poor from working, and middle class Americans, and also creates sharp divisions among the poor. And once categorized by the programs, the poor are then denigrated by the treatment accorded them. Benefits in the poor-serving programs are less likely to be a matter of right and more likely to be discretionary, subject to the successful hurdling of bureaucratic inquisitions and runabouts, and continuing bureaucratic surveillance, all of which shapes the understandings both of the people who endure this treatment, and the people who in a sense are the public audience for these rituals. Finally, and very important, recipients receive benefits which keep them very poor, ensuring their marginalization in an affluent and materialistic society.[28]

In fact, we might say that each social welfare entitlement has its own psychic life.[29] The psychic life of welfare, for instance, is tied to aligning its practice with the dominant norms of work and family, as welfare reform repeatedly does. Welfare must of necessity continually distinguish itself from the specter of the other—the "bad welfare," we might say—that haunts it. Welfare must continually prevent itself from appearing to pose a threat to the dominant norms of work and family. It must continually prove itself to be the "good welfare" that promotes work and family norms, or it will lose legitimacy and disentitlement politics will accelerate. In the process of trying to be consistent with the dominant norms of society, welfare becomes much less than universalistic.

The difficulties of norm-based welfare therefore are not that we have the wrong norms, or lack norms but that invariably we have too many conflicting norms. In the real world of welfare policy, norm-based policies collapse under their own normative excess. The profound contradictions between work and family they have intensified in the postindustrial era of dual wage-earning families, mother-only families, and children born outside marriage. Of necessity, therefore, welfare is a schizoid practice, whose problems cannot be solved in a satisfactory way. It cannot but remain an anxious, vexed flashpoint for thinking about the contradictions that plague work and family. Rather than punishing people for failing to resolve these contradictions on their own, we can support people in their attempts to negotiate them. While this might not simply mean giving everybody more money under any circumstance, it surely should mean being less punitive and more supportive of mother-only families than we are currently being.

The current ethic of exclusionary social provision, as developed under the 1996 welfare reforms, has intensified the focus on punishing families for failing to live up to what has become an unsustainable ideal. We need an alternative ethic better geared to the social and economic realities of postindustrialism. However, given the foregoing argument, we should readily acknowledge that every norm for determining redistribution will imply recognizing some identities over others. Norm-based social provision will implicitly or explicitly privilege some subject position at the expense of others, whether it is the "breadwinner" or the "homemaker," whether it is the productive worker or those who are primarily responsible for reproduction, and so on. Therefore, nothing is to be gained by delaying the recognition that every normative standard for determining the basis for redistribution is vulnerable to amendment for exceptions and exemptions. "Innocents" who are "truly needy," but not the "undeserving," will qualify for inclusion in social provision to varying degrees, as the strict adherence to the norm is seen to do an injustice in specific instances.[30] Widows, yes, unmarried teen mothers, no. The mentally ill, yes; drug addicts, no. Subject positions proliferate and deviance is demarcated when the normative basis of the welfare state is made explicit.

This can never be done in a clean fashion. All social policy makes invidious distinctions that cannot be definitively defended philosophically and are in need of political supplementation in order to survive challenge. Some defy their own logic faster than others. All normative orders leak and the need for compensating action is never ending. Only the contingencies of any one policy will provide the basis for what reforms would best reduce hardship in a particular instance. The normative basis for social welfare provision is never airtight. It may well be that our time is better spent attending to the leaks than to the norms, to breathing life into the welfare state than to stabilizing it as a suffocating normative order that is inattentive to the violence its exclusions inflict.

The answers to the questions of social welfare can never be answered entirely in the abstract. The specifics of policy require their own attention. The contradictions of the welfare state intensify this predicament. Universal programs will never be complete; they will always leave some people out. Compensatory targeted programs will follow. And with the proliferation of compensatory programs, calls for the consolidation of a universalistic policy will subsequently ensue. The choice between universalism and targeting is a false one, given that the one begets the other. Under these conditions, no norm of social provision is self-sustainable in the real world of welfare state contradictions.

A Nonfoundational Ethic

Iris Marion Young provides us with an opportunity to consider a nonfoundational approach to social provision. I therefore want use Young here to counter Fraser. This encounter has already been staged by Young and Fraser. Their debate, however, is ostensibly about political economy versus identity politics; that debate is less important to me than what I want to discuss here. But first, Young has complaints about Fraser that are worth mentioning.[31] Young suggests that Fraser engages in dichotomous thinking in that she is too rigid in distinguishing a political economy of redistribution from a cultural project of recognition. Young argues that recognition and redistribution are entwined. She finds a tremendous overlap between an identity politics that fights against the marginalization of people based on group identity and a political and economic struggle that fights for the class-based reallocation of material resources. Race and gender conflicts are class conflicts, and vice versa. Young feels that Fraser falsely segregates cultural and politico-economic conflict while privileging the latter. Clearly however, Fraser is trying to find a way to avoid marginalizing cultural issues, even if Young's complaints have some merit.

Fraser has her own position. Fraser reads Young's work as suggesting that all the important forms of oppression associated with identity that Young identifies are really forms of economic exploitation. Yet, to my mind Young has clearly helped us see that there is more to the struggle than fighting class inequity, that identity politics is directed at forms of oppression which are not reducible to economic exploitation, and that class position is not a universal subject position for resisting all oppression.

For my purposes, I want to restage the Young-Fraser encounter from another, more mutually supporting, vantage point. Combining concern for recognition with concern for redistribution points toward how norm-based social policy is exclusionary. Using these categories separately makes for analysis that is too stark and dichotomous. The alternative sort of analysis enables us to raise the issue of how a norm-based ethic of social provision unavoidably makes distinctions that privilege some identities over others. It alerts us to how the policy process transforms difference into otherness, and how otherness easily gets alienated and subjugated.

What then is the alternative ethic implied in the concern to compensate groups for the way have been othered? How is a nonfoundational ethic possible? Not all ethics need be command ethics grounded in categorical imperatives of a priori premises and foundational theories that specify the needed conditions for right conduct ahead of time.[32] An ethic of contingency, equipping us to respond as circumstances change, is one way of talking about alternatives. This is the beginning of what I would call a postmodern ethic.[33] In social policy, such an ethic would continually correct the harms and injuries caused by exclusions and limitations in social policy.

With such an ethic, we would forgo trying to stabilize families in terms of "social security," which often involves marginalizing, if not punishing, those that do not conform to normative standards. We would move beyond a normative approach that prioritizes a particular version of the family over others. Instead, we would have a system of "compensation" to attend to the needs of families that have been marginalized by the operative exclusionary standards. The social security "state" would be replaced by a compensatory "process." While social security tries to arrive at a stabilized "state," compensation enacts a dynamic "process" that responds to contingent circumstances and redresses the needs of those who have been left behind. Social security fixes distinctions of deservingness, while compensation seeks to correct them.[34]

Social provision consistent with this alternative compensatory perspective would still be tied to philosophy, if not to foundations. It would be based on an alternative "ethic of alterity" that attends to constantly being attentive to the "others" who have been discriminated against and left behind in the face of social and economic change.[35] Such an ethic of alterity would not align itself with an epistemology of interpreting the unknown in terms of the known and it would resist an ontology of sameness that evaluates the other in terms of the self.[36] Instead, an ethic of alterity would encourage us to learn to work with what Homi Bhabha calls the "anxiety of signification." Its pedagogy would teach us to live with the liminal state of being "in between." It would attend to the way the normative standards of, say, the self-sufficient self "other" (as in the verb "to other") some people and leave out alternative identities and practices that are nonetheless worth affirming and supporting in their own right.[37] In such cases, people whose contributions to society take the form of child rearing or caregiving more generally, can be seen to be engaged in productive work, and vice versa. We can then begin to appreciate how each can be supported under another's rationale in particular instances. A work ethic and a care ethic need not be treated as mutually exclusive and what counts as work or care will be recognized as changeable and in need of constant reconsideration under a dynamic compensatory process.[38]

Rather than trying to treat "like cases alike" according to liberal notions of equality of opportunity, fairness, and procedural due process, the compensatory process would be willing to continually make exceptions and account for anomalies, especially when those exceptions are a product of broader societal forces that discriminate against those who are so "othered." Such a process would recognize that inequalities or relative deprivation can translate into inequities or absolute deprivation, especially when such distinctions are exacerbated under conditions of rapid social and economic change. The compensatory process would be prepared to bring forward those left behind in appreciation of the fact that their relative access to specific social goods has been affected by their "othered" status and that this will affect their ability to provide for their families in the future in real terms.

The False Binary: Social Insurance versus Public Assistance

The move from an ethic of universalism to an ethic of compensation could be an effective approach to confronting the inadequacies of the "industrial system of social provision" as it collides with the social casualties of the postindustrial economy. One could and probably should argue that the move to a nonfoundational ethic is a timeless strategy worthy of consideration throughout the ages. I am not sure how many votes you would get for that one. However, given the current disjuncture between the industrial system of social provision and postindustrial economic change, this is a particularly propitious time to consider such a move.

The timing may also be right because "social security" is no longer the secure linguistic home for social provision it once was. With social provision on the road in search of a new home, it might be time to consider replacing the falsely stable social security state with the more flexible and contingent compensatory process. In fact, we might start by recognizing that social security had its own process of othering that produced stability for some, such as middle-class retirees, while continuing to create instability for others, such as poor single mothers with children. Perhaps once we see social security not as a welfare state but as its own, if discriminatory, process, we can start to find ways to compensate people who have been determined to have been unfairly othered by that process. We might then begin to find ways to empower families regardless of their circumstances rather than punishing them for failing to live up to preset, falsely neutral, universal, industrial standards that are a growing number of postindustrial families are unable to meet.

The possibility of countering "social security" with "compensation" as the preferred discursive and institutional practice starts by examining how Social Security has operated in text and policy. Barbara Nelson and others have effectively argued that since the passage of the Social Security Act in 1935 the U.S. welfare state has been a two-tiered or dual-track system of cash assistance.[39] The programs on the upper track have tended to be nationally funded and administered, with more generous benefits. Beneficiaries of such programs have been seen as having earned their benefits by virtue of their relationship to the wage-labor market. This top tier is reserved for the rhetorically designated "insurance" programs, as they have been somewhat pseudonymously called. The term "insurance" was designed to suggest that the recipients of these programs were only getting back what they had paid in and earned.

But there is no such program, not even the primary example of a top-tier program, old age and survivors' retirement benefits, popularly known by the title of the entire 1935 legislation—Social Security. Given its popularity as a program for the deserving, it is probably no accident that this program came to take on the name of the entire 1935 legislation. It was popularly touted as being thoroughly consistent with the basic American values of individualism and the work ethic. The reality is something else.

Actually, for most of its history Social Security has not operated as an insurance program wherein each person only gets back what his or her payments have earned.[40] It does have a Social Security Trust Fund and each contributor has her or his own individual retirement account; however, these are best understood as accounts documenting what people are eligible to receive rather than accounts that actually hold money. For years the Trust Fund has loaned what surplus it has had, when it has had it, to the rest of the federal budget. Instead, it shares a fundamental feature with the public assistance programs of the second tier that operated as welfare programs.

Welfare programs are income-transfer programs that transfer income from one group to another. Rather early on, Social Security unavoidably became an income-transfer program in that, like other welfare programs, it could not finance itself unless it was able to transfer income from one group to another. For years, the money simply changed hands; the working generation transferred income to the retired generation and as the ratio of workers to retirees shrank, surpluses that had been built up were depleted. In preparation for future shortfalls, after being reformed Social Security has in recent years again operated with a surplus left over, which is used to buy U.S. treasury bonds. Still, no matter how you look at it there is not really money in the Social Security Trust Fund to cover all obligations. It still cannot cover all outstanding obligations even if it were to cash in its bonds. It is not actuarially sound in this strict sense. It will soon barely bring in enough each month to pay out benefits and will have to start drawing down its current surplus by cashing in the government securities it has purchased. If current policies and economic assumptions hold, starting in 2032 it will not have enough funds to cover all benefits for that year.[41] Under these conditions, it is difficult to insist that Social Security is an insurance program rather than an income-transfer program.

However, Social Security has been a special case of an income-transfer program. It has undoubtedly been a privileged program benefiting from its top-tier insurance designation, allowing it to receive much legitimacy and popularity as a program consistent with American values. Its beneficiaries too have benefited by being called beneficiaries rather than recipients, by being seen as having earned their benefits, by not having to meet means tests or low-income eligibility requirements for the most part, and by avoiding the surveillance that harasses recipients of second-tier public assistance programs. Over the years these beneficiaries have gained cost-of-living adjustments and other enhancements in benefits. From the early 1970s, cost-of-living adjustments have been automatic, first twice a year and now annually. As a result, poverty among the elderly has been halved over the last twenty-five years while poverty among children has increased sharply in the last fifteen. It is important to add that Social Security Disability Insurance has also benefited from its being seen as an insurance program. It has also been nationally administered and funded with better benefits.[42]

While the first tier was mislabeled insurance, the second tier programs can be called compensation. In theory, the second tier compensates people who are left out of the categories of inclusion in the first tier. Those of the elderly who did not work and did not qualify for Social Security, for instance, could often qualify for second-tier benefits under programs that provided aid to the aged. However, the second tier has been no more grounded in reality than the first; its benefits were almost always inadequate and its standards for eligibility highly exclusionary, whether for aid to the aged or aid to single mothers with children. Compensation for the injustices of the broader political economy were not what the second tier provided.

The tiering of social programs has been gendered, with single mothers in need of income support often having to rely on inferior second-tier benefits.[43] Jill Quadagno and Robert Lieberman have noted that the tiering of programs has occurred along racial lines, with white workers and their dependents more likely to be covered by the top-tier insurance programs.[44] Frances Fox Piven and Richard Cloward have shown that programs have been tiered in terms of one's attachment to the labor market, thereby reinforcing class relations.[45] However, while the class, race, and gender biases of the social order have undoubtedly been reflected in the tiering of social policies, something more basic has also been at work. The textual positioning of the second tier as categorically different has itself done much for its fortunes—just as the insurance myth has for Social Security, if in the other direction.

Since 1935 the second tier of the social security state has consisted of public assistance programs for people who are not viewed as having earned their benefits and who are therefore considered undeserving of first-tier insurance benefits. While they may have worked as hard as anyone else, usually harder, and may be as innocent in terms of why they are now without a wage income, by definition their exclusion from the first tier suggests otherwise. In particular, single mothers who have been abandoned rather than widowed are considered not to be deserving of first-tier insurance support. All second-tier recipients are nonetheless treated suspiciously by the public as well as welfare administrators.

Quite logically within the existing federal system, the programs that provide second-tier recipients with benefits have therefore been only partially federally funded, are state-administered, offer lower benefits, require means tests for determining eligibility, and have had extensive surveillance procedures to ensure that recipients qualify for benefits. People who were kept out of primary labor markets because of their skin color, or lost the support of a spouse who deserted them, or were unable to accumulate much in retirement due to their low wages were denied the benefits of the first tier when they needed that support. In addition, just as the discriminations of the broader society were reflected in the tiering of benefits, and the tiering of benefits in turn helped reinforce those discriminatory practices.[46] While the discriminated against were marginalized in the development of social policy and relegated to relying on second-class protections, defining them as undeserving and withholding needed assistance was critical to making them unable to demonstrate their worthiness. Programs for poor people have made for poor programs, and vice versa.

The federally established entitlement of Aid to Families with Dependent Children (AFDC) was the primary example of a second-tier program until it was superseded by the Personal Responsibility and Work Opportunity Reconciliation Act of 1996 and replaced with the block-grant program, Temporary Assistance for Needy Families (TANF).[47] This is the program commonly referred to as welfare, primarily received by single mothers with children. The way AFDC—and now TANF—has been structured is devoid of any sort of informed understanding of the material circumstances of most welfare recipients. Second-tier programs have historically lacked legitimacy because their recipients are said to lack the "innocence" associated with the worthy poor who are in need through no fault of their own.[48]

Yet, the single motherhood that causes most women on public assistance to be poor has been tendentiously constructed in welfare policy discourse to approximate a bad "lifestyle choice" that must not be rewarded. The factual basis for this position is itself suspect. Indeed, public assistance programs for single mothers have tended to be based on rumor, stereotype, and prejudice about promiscuous young women, irresponsible parents, and income-maximizing adults—in other words, about the "Welfare Queen" who is seeking a free ride.

However, welfare benefits have never paid well and have been in precipitous decline for two and a half decades. The desperate, deserted, and divorced, but also the abused, traumatized, and unemployable make up the bulk of mothers who must rely on welfare. Many of those receiving welfare for shorter periods of time only need only a temporary form of assistance until they can get their lives back together after being left on their own with their children. Others, often younger, never married, undereducated, without much support from family and friends, and often from poorer minority communities need more time before they can handle single motherhood on their own without help from the state. And even among this needy group, only the most desperate will endure the stigmatization and punishment associated with trying to eke out an existence on welfare. The second tier, therefore, is for people who are considered second-class citizens.

It is no accident, then, that the prevailing biases of welfare policy discourse make welfare a hostage, if not an orphan, to the need to universally enforce the work ethic and family values regardless of individual circumstances and how people got there. Rather than helping welfare families to meet societal standards of work and family, welfare provides them a meager form of assistance while punishing them for failing to live up to those standards in the first place. Although second-tier programs like AFDC or TANF are said to exist to help those who do not qualify for first-tier programs, their primary purpose seems to be to remind everyone that they will suffer if they do not adhere to the dominant values in society regarding work and family. Second-tier programs make the idea of compensation suspect. They provide inferior benefits to people whose particular needs are seen as less deserving than those whose needs are met by first-tier programs.

It may be no accident then that first-tier programs also tend to be based on the assumption that the white male head of a middle-class, two-parent family is the modal beneficiary or person whose labor qualified the family for assistance. For years, many occupations in which women, persons of color, or low-skilled workers predominated were excluded from Social Security coverage and some still are. Second-tier programs, however, are disproportionately populated by single mothers, racial minorities, and low-wage workers. The two-tier welfare state not only makes a fictitious distinction between those who earned their benefits and those who did not, but it does so in ways that reinforce gender, race, and class privileges in society.

The tiering of cash income programs is mirrored in the area of health policy as amended by the Social Security Act of 1965. These amendments provided health insurance for the retired elderly under Medicare, and free health care for low-income families under Medicaid. Yet, much like welfare under AFDC, Medicaid, with its national-state system of financing and administration, is subject to constant cutbacks and underfunding. Aggressive efforts have been made to limit services through managed care. In spite of its failure to cover its own costs, Medicare, on the other hand, continues to operate like Social Security as a fictional insurance program and, more important, it continues to provide better coverage than Medicaid.

For years, the goal of many who struggled with social policy was to help those sequestered in the second tier to qualify for first-tier benefits, that is, to replace compensatory programs with insurance programs.[49] This goal was based on the appreciation that second-tier programs were in fact compensatory programs that failed to compensate effectively those excluded from the dominant categories of deservingness. Efforts were made at various levels, from helping disabled individuals move up from inferior welfare programs to disability insurance, to revising categories upward to the first tier—again disabilities would be a good example—to proposing reforms such as divorce or family insurance, or even allowances for children, to protect families with children from the income limitations associated with single-parent families. However, despite incremental successes of some of these efforts over the years, the strategy of incorporating individuals, categories, and programs into the first tier has become more difficult to sustain. This is because the first tier itself is under assault. In late-twentieth-century America, after the disentitlement in the second tier, we live to see that there is no security in Social Security at any level. Neither tier is secure. The assault on entitlements continues with the "contracting of America." With the passage of the welfare reform of 1996 welfare has ended as an entitlement. And now Social Security is under attack so the need to consider strategic alternatives is very much upon us.

Although the reactionary rhetoric against Social Security is disturbing, it arises in part because Social Security has been shrouded in myth. Its own disingenuous rhetorical distinctions have made it vulnerable to attack.[50] For instance, a good part of the assault on Social Security comes from the misapprehension that it is an insurance program. Rumors have been rampant for years that Social Security is bankrupt and will not be able to pay out benefits when they are due.[51] While the rumors are the product of hyperbole, and economists such as Robert Eisner and others have demonstrated convincingly that Social Security is entirely fixable with minor changes, nonetheless the demand to make fundamental changes in Social Security has been hard to quell.[52] This is in part due to the fact that before it came under attack via misleading characterizations, for years Social Security benefited from other misleading notions. In this sense, the chickens have come home to roost. For years, it was touted as an actuarially based insurance program; now it suffers because it cannot live up to the lie.

Social Security is not bankrupt and it need not go broke if policy makers are willing to make adjustments.[53] But powerful and wealthy interests do not want that to happen and they are using the insurance myth against Social Security to undermine its credibility with the population at large. The myth of insurance has been replaced by the equally misleading myth of insolvency. Of course, Social Security is bankrupt in the sense that it is not an actuarially based insurance program. But that could be remedied with continued growth in the economy or minor changes in the contribution rate and other features of the program. Nonetheless, as rumors have spread, the idea that Social Security has been ripped off has taken on a life of its own.

However, the real issue for Social Security is whether it will pay out benefits as scheduled irrespective of the availability of funding to cover all future obligations. This is an issue of public policy, not of insurance. Are policy makers and taxpayers willing to pay off the bonds when they come due and to raise taxes and do other things to maintain benefits to retirees at a sufficient rate? From five workers paying Social Security taxes for every retiree to receive benefits at the outset, Social Security is heading toward a projected ratio of a mere two workers per retiree by around the year 2025, making policy change a necessity. More significantly, retirees are living longer.[54] Nevertheless all policy makers have to do for Social Security to survive is either raise taxes slightly or reduce benefits for some or all retirees, or some combination of both. Then again, the economy could perform better than expected, making the program's survival possible with even smaller changes in either taxes or benefits. The question of why there are not enough government treasury bonds in the Social Security Trust Fund is therefore not really relevant. It reflects the insurance myth that once made the program popular and now makes it vulnerable to abolitionists who want their money back so they can invest it privately.

The push in the 1990s to privatize Social Security is therefore based on a fictitious distinction between insurance and public assistance. The most likely means to save Social Security is to end the "myth of tiers." Instead of privatizing Social Security it should be made into an income transfer program that transfers income from workers to needy retirees, eliminating some benefits from the well-off elderly. This could save billions of dollars and make Social Security solvent for decades. It is likely to be a major part of the response to the current Social Security "crisis." Public policy makers have been incrementally moving in this direction for over twenty years, reducing benefits to the well-off elderly slowly, revising the formula for calculating benefits, and initiating taxes on Social Security benefits based on income. As a result, the higher the retiree's income the less of each Social Security dollar he or she gets to keep. The means-testing of Social Security has been an incremental policy change for years. Should Social Security go the way of public assistance programs the distinction between the first and second tiers will evaporate, and with it the strategy of moving everyone into the first tier. I would therefore suggest that it is time to consider alternative linguistic moves that might engender new political possibilities.

The need to consider alternatives in order to structure social provision in more equitable ways is however not necessarily a desperate move brought about by the collapse of the insurance myth. This was an invidious myth that discriminated against particular families, including poor single women with children. Social Security discourse used the pretext of guilt to construct the ground on which the innocent were positioned. The elderly got to be the innocents, deserving their earned benefits, because they were not like the single mothers whose deviant behavior had brought them down into poverty. The idea that the elderly had earned their benefits was always a lie, in large part because they received much more than what a private retirement plan would have paid them. The back up position that older people have paid taxes overlooks the fact that most poorer recipients have paid taxes too—though not always taxes earmarked for the program they needed. The real question is why Social Security taxes are earmarked in the first place. Why are the taxes used to finance public assistance not so designated? In other words, why is Social Security protected but not public assistance?

These are not questions of deservingness as much as questions of power. They are about how symbolic distinctions translate into material consequences. Since the elderly are seen as adhering to white, male, middle-class norms of work and family, and more importantly, because the original beneficiaries were disproportionately white, male and middle class, once adopted their program was privileged.[55] Subtextually, both the program's privileged status and male whiteness were written into law, at the same time. Social Security would be a program for white, male, middle-class recipients and would therefore be privileged. Of course, in order to maintain that privileged status while it simultaneously extended coverage to other occupational groups who were not always middle class, male, and/or white, Social Security had to insist on policing its border with public assistance programs to reassure all concerned that it was not turning into a welfare program that irresponsibly doled out benefits to the undeserving. Therefore, the less Social Security worked as an insurance program—especially as it gave people more than they had earned—the more policy makers had to insist on the insurance myth and on Social Security's separation from public assistance programs. When the Social Security Administration did take on public assistance programs like Supplemental Security Income, it acted as if it had been infected by a virus and become dysfunctional.[56]

It is important at this point to note the most critical chiasmus of Social Security. Social Security ironically reinscribed the desire to be secure from the social, and to be an isolated individual who provided for him or herself in a self-sufficient fashion. Social Security practiced its own "politics of incorporation," making sure its collective program for ensuring well-being would be seen as entirely consistent with the individualistic ethos of the country. The insurance myth helped Social Security get incorporated into "America, Inc." It became as American as any trust fund. Wrapping Social Security in the insurance myth not only made it politically feasible but also forestalled further efforts to provide "social security" in a more social and collective sense. In fact, wrapping the program in this myth has now legitimized the push to privatize Social Security in its time of public turmoil.

Here is the warped logic that derives from the discursive politics of Social Security: since the program is designed to be consistent with the individualistic ethos, and since the program is now incapable of ensuring that the benefits it can pay individuals are as good as before or as good as what they could make by investing in the stock market, people should be able to privatize the program. Consistent with this logic, they should be able to do so by individual choice, one person at a time, each with his or her own investment account. The irony is bitter: a program designed to serve social purposes was legitimized in such a way that it reinscribed antisocial tendencies and set itself up for privatization.

But wrapping Social Security in the insurance myth had another, perhaps even more critical, chiasmatic reversal. Social Security was christened as a separate insurance program in ways that discouraged the elderly from building coalitions with other welfare state recipients. While Social Security was undoubtedly a product of effective national advocacy by such groups as the Townsend Movement and others, in the 1990s it represents an example of the reverse.[57] While it once illustrated how advocacy groups could influence public policy, in the 1990s it represents the quintessential case of public policy influencing advocacy groups. The insurance myth was originally promoted to make Social Security politically palatable and to allow upper-income groups to forgo having all their income taxed to finance their benefits. But the insurance myth also helped separate Social Security from other welfare programs and over time engendered an old-age movement that has aggressively resisted aligning itself with other social welfare constituencies.

It is the height of irony that over time this has led the allegedly most deserving group to act in the most blatantly self-serving way when it comes to social welfare policy issues. Led by the American Association of Retired Persons, which is first and foremost an organization that sells insurance and other consumer-products tailored to the retired, the old-age lobby trades in its good name every day in order to protect its exclusive benefits at the expense of building alliances with other welfare programs. In welfare policy discourse, Social Security has made the elderly, as much as the other way around.

Social Security exploited the relative symbolic distinction between insurance and public assistance and prefigured the absolute, material distinction between good and bad benefits. The most needy often became the least deserving, at risk of being "remaindered" for not fitting into the categories of innocence and worthiness reserved for the upper tier. The wrong gender, the wrong race, the wrong job, the wrong disability, the wrong social problem, the wrong family formation, and so on, could remainder the recipient and reinscribe her or his subordination in second-tier public assistance programs. Over the years, remaindering worked its rhetorical magic to produce real deprivation—migrant workers and sharecroppers would not get Social Security; alcoholics would not get disability insurance; unwed mothers could be sterilized; abused single mothers could be penalized for not working, even if their abusers only hurt them more when they worked. Guilty of not fitting into first-tier categories, these misfits of policy discourse were unfortunately not figments of textual practice. They were not Welfare Queens or other rhetorical realities. They were real people who had to live out the consequences of being left out by the tiered system of welfare-policy discourse.

Therefore, perhaps it is not the greatest social policy tragedy of all time that the tiered system has begun to collapse of its own rhetorical weight. Its demise will offer both opportunities and dangers for the most needy in our society.[58] The worthwhile strategy of trying to get everyone into the first tier is conceivably ending. That tiered system was always inventing ways to leave some people behind in spite of all the real pain such rhetorical "remaindering" caused. Although Social Security did provide needed aid to many families, there never was real "social" security in social security discourse.

Compensation in Word and Policy

One alternative to the failure to provide "social security" to all who need it is to give up on a universalistic social insurance system and turn to securing special benefits for each group as its needs are legitimated by the political process. Give up the quest for some unrealizable stable security in favor of a flexible system that allows us to respond to needs as they arise due to the contingencies of the changing economy. This proposal has particular merit when a good case can be made that the people in question were disadvantaged by preexisting practices that discriminated against them.

In order to make this linguistic turn, I employ a category that is already well established in the lexicon of the welfare state. It offers neither the false stability and security of "social security" nor the demeaning patronage of "public assistance." It is the repudiated idea of "compensation," which I want to resuscitate as a space from which to reposition social provision. I want to see if using compensation in new ways can help promote the idea that social provision is a dynamic process of compensating people, identities, and practices that have been excluded from the categories of privilege.

Some programs were explicitly called compensation. Unemployment Compensation was part of the Social Security of 1935. It was eventually renamed Unemployment Insurance. However, it has had problems in recent years, proving woefully inadequate to its task. A dwindling proportion of the unemployed are covered by the program, largely because the unemployed often need protection beyond the time it covers. In 1995, in any one month less than 40 percent of the persons listed by the federal government as unemployed were receiving unemployment compensation.[59] Unemployment insurance is becoming an exclusive income maintenance program for a declining number of primary sector workers. In this case, renaming unemployment compensation as insurance went unnoticed and in recent years did not have the salubrious effect it had had on Social Security. Unemployment remained mired in its past and merely renaming it changed nothing.

Nonetheless, let us consider a "compensatory process" that does more than merely rename, but actually covers people who are being left out by political and economic change. In lieu of a welfare state that guarantees a level of well-being to those who measure up to normative standards, this process would compensate those who had been left out and who in retrospect were seen to have been unfairly marginalized by those standards. While the Contract with America seeks to determine access to benefits based on whether a person measures up to standards of personal responsibility in matters of work and family, a compensatory public policy would provide benefits to those unfairly marginalized or disadvantaged by virtue of normative standards.

People receiving public assistance already get compensation as part of the current social security regime. However, this compensation is marginalized not only in second-tier but even in third-tier or no-tier programs. In the current system benefits in kind and vouchers reflect an appreciation of the need to compensate some families for inequities. Benefits in kind, particularly food from the charitable sector, have become increasingly prevalent over the last twenty years as public assistance has been slashed. That the private sector must grow to compensate for the retrenchment of the public sector has been the constant refrain of presidents and just about everyone else. Compensation levels have been grossly inadequate to make up for the cutbacks, but the idea continues to be emphasized. Benefits in kind are a particularly effective form of compensation as they put back only what is seen as having been taken away. Benefits in kind also give greater control over the compensation, as they can only be used for a specific purpose—as with food stamps, which can only be used for food and only certain kinds of food, at that. Vouchers for poor families for food and more commonly for housing operate in a similar way. The paternalism of these programs makes them suspect to many people, especially when they offer inferior benefits under stigmatizing conditions. However, given contemporary social welfare politics it is not only their paternalism that has led them to be marginalized. Instead, the idea of compensation is unpopular across the political spectrum, with the left objecting to its inadequacy and the right objecting to its proliferation in the face of the repeal of entitlements.

Despite these problems, the very existence of these programs tells us that compensation is not an alien idea and that it has a strategic appeal that resonates with the existing system of social provision. However, my interest in compensation is not to defend the provision of inferior and stigmatizing services for the allegedly undeserving. Instead, I want to argue that compensation points to an important dimension of social policy—the process of addressing the needs of the excluded. We need to take compensation seriously and devise better ways of dealing with the consequences of marginalization.[60]

Postindustrial Social Provision: Incremental Universalism

Once compensation is seen as a necessary part of social provision, the issue of criteria begins to reemerge. Who gets compensated for what and how? Aimless efforts of compensation are not good enough—as the inadequacy of existing second-tier programs indicates. Without a normative foundation they lack the legitimacy to move beyond being marginal programs. Therefore, neither a strictly norm-based social policy nor a nonfoundational compensatory process suffices in and of itself. What then?

In the real world of contradictions wrought by that hybrid of "welfare capitalism," we currently have no option but to try to develop social insurance while compensating those who do not qualify for such programs. But rather than accepting things as they are or identifying an alternative normative basis for extending social insurance, perhaps we should push the incremental strategy of trying to get more people, more problems, and more risks covered under the banner of social insurance. This would not repeat our current system's inadequacies. Here compensation becomes the means and insurance becomes the goal. Or vice versa. Insurance and compensation combine. So we get compensatory insurance, provided on a piecemeal basis, one group at a time, each justified according to a principle that legitimates their deservingness and invalidates their being left out. When that happens such programs are given the preferential treatment accorded insurance treatment. The best example of such an approach would be if we were to decide to insure all women with children against the loss of a wage-earning spouse—divorced and deserted mothers as well as widows with children. These other single mothers would get benefits as good as widows' benefits under survivors' insurance in the first-tier Social Security program. Each such program would be justified on its own grounds as covering a risk that merits insurance protection.

These compensatory insurance programs would not be limited to socializing the risks of workers as under the current patriarchal welfare state. Insurance need not be limited to protecting people from the risks arising out of inability to engage in the wage work associated with production. Linking insurance to what the existing political economy considers "productive work" reflects the biases of the culture of capitalism.[61] Pushing for an expansion of the insurance concept, even on an incremental basis, would involve challenging those biases. Insurance must be extended to cover the risks associated with "reproductive work" as well as production. Care as well as work must be compensated by ensuring that those who provide care are insured against the risks associated with the loss of income and support. Moving from one group to the next, such an incremental strategy would involve establishing care as a basis for qualifying for insurance against the loss of income and the risk of impoverishment.

This then would not be a status quo reinforcing incrementalism but a "radical incrementalism" that would challenge the existing biases of the culture of capitalism. It is also an "incremental radicalism": many small programmatic changes could be initiated with the cumulative effect of creating a more universalistic welfare state.[62] For instance, divorce insurance could be followed by pregnancy insurance or child insurance, each defending itself in terms of its own normative foundation while creating the possibility for the next. These insurance programs would fulfill the principle of compensation. However, one danger is that incremental insurance or compensation program development would only socialize the risk of those admitted to each insurance pool. Like bad drivers, allegedly "bad" wives and mothers would therefore still be left out or left to make do with their own marginal insurance pools.[63] Therefore, incrementalism must proceed on several fronts, seeking to expand the pool of people covered while adding new pools of coverage for the deserted and divorced, the abused and the neglected, while guarding against the re-creation of a new second tier of inferior insurance pools for people who are deserving but not seen as being so. With time, more and more people will be found to be deserving—not according to some universal principle but according to the political struggles that enable them to be incorporated into the welfare state, each on their own terms.

Some risks will be more difficult to cover than others. It will be more difficult to include some groups than others. Insurance for unwed teen mothers, for instance, will be extremely difficult politically. Yet here too mitigating circumstances can be used to show that a pregnancy was not due to personal irresponsibility as much as to poverty, lack of information, an abusive relationship, and the like. Undoubtedly some cases will be harder than others but that should not stop the effort to prove the deservingness of single women with children.

One significant risk of such an approach is that if you win at this game you actually lose—that is, winning gives you the status of a protected class of people who therefore deserve to be compensated for their injuries. But acquiring insurance as compensation need not make one a ward of the state in this dependent sense. In fact, this is where the power of the myth of insurance lies. It legitimates state entitlement without requiring beneficiaries to take on the identity of a dependent in need of protection from those who have harmed them. Instead, the idea of insurance is that you have legitimately earned your benefits and need not apologize for invoking your right to use them as needed. If divorce necessitates use of your insurance benefits, you need not explain that you have been especially wronged; instead, in providing an insurance benefit the state is explicitly accepting its responsibility to provide benefits a routine response to such circumstances. And adequate minimum benefits can protect those who have not made or have had contributions made on their behalf. While routinizing the protection against impoverishment from divorce will be criticized by some as an immoral policy that makes divorce acceptable, other people in contemporary America are just as likely to view it as a necessary development for most families with children, not just for particular women who need special protection.

Another risk is that such a strategy works within the limited categories of the existing political economy. "Insurance" reinscribes the ethos of exclusive individualistic consumption that is the hallmark of the dominant culture. Propagating insurance schemes might reinforce the idea of "each according to their ability" rather than "each according to their need." "Social insurance" can as quickly lead to a "politics of co-optation." A "politics of co-optation" comes into play when marginalized groups are incorporated into the insurance state but in ways that ensure the continued marginalization of other disadvantaged groups.

However, there can also be a "politics of incorporation" wherein marginalized groups are shown to be no different from those included in the insurance state. Divorced and deserted mothers become like widowed mothers. Those who have been left out are shown to be as deserving as those currently receiving benefits. Impoverishment due to the absence of a wage-earning spouse becomes something to be insured against regardless of whether that spouse died, became disabled, or abandoned the family. It is true that we might want to build in ancillary procedures to garnish the wages of absent parents who are not supporting their families when they can. Yet even these procedures would need to be supplemented by others that recognized that most poor single mothers who have needed welfare for extended periods in the past had given birth to children whose fathers did not earn enough to enable them to leave welfare.[64] We might want to have a variety of ancillary procedures. But a politics of incorporation would proceed by first using the available "cultural software" to demonstrate that parents who have been deserted deserve insurance protection against impoverishment just as widows do.[65]

Still another risk is that in an act of exclusive political consumption each group will close the door behind it, making it harder for those left behind to have their risks socialized through a public insurance program. Each group will be potentially the last, leaving the others to second-class compensatory programs. Yet, groups need allow the insurance state to organize them as the elderly in the United States have done. Each group can consciously see itself as a forerunner, linked to the others, acting in concert even as they achieve policy transformation on a piecemeal basis. Conservative, exclusionary incrementalism is only one kind of incrementalism. The issue is not incrementalism versus something else. It is what kind of incrementalism. Will it be "top-down" or "bottom-up" incrementalism? Will it be "bottom-up" incrementalism that challenges the existing biases of the systems of social provision as the most dramatic changes in the past have done?

The table below suggests a typology for social policy politics. We can choose first-class insurance programs—universal in scope—or second-class compensatory programs—targeted in scope. We can approach them incrementally or comprehensively. The dream of social policy politics is the upper left-hand cell—"comprehensive insurance." This approach holds out for the ideal of a universal welfare state. However, apart from being excessively controlled, with time it becomes maddeningly unrealistic. Why accept such dichotomous thinking as a blueprint for social policies that will never be? Why not transgress those boundaries? We then can do some good by exploiting the opportunities for change that exist under current conditions. Such an approach will elaborate an extensive social safety net piecemeal, providing needed social assistance for each group in response to the way it has been disadvantaged. Momentum can be built up by expanding the support base for such revisions through an articulation of affinities across different groups. The process need not involve successive mobilizations or people breaking up into splinter groups. Instead, the process involves extending state support to needed groups as their needs are legitimated. It also involves pushing for a variety of supports to particular groups that need them, such as single mothers, and doing so across a variety of areas: income, housing, child care, education, training, and the like. In other words, the ethic is universalist but the method is incremental. This way we achieve meaningful compensation even in the questionable normative order that operates in the United States today where serious constraints are imposed on social provision to the most needy.

Typology of Social Policy Politics

	Political Strategy	
Comprehensive		Incremental
Comprehensive Insurance (Universal Welfare State)		Incremental Insurance (Elaborated Social Safety Net)
Comprehensive Compensation (Paternalistic Welfare)		Incremental Compensation (Emergency Assistance System)

Top Row Across: Insurance Policies
Bottom Row Across: Compensatory Policies

The typology need not clarify but can blur the boundaries between insurance and compensation. Therefore it might be time to give up the equally limited debate over whether we should promote universal or targeted social policies. In this debate universal policies are defined as providing broad coverage, offering categorical eligibility, with better benefits. They are often touted as insurance programs. Social Security is the prime example. Targeted programs are defined as providing limited coverage, means-tested eligibility, and lower benefits. These programs are seen as welfare, not insurance. TANF would be the primary example today. Analysts such as Theda Skocpol or William Julius Wilson have emphasized that targeted programs fit the old saying: Programs for poor people make for poor programs.[66] Narrowly focused on the poor, these programs lack wide support and are often tightly surveilled to ensure that only those people who absolutely need the program will apply. However, analysts such as Robert Greenstein have defended targeted programs as enabling resources to be concentrated where they are most needed, while reassuring the broader taxpaying public that benefits will only be used for the legislated purpose.[67] He offers food stamps as an example of a successful targeted program. In practice, however, there really are no programs that are completely targeted or universal. The distinction is overdrawn. Instead, all programs are somewhat targeted if they qualify people according to some general category like poor families with children. In addition, in recent years the insistence on holding out for universal programs has done much to undermine the already weak support for welfare. It has given the impression that even liberals did not support welfare (and in many cases, they did not). This can be dangerous and can lead to exactly what has happened—the termination of programs on the grounds that they were too limited as well as ineffective. The incremental process of social inclusion outlined above would help avoid these pitfalls. It would transcend the limitations of universalism versus targeted programs by incrementally extending social insurance to cover all the social risks that need to be covered.

The foregoing points toward an important distinction. It is one thing for advocates to know in their heads, and to feel in their hearts, what social justice is; it is another thing to make it happen. Social justice cannot be legislated by some founding ethic that specifies the right normative standard we all must adhere to. Instead, advocates must take seriously both parts of the term social justice. It is a human creation; it is social. It is political; it is messy and always incomplete. No normative foundation by itself can identify the just order. All norms are in need of supplementation. Just as justice needs to be supplemented with mercy, so all norms need to be adjusted to reflect the everyday struggles of real people. While normative considerations give rise to questions about whom we should insure, we need to add a compensatory process to address the needs of those left behind. Just as norms need to be supplemented by the interrogation of categorical distinctions, insurance needs to be supplemented by compensation; otherwise norms will continue to marginalize and insurance will continue to put some people at risk. In the current welfare state, this means that single mothers will continue to be marginalized with increased risks for the well-being of their children.

In the end, these considerations remind us that social justice is still contingent on all families being able to access basic social welfare entitlements. All families should be able to practice a "politics of survival." Parents should have access to the basic services needed to raise their children: health care, nutritional assistance, housing, schooling, and the like. Parents should be able to receive the education and job training they need not only to be effective parents but also productive citizens. Whether these universal entitlements should be guaranteed all at once under some comprehensive family policy or whether they should be built up one after another was decided a long time ago. The time for incrementalism to get radical and radicalism to get incremental is long overdue.

In other words, while the goals of social justice remain the same, the pragmatics of how to get there need renewed attention. These goals, as Wendy Sarvasy has stated, are: "the public alleviation through social policy of the unjust social inequalities created by class, race, ethnic, and gender power relations."[68] The road there requires continual struggle, by and for real people in terms that address real needs in all their diversity.

Conclusion

The current *fin de siècle* rush to remake social policy aims to return it to a simpler time. It seeks to ground it more firmly in the traditional norms of work and family. But this is a postindustrial ethic only in the most unreflective sense. It becomes an excuse to deny having to deal with the burgeoning social problems associated with a changing economy and an opportunity to "contract" America as a leaner, meaner, more efficiently managed, less inclusive society. In the process, the social security state has come under increased scrutiny and attack.

But the "social security state" has never been the safe, stabilized space it was hoped it would be. Social security was a discursive and institutional practice that created safety and stability for some, particularly the middle-class elderly, by paternalistically reinforcing the stigmatization and insecurity of others, particularly single women with children. Social security was also premised on categorical distinctions, as between those who "earned" their benefits and those who did not. These distinctions reflected a foundationalism grounded in the work ethic and the traditional family. All families were to be evaluated and treated according to allegedly neutral, universal standards to which they had to measure up. Such a system of social provision sets up some families for punishment for failing to adhere to established standards and to achieve self-sufficiency, instead of empowering them to meet those standards and become self-sufficient in the future.

Critics of the current social policy politics are therefore strongly tempted to ground the welfare state in an alternative ethic. However, all norm-based social policy is at risk of having to compensate those it excludes. On the other hand, simply trying to compensate all disadvantaged groups and individuals is a rudderless process that can lead nowhere. Rather than trying to either stabilize social security in some fixed delimited and bounded way or to aimlessly respond to disadvantaged groups in an ad hoc fashion, it might be better to return to the struggle to include more marginal groups in the first tier. However, it is time to recognize that this is a never-ending process. Rather than pursuing the ghost of a never attainable "social security," we should incrementally extend the same social security protection afforded retirees to other economically vulnerable groups. Divorce insurance is one possible option, to be followed by others, each legitimated by demonstrating how the people in that group have been arbitrarily marginalized as not deserving.

In the idiom of the American political economy, this sort of insurance incrementalism deploys its own "cultural software" and enacts its own "politics of incorporation," enabling excluded groups to receive the insurance protections that are currently provided to others as a matter of right. Piece by piece, such a politics of incorporation will address the needs of groups like divorced or unmarried mothers with children who have been left out of the insurance system. It will work for their incorporation into the insurance state by demonstrating how they are as deserving of having their risks socialized as retirees or widows.

In the real world of politics, if there is to be a universal welfare state at all, it will be by way of an incremental universalism in which each new program paves the way for larger changes. André Gorz once argued for what he called "non-reformist reform" over the more common "reformist reform" that reinforced the existing structures of inequalities. "Non-reformist reform" created the capacity to cumulatively transform the existing system.[69] A radical incrementalism dedicated to step-by-step expansion of the first tier of insurance programs could lead to "non-reformist reform." In the late 1990s, it is politically the most feasible way to proceed. The product of word play, this strategy reverses the meanings of compensation and insurance. In the process, it stretches the terms of insurance to cover each new program. It becomes its own politics of incorporation, including marginalized groups as deserving members of the insurance state. Such a process of social inclusion would be a postindustrial ethic worth taking seriously.

Notes

NOTES TO THE INTRODUCTION

1. Francis Fukuyama, *The Great Disruption: Human Nature and the Reconstitution of Social Order* (New York: Free Press, 1999). For an alternative perspective, see Jean Baudrillard, *The Illusion of the End*, trans. Chris Turner (Stanford: Stanford University Press, 1994), pp. 122–23.

2. See Nancy Fraser, "After the Family Wage: Gender Equity and the Welfare State," *Political Theory* 22 (November 1994): 591–618; and Linda Gordon, *Pitied but Not Entitled: Single Mothers and the History of Welfare* (New York: Free Press, 1994), pp. 53–59.

3. Lawrence M. Mead, *The New Paternalism: Supervisory Approaches to Poverty* (Washington, D.C.: Brookings Institution Press, 1997).

4. See Judith Stacey, *In the Name of the Family: Rethinking Family Values in the Postmodern Age* (Boston: Beacon Press, 1996).

5. See Andrew Ross, *Real Love: In Pursuit of Cultural Justice* (New York: New York University Press, 1998).

6. Ibid., p. 3.

7. See Michael J. Shapiro, *Reading "Adam Smith": Desire, History and Value* (London: Sage, 1993), pp. 69–83.

8. See Frances Fox Piven and Richard A. Cloward, *Regulating the Poor: The Functions of Public Welfare*, updated ed. (New York: Vintage Books, 1993), pp. 415–16.

9. J. M. Balkin, *Cultural Software: A Theory of Ideology* (New Haven: Yale University Press, 1998), p. 217.

10. See Ibid., p. 234.

NOTES TO CHAPTER 1

1. See Frances Fox Piven and Richard A. Cloward, *The Breaking of the American Social Compact* (New York: New Press, 1997), pp. 59–77.

2. "In Their Own Words: The Republican Promises," *New York Times*, November 11, 1994, p. A26. Also see Ed Gillespie and Bob Schellhas, eds., *Contract with America: The Bold Plan by Rep. Newt Gingrich, Rep. Dick Armey and the House Republicans to Change the Nation* (New York: Times Books, 1994).

3. See John Fiske, *Power Plays, Power Works* (London: Verso, 1993), pp. 206–23.

4. See J. M. Balkin, *Cultural Software: A Theory of Ideology* (New Haven: Yale University Press, 1998).

5. Ibid., pp. 60–61.

6. Ibid., pp. 216–41.

7. See Lawrence M. Mead, *The New Paternalism: Supervisory Approaches to Poverty* (Washington, D.C.: Brookings Institution Press, 1997), p. 5.

8. On "contract" as constituting the liberal individual as a reliable agent of exchange, see Anne Norton, *Republic of Signs: Liberal Theory and American Popular Culture* (Chicago: University of Chicago Press, 1993), p. 130. On the contractual self, see William M. Reddy, "Postmodernism and the Public Sphere: Implications for an Historical Ethnography," *Cultural Anthropology* 7 (May 1992): 134-68. Also see Michael J. Shapiro, *Reading "Adam Smith": Desire, History and Value* (London: Sage, 1993), pp. 45–86.

9. Norton, *Republic of Signs*, pp. 160–61.

10. On how texts, whether diaries or contracts, construct the subject positions of author and audience, writer and reader, see Paul Smith, *Discerning the Subject* (Minneapolis: University of Minnesota Press, 1988); Roland Barthes, "The Death of the Author," in *Image/Music/Text*, trans. S. Heath (London: Fontana, 1977); and Michel Foucault, *The Archaeology of Knowledge* (New York: Pantheon, 1972), pp. 92–95.

11. "Contracting America" has parallels with "contracting colonialism," where colonialism is negotiated in a discourse that constructs the colonizer and the colonized as subject positions existing in reciprocal relations producing rights and responsibilities. On the contractual nature of colonialism, see Vicente L. Rafael, *Contracting Colonialism: Translation and Christian Conversion in Tagalog Society under Early Spanish Rule* (Ithaca, N.Y.: Cornell University Press, 1989).

12. The term "two-thirds society" refers to the disentitlement of the bottom third of society. It comes from Michael K. Brown, ed., *Remaking the Welfare State: Retrenchment and Social Policy in America and Europe* (Philadelphia: Temple University Press, 1988), p. 8.

13. While the right has been accused of taking out a Contract *on* America, not too long ago the left was suggesting that the United States needed a new social contract that better ensured the fulfillment of citizen entitlements.

14. For the idea that modernism promotes pure categories that diminish the recognition of hybridity and the fact that most things are neither purely cultural nor natural, see Bruno Latour, *We Have Never Been Modern* (Cambridge: Harvard University Press, 1993). For the idea that discursive practices like "contract" are neither strictly symbolic nor material, see Fiske, *Power Plays Power Works*, pp. 206–23.

15. Representation as a "processing" of that which is then re-presented in a commodifiable and therefore exchangeable form is discussed in Nina Cornyetz,

"Fetishized Blackness: Hip Hop and Racial Desire in Contemporary Japan," *Social Text* 41 (winter 1994): 114-39.

16. Articulation as doubled in meaning, suggesting both to express and to connect, is discussed by Stuart Hall and John Fiske. See Stuart Hall, "On Postmodernism and Articulation: An Interview with Stuart Hall," *Journal of Communication and Inquiry* 10 (1986): 45–62; and John Fiske, *Understanding Popular Culture* (Boston: Unwin Hyman, 1989), p. 146.

17. See J. L. Austin, *How to Do Things with Words* (Cambridge: Harvard University Press, 1962).

18. See Judith Butler, *Excitable Speech: A Politics of the Performative* (New York: Routledge, 1997), pp. 1–4.

19. Ibid., p. 3.

20. Charles Noble, *Welfare as We Knew It: A Political History of the Welfare State* (New York: Oxford University Press, 1997), pp. 125–26.

21. Only what Jacques Derrida calls a metaphysics of presence, whereby volitional speaking subjects are assumed to be the originating source for what they take to be their own ideas, creates the ground to deny that the representations of discourse indefinitely defer meaning by delegating that responsibility to intertextual exchanges. See Jacques Derrida, *Of Grammatology*, trans. Gayatri Chakravotry Spivak (Baltimore: Johns Hopkins University Press, 1977), chapter 3.

22. Bonnie Honig, "Declarations of Independence: Arendt and Derrida on the Problem of Founding a Republic," *American Political Science Review* 85 (March 1991): 97–113; and Jacques Derrida, "Declarations of Independence," *New Political Science* 15 (1986): 10.

23. Jacques Derrida, "Signature Event Context," in *Margins of Philosophy*, trans. Alan Bass (Chicago: University of Chicago Press, 1982), pp. 309–11, suggests that "communication" is the quintessential term of phonocentric thinking (i.e., it is centered on belief in the intentional, volitional, speaking subject). It assumes the self as an intentional act while nonetheless leaving the contaminating trace that speech acts refer back not to their speakers but to the discourses from which they are borrowed, especially the ones that make intentionality intelligible. Communication is made possible by the deferrals of intertextuality rather than the intentions of actors. Communication is the contagion of interpersonal discourse just as contract is the contagion of liberal policy discourse. Both reinscribe "personal responsibility" even as they erase the ways in which they have confined it.

24. Balkin, *Cultural Software*, pp. 74-97.

25. For an examination of how the liberal political discourse of contract necessarily invokes property relations even to the point of constructing persons as property, see Patricia Williams, *The Alchemy of Race and Rights* (Cambridge: Harvard University Press, 1991). The liberal political discourse of contract creates a hierarchy of personhood based on the extent to which people are seen as deserving of

contractual rights to their own persons as property. From indentured servitude to enfranchised citizen, personhood in the contractual society is a question of possession of the self as a propertied entity.

26. See Paul de Man, *The Resistance to Theory* (Minneapolis: University of Minnesota Press, 1986), pp. 3–20, where his discussion of John Keats's epic poem "The Fall of Hyperion" is suggestive of the problems of Gingrich's Contract with America.

27. See George Kateb, *Inner Ocean: Individualism and Democratic Culture* (Ithaca, N.Y.: Cornell University Press, 1992), pp. 172–98; and Stewart R. Clegg, *Frameworks of Power* (New York: Sage, 1989), pp. 265–71.

28. Jacques Derrida, *Dissemination*, trans. Barbara Johnson (Chicago: University of Chicago Press, 1981).

29. Jean Baudrillard, *For a Critique of the Political Economy of the Sign*, trans. Charles Levin (St. Louis: Telos Press, 1981), pp. 155–63.

30. Norton, *Republic of Signs*, pp. 166–68.

31. Mark Poster, *Critical Theory and Poststructuralism: In Search of a Context* (Ithaca, N.Y.: Cornell University Press, 1989), p. 133.

32. Jean Baudrillard, *Simulations*, trans. Paul Foss, Paul Patton, and Philip Beitchman (New York: Semiotext[e], 1983), pp. 125–33.

33. Norton, *Republic of Signs*, pp. 166–68. Norton uses Roland Barthes's notion that mythology is necessarily conservative. See Roland Barthes, *Mythologies*, sel. and trans. Annette Lavers (New York: Hill and Wang, 1957), pp. 146–48. Barthes concedes that there is a left-wing myth but believes that it is "inessential and therefore undecidable."

34. See John Rawls, *A Theory of Justice* (Cambridge: Harvard University Press, 1971), pp. 11–17.

35. For meditations on the violence done in the name of constituting some Americans as the United States, see Thomas L. Dumm, *united states* (Ithaca, N.Y.: Cornell University Press, 1994), pp. 33–40 and elsewhere.

36. See R. B. J. Walker, *One World, Many Worlds: Struggles for a Just World Peace* (Boulder, Colo.: Lynne Rienner, 1988), pp. 21–25. Also see Benedict Anderson, *Imagined Communities: Reflections on the Origin and Spread of Nationalism* (London: Verso, 1983); and Homi Bhabha, "DissemiNation: Time, Narrative, and the Margins of the Modern Nation," in Homi Bhabha, ed. *Nation and Narration* (London: Routledge, 1995), p. 301.

37. See Russell Banks, *Continental Drift* (New York: Ballentine Books, 1985), pp. 61–68, for a story that problematizes the idea that the nation is some primordial, preexisting reality that can serve as the legitimating foundation for either a "people" or a "polity." Also see Michael J. Shapiro, *Violent Cartographies: Mapping Cultures of War* (Minneapolis: University of Minnesota Press, 1997).

38. Honig, "Declarations of Independence," pp. 97–113.

39. Derrida, "Declarations of Independence," p. 10.

40. See Michel Foucault, *The Order of Things: An Archeology of the Human Sciences* (London: Tavistock, 1970), p. 26, where he states, "there are no resemblances without signatures."

41. Myra Jehlen, *American Incarnation: The Individual, the Nation and the Continent* (Cambridge: Harvard University Press, 1986).

42. Norton, *Republic of Signs*, p. 139.

43. Ibid., p. 130.

44. Richard A. Fenno, Jr., "If, as Ralph Nader Says, Congress Is 'The Broken Branch,' How Come We Love Our Congressmen So Much?" in Peter Woll, ed., *American Government: Readings and Cases*, 8th ed. (Boston: Little, Brown, 1984), pp. 477–84.

45. See Graham Fraser, "1978 Book Laid Out a Scenario Just Like Oklahoma City," *Minneapolis Star Tribune*, April 26, 1995, p. 12A.

46. Elizabeth Kolbert, "The Vocabulary of Votes: Frank Luntz," *New York Times Magazine*, March 26, 1995, pp. 46–49.

47. See ibid., p. 48.

48. Frank Luntz was Perot's pollster before he became the strategist behind the Contract with America. Perot's own preference for a business discourse for articulating the problems of politics was filmic in a particularly Hollywood sense. He exhibited an uncanny capacity to perform this discursive practice in ways already scripted in Hollywood films that privileged the common sense of businessmen as in "Meet John Doe" and "Mr. Smith Goes to Washington." See Linda Schulte-Sasse, "Meet Ross Perot: The Lasting Legacy of Capraesque Washington," *Cultural Critique* 25 (fall 1993): 91–119.

49. See Robin Toner, "GOP Gets Mixed Reviews from Public Wary on Taxes," *New York Times*, April 6, 1995, p. A1.

50. Reddy, "Postmodernism and the Public Sphere," pp. 154-55.

51. Barbara Cruikshank, *The Will to Empower: Democratic Citizens and Other Subjects* (Ithaca, N.Y.: Cornell University Press, 1999), p. 20.

52. For what is still the most compelling analysis of the regulatory character of public assistance, see Frances Fox Piven and Richard A. Cloward, *Regulating the Poor: The Functions of Public Welfare* (New York: Vintage Books, 1971). For Cruikshank, welfare does not so much *regulate recipients* as much as it collaborates with other "technologies of citizenship" inside and outside of government to *constitute citizens* as subordinated subjects. See Cruikshank, *The Will to Empower*, pp. 24-42. The emphasis on regulating as a form of social control is a more structural orientation, while the emphasis on constituting as a form of character building is a more poststructural orientation.

53. See *Personal Responsibility and Work Opportunity Reconciliation Act of 1996*, P.L 104–193, 110 STAT. 2153, 42 U.S.C. sec. 601 et seq. (Supp. 1996).

54. *Personal Responsibility and Work Opportunity Reconciliation Act of 1996*, P.L 104-193, sec. 408(b), 110 STAT. 2153, 42 U.S.C. sec. 601 et seq. (Supp. 1996).

55. These contracts had appeared earlier in some states under the Family Support Act of 1988. See Catherine Pelissier Kingfisher, *Women in the American Welfare Trap* (Philadelphia: University of Pennsylvania Press, 1996), p. 21.

56. Mead, *The New Paternalism*, p. 5.

57. Wendell Primus, et al., *The Initial Impacts of Welfare on the Incomes of Single-Mother Families* (Washington, D.C.: Center on Budget and Policy Priorities, 1999); and Peter Edelman, "Clinton's Cosmetic Poverty Tour," *New York Times*, July 8, 1999, p. A27.

58. Linda Gordon, *Pitied but Not Entitled: Single Mothers and the History of Welfare* (New York: Free Press, 1994), pp. 53–59.

59. See Stephanie Coontz, *The Way We Never Were: Family and the Nostalgia Trap* (New York: Basic Books, 1993).

60. See Nancy Fraser, "After the Family Wage: Gender Equity and the Welfare State," *Political Theory* 22 (November 1994): 591–618.

61. See Gordon, *Pitied but Not Entitled*, pp. 287–306.

62. Nancy Fraser, *Unruly Practices: Power, Discourse and Gender in Contemporary Social Theory* (Minneapolis: University of Minnesota Press, 1989), pp. 144–60.

63. Ibid., p. 155.

64. See Frances Fox Piven and Richard A. Cloward, *The New Class War: Reagan's Attack on the Welfare State* (New York: Pantheon Books, 1983), pp. 98–99.

65. See Martha F. Davis, *Brutal Need: Lawyers and the Welfare Rights Movement, 1960–1973* (New Haven: Yale University Press, 1993), pp. 81–98.

66. On the implications of contractual discourse for social welfare policy, see Nancy Fraser and Linda Gordon, "Contract versus Charity: Why Is There No Social Citizenship in the United States?" *Socialist Review* 22 (July-September 1992): 45–68.

67. Gordon, *Pitied but Not Entitled*, p. 295.

68. Ibid.

69. See Linda Gordon, "Social Insurance and Public Assistance: The Influence of Gender in Welfare Thought in the United States, 1890–1935," *American Historical Review* 97 (February 1992): 21; and Alan Wolfe, *Marginalized in the Middle* (Chicago: University of Chicago Press, 1996), pp. 153–70.

70. Gordon, *Pitied but Not Entitled*, pp. 303–6.

71. Cruikshank, *The Will to Empower*, p. 17.

72. Ibid., p. 34–42.

73. Steve Berg, "Can Congress Really Fix Welfare?" *Minneapolis Star Tribune*, March 26, 1995, p. 10A.

74. Interstate enforcement is still lagging, but President Clinton did sign into law the "Deadbeat Parents Punishment Act of 1998." This law increased the penalty in interstate nonsupport cases to a felony and increases jail time to a possible two years plus fines. Richard Casey Hoffman, past president of the National Child Support Enforcement Association, noted that while funding for arresting violators of

this law was being used by the federal government, states fail to apply enough available resources to increase interstate collections. Personal communication, July 14, 1999.

NOTES TO CHAPTER 2

1. See Kathleen O. Kane, "Hidden in Plain Sight: Gender and Death," (Ph.D. dissertation, University of Hawai'i, Honolulu, 1994; and Kathy E. Ferguson and Phyllis Turnbull, *Oh, Say, Can You See? The Semiotics of the Military in Hawai'i* (Minneapolis: University of Minnesota Press, 1998), p. xiii; and Micaela di Leonardo, *Exotics at Home: Anthropologies, Others, American Modernity* (Chicago: University of Chicago Press, 1998), prologue.

2. For an incisive critique of current welfare policies as reinforcing gender, race, and class biases, see Randy Albelda and Chris Tilly, *Glass Ceilings and Bottomless Pits: Women's Work, Women's Poverty* (Boston: South End Press, 1997), pp. 79–146. Among those who share the view that welfare is structured to be consonant with the dominant biases of the broader society, there is debate over which type of bias—class, gender, or race—is more pronounced. For an emphasis on class, see Frances Fox Piven and Richard A. Cloward, *Regulating the Poor: The Functions of Public Welfare,* updated ed. (New York: Vintage Books, 1993). For the argument that welfare regulates not merely class relations, but race and gender as well, see Linda Gordon, "What Does Welfare Regulate?" *Social Research* 55 (winter 1988): 609–30.

3. Nancy Fraser, "After the Family Wage: Gender Equity and the Welfare State," *Political Theory* 22 (November 1994): 591–618.

4. Lawrence M. Mead, "The Rise of Paternalism," in Lawrence M. Mead, ed., *The New Paternalism: Supervisory Approaches to Poverty* (Washington, D.C.: Brookings Institution Press, 1997), pp. 1–38.

5. See Michael B. Katz, *The Undeserving Poor: From the War on Poverty to the War on Welfare* (New York: Pantheon, 1989), pp. 121–22.

6. For a related genealogy of "dependency," see Nancy Fraser and Linda Gordon, "A Genealogy of *Dependency:* Tracing a Keyword of the U.S. Welfare State," *Signs* 19 (winter 1994): 309–36.

7. See Albelda and Tilly, *Glass Ceilings and Bottomless Pits,* pp. 122–30.

8. Ibid., pp. 45–64.

9. On transmission, see J. M. Balkin, *Cultural Software: A Theory of Ideology* (New Haven: Yale University Press, 1998), pp. 74–97. On relays, see Patricia Clough, *The End(s) of Enthography: From Realism to Social Criticism* (Newbury Park, Calif.: Sage, 1992), pp. 26–27.

10. For a related reading, see Barbara Cruikshank, "Welfare Queens: Policing by the Numbers," in Sanford F. Schram and Philip T. Neisser, eds., *Tales of the State: Narrative in U.S. Politics and Public Policy* (Lanham, Md.: Rowman & Littlefield,

1997), pp. 113–24; and Barbara Cruikshank, *The Will to Empower: Democratic Citizens and Other Subjects* (Ithaca: N.Y.: Cornell University Press, 1999), pp. 104—21.

11. See Irene Lurie, "Temporary Assistance for Needy Families: A Green Light for the States," *Publius: The Journal of Federalism* 27 (spring 1997): 73–89.

12. See Lawrence M. Mead, "Citizenship and Social Policy: T. H. Marshall and Poverty," *Social Philosophy and Policy* 14 (summer 1997): 197–230.

13. See Charles Tilly, *Durable Inequality* (Berkeley: University of California Press, 1998), pp. 229–33; and Sheldon Danziger and Peter Gottschalk, *America Unequal* (Cambridge: Harvard University Press, 1995), pp. 151–58.

14. See Anne Norton, *Republic of Signs: Liberal Theory and American Popular Culture* (Chicago: University of Chicago Press, 1993), p. 130.

15. See Michael J. Shapiro, *Reading "Adam Smith": Desire, History and Value* (London: Sage, 1993), pp. 1–44.

16. Friedrich Nietzsche, *On the Genealogy of Morals*, in *On the Genealogy of Morals and Ecce Homo*, trans. Walter Kaufmann and R. J. Hollingdale (New York: Vintage Books, 1967), II, 1: 57; and II, 2: 59.

17. Ibid., II, 2: 59.

18. Slavoj Žižek, *The Plague of Fantasies* (London: Verso, 1997), p. 27. Emphasis in the original.

19. See Balkin, *Cultural Software*, pp. 226–41, especially p. 229, where he suggests that "cultural software is the product of conceptual bricolage. It is not a rationally designed structure of conceptual relationships, but a historical jerry-built product."

20. On how both therapeutic and economic discourses reinforce the idea of "welfare dependency," see Fraser and Gordon, "A Genealogy of *Dependency*," pp. 309–36.

21. Lurie, "Temporary Assistance for Needy Families," pp. 73–89.

22. *Personal Responsibility and Work Opportunity Reconciliation Act of 1996*, 110 Stat. 2159, 42 U.S.C.S. § 601. (Supp. 1996).

23. There is no evidence that single parenthood declines when single mothers on welfare are required to work. The work requirement may very well increase it by enabling some single mothers who do find jobs to become self-supporting without having to get married. The work and family commitments in the 1996 law may be at cross-purposes. Liberals are not the only ones who worry that the welfare reform law of 1996 may undermine the ability of some single mothers to be good parents by requiring them to work to the point where they do not have the time to tend to their children adequately. In a widely read opinion piece, conservative political scientist James Q. Wilson said as much. See James Q. Wilson, "A GI Bill for Mothers," *Newsweek*, December 22, 1997, p. 88.

24. *Personal Responsibility and Work Opportunity Reconciliation Act of 1996*, P.L 104-193, Sect. 408(b), 110 STAT. 2153, 42 U.S.C. sec. 601 et seq. (Supp. 1996).

25. U.S. Department of Health and Human Services, Administration on Children and Families, *Temporary Assistance for Needy Families (TANF): 1936–1998*, Updated September 1998 (http://www.acf.dhhs.gov/news/3697.htm).

26. On sanctions, see Barbara Vobejda and Judith Havemann, "Sanctions: A Force behind Falling Welfare Rolls," *Washington Post*, March 23, 1998, p. A1. Also see Robert E. Recor and Sarah E. Youssef, "The Determinants of Welfare Caseload Decline," Report #99-04 (Washington, D.C.: The Heritage Center for Data Analysts, Heritage Foundation, May 1999). On the condition of families that have left the rolls, see "CDF, New Studies Look at Status of Former Welfare Recipients," *CDF Reports* (April/May 1998); and "Tracking Recipients after They Leave Welfare: Summaries of State Follow-Up Studies" (Denver: National Conference of State Legislatures, February 1998). See Kathryn Edin and Laura Lein, *Making Ends Meet: How Single Mothers Survive Welfare and Low-Wage Work* (New York: Russell Sage Foundation, 1997), for evidence that most women receiving welfare supplement their cash benefits by engaging in unreported work and with income support from family and friends, but do not resort to selling drugs or sex.

27. Edin and Lein, *Making Ends Meet*, pp. 234–35, found that poor single mothers who worked were *worse off* financially, were *more* harried, and had *less* time for their children than those who relied primarily on welfare for an income.

28. Charles Murray, *Losing Ground: Social Policy 1950–1980* (New York: Free Press, 1984); and Lawrence M. Mead, *The New Politics of Poverty: The Non-Working Poor* (New York: Free Press, 1992).

29. See Fred Siegel, *The Future Once Happened Here: New York, D.C., LA, and the Rate of American Big Cities* (New York: Free Press, 1997).

30. Michael Wines, "White House Links Riots to Welfare," *New York Times*, May 5, 1992, p. A1.

31. Myron Magnet explicitly connects welfare dependency and the liberalism of the 1960s in *The Dream and the Nightmare: The Sixties' Legacy to the Underclass* (New York: Morrow, 1993).

32. An equally curious connection between the 1960s and contemporary policy is made by some disenchanted leftists who claim that the "crisis strategy" developed by Frances Fox Piven and Richard A. Cloward in the 1960s to overload the welfare system and force reform finally backfired in the 1990s when conservatives struck back against welfare dependency and were able to end the welfare entitlement. See Michael Tomasky, *Left for Dead: The Life, Death, and Possible Resurrection of Progressive Politics in America* (New York: Free Press, 1996), pp. 105–17; and Jim Sleeper, *Liberal Racism* (New York: Viking, 1997), pp. 58–60.

33. Murray, *Losing Ground*, p. 33.

34. Gertrude Himmelfarb, *The De-Moralization of Society: From Victorian Virtues to Modern Values* (New York: Knopf, 1995).

35. Mead, *The New Politics of Poverty*, pp. 260–61.

36. Mead, "The Rise of Paternalism," in Mead, *The New Paternalism*, pp. 1–38.

37. Mead, "Citizenship and Social Policy," pp. 220, 229–30. Emphasis in the original.

38. In particular, see Edin and Lein, *Making Ends Meet,* pp. 127–36.

39. See Amy Ansell, *New Right, New Racism: Race and Reaction in the United States and Britain* (New York: New York University Press, 1997), pp. 74–141; Etienne Balibar, "Is There a 'Neo-Racism'?" in Etienne Balibar and Emmanuel Wallerstein, eds., *Race, Nation, Class,* trans. Chris Turner (London: Verso, 1991), p. 43; and Patricia J. Williams, "Of Risk and Race," *Nation.,* December 29, 1997, p. 10.

40. Melvin L. Oliver and Thomas M. Shapiro, *Black Wealth/White Wealth: A New Perspective on Racial Inequality* (New York: Routledge, 1995), pp. 91–126.

41. For a discussion of the hoarding of "social capital," see Tilly, *Durable Inequality,* pp. 147–69.

42. Frances Fox Piven and Richard A. Cloward, *The Breaking of the American Social Compact* (New York: New Press, 1997), pp. 113–30.

43. See Albelda and Tilly, *Glass Ceilings and Bottomless Pits,* pp. 1–44.

44. Martin Gilens, *Why Americans Hate Welfare: Race, Media, and the Politics of Antipoverty Policy* (Chicago: University of Chicago Press, 1999), pp. 102–53.

45. Ibid., pp. 70–71. For an account of how social programs get marginalized when they are seen as "black" programs, see Jill Quadagno, *The Color of Welfare: How Racism Undermined the War on Poverty* (New York: Oxford University Press, 1994); and Michael K. Brown, *Race, Money, and the American Welfare State* (Ithaca, N.Y.: Cornell University Press, 1999).

46. Frances Fox Piven and Richard A. Cloward, "The Contemporary Relief Debate," in Fred Block, Richard A. Cloward, Barbara Ehrenreich, and Frances Fox Piven, eds., *The Mean Season: The Attack on the Welfare State* (New York: Pantheon, 1987), pp. 45–52.

47. See Jason DeParle, "Shrinking Welfare Rolls Leave Record High Share of Minorities," *New York Times,* July 27, 1998, p. A1.

48. See Margaret Weir, "Is Anybody Listening," *Brookings Review* 15 (winter 1997): 30–33.

49. DeParle, "Shrinking Welfare Rolls Leave Record High Share of Minorities," p. A1.

50. See Albelda and Tilly, *Glass Ceilings and Bottomless Pits,* pp. 107–13.

51. Jody Raphael and Richard M. Tolman, "Trapped in Poverty/Trapped by Abuse: New Evidence Documenting the Relationship between Domestic Violence and Welfare" (Ann Arbor: School of Social Work, University of Michigan, 1998) (http://www.ssw.umich.edu/trapped/).

52. See Alan Wolfe, *Marginalized in the Middle* (Chicago: University of Chicago Press, 1996), pp. 153–70.

53. Edin and Lein, *Making Ends Meet,* pp. 147–80.

54. Lurie, "Temporary Assistance for Needy Families," pp. 73–87.

55. Piven and Cloward, *The Breaking of the American Social Compact,* pp. 72–77.

56. See Diana Pearce, "Welfare Is *Not* for Women: Why the War on Poverty Cannot Conquer the Feminization of Poverty," in Linda Gordon, ed., *Women, the State, and Welfare* (Madison: University of Wisconsin Press, 1990), pp. 265–79.

57. Balkin, *Cultural Software*, p. 229.

58. Ansell, *New Right, New Racism*, pp. 69–73.

59. Lawrence Bobo, James R. Kluegel, and Ryan A. Smith, "Laissez-Faire Racism: The Crystallization of a 'Kindler, Gentler' Anti-Black Ideology" (New York: Russell Sage Foundation: June 1996 [http://epn.org/sage/rsbobo1.html]).

60. Sanford F. Schram, *Words of Welfare: The Poverty of Social Science and the Social Science of Poverty* (Minneapolis: University of Minnesota Press, 1995), pp. 15–16.

61. Ansell, *New Right, New Racism*, pp. 266–67.

62. Balibar, "Is There a 'Neo-Racism'?"

63. On the distinction between ideology and discourse, Wendy Brown writes:

Liberalism will appear here as both a set of stories and a set of practices, as ideology *and* as discourse, as an obfuscating narrative *about* a particular social order as well as a narrative *constitutive of* this social order and its subjects. These two apparently antagonistic formulations—the former associated with a Marxist theory of ideology and the latter with Foucault's critical replacement of that theory with the notion of discourse—are both important to apprehending the operation of gender in liberalism. . . . To my knowledge, no one has yet satisfactorily articulated a relationship between discourse and ideology as terms of critical theory. . . . What does each term "do" that implicates or requires the other? In Foucault's formulation of power in and as a regime of truth, the ideological element of discourse appears not in opposition to materiality but in relation to the effects of power that it naturalizes or ontologizes. Thus, the discursive production of the subject can be conceived as ideological not in relation to some "real" subject or nondiscursive account of the subject, but insofar as this discourse naturalizes itself and thereby renders effects of power—subjects—as objects in the prediscursive world.

Wendy Brown, *States of Injury: Power and Freedom in Late Modernity* (Princeton: Princeton University Press, 1995), p. 142. Emphasis in the original.

64. William Julius Wilson, *When Work Disappears: The World of the New Urban Poor* (New York: Knopf, 1996), pp. 183–206.

65. Douglas S. Massey and Nancy A. Denton, *American Apartheid: Segregation and the Making of the Underclass* (Cambridge: Harvard University Press, 1995), pp. 234–36.

66. Richard J. Herrnstein and Charles Murray, *The Bell Curve: Intelligence and Class Structure in American Life* (New York: Free Press, 1994), pp. 269–553. It is important to ask whether *The Bell Curve* is an example of the old or the new racism. There are parallels with eugenic literature that spoke of such things as "racial cleans-

ing." This represents an explicit appeal both to ideologies of racial hierarchy and to the scientific theories of genetics. I would argue that the new and old racism both appeal to these two sources but in reverse order—the old racism relied primarily on ideology, while the new racism avoids explicit references to an ideological position and relies more on allegedly neutral scientific discourse. On the basis of this comparison, *The Bell Curve* is an example of the new racism more than the old.

On the old racism and its relationship to eugenics, see Schram, *Words of Welfare*, pp. 14–15; and Michael J. Shapiro, "Winning the West, Unwelcoming the Immigrant: Alternative Stories of 'America,'" in Schram and Neisser, *Tales of the State*, pp. 17–26.

67. Žižek, *The Plague of Fantasies*, pp. 179–82.

68. Ibid., pp. 55, 56, 73. Emphasis in the original.

69. On individuation, see Michel Foucault, "Governmentality," in Graham Burchell, Colin Gordon, and Peter Miller, eds., *The Foucault Effect: Studies in Governmentality* (Chicago: University of Chicago Press, 1991), pp. 98–104.

70. Tilly, *Durable Inequality,* pp. 193–228.

71. Ibid., pp. 236–40.

72. The 1996 law does make concessions such as allowing states to grant exemptions for up to 20 percent of their caseload, most prominently for women at risk of domestic violence. These are intended to be temporary exemptions and women are still not eligible for federally funded assistance for more than five years, discounting exempted time. See Lurie, "Temporary Assistance for Needy Families," p. 82.

73. On "surplus whiteness," see Jacques Derrida, "White Mythology: Metaphor in the Text of Philosophy," in *Margins of Philosophy*, trans. Alan Bass (Chicago: University of Chicago Press, 1982), pp. 207–29.

74. See Tilly, *Durable Inequality,* pp. 229–34.

75. Peter Passell, "Benefits Dwindle for the Unskilled along with Wages," *New York Times,* June 14, 1998, p. A1.

76. See Andrew Ross, ed., *No Sweat: Fashion, Free Trade, and the Rights of Garment Workers* (London: Verso, 1997).

77. Linda Gordon, *Heroes of Their Own Lives: The History and Politics of Family Violence* (New York: Viking, 1988).

78. John Mowitt, Foreword to Paul Smith, *Discerning the Subject* (Minneapolis: University of Minnesota Press, 1988), p. xxii. Also see Paul de Man, *Resistance to Theory* (Minneapolis: University of Minnesota Press, 1986), pp. 3–20.

79. See Marita Sturken, *Tangled Memories: The Vietnam War, the AIDS Epidemic, and the Politics of Remembering* (Berkeley: University of California Press, 1997).

80. See Maureen Dowd, "From the Bush Library Dedication Comes News of Hot Mugs, Mad Dogs and the Early Republican Hopefuls for 2000," *Cleveland Plain Dealer,* November 17, 1998, p. 9B.

81. Raphael and Tolman, "Trapped in Poverty/Trapped by Abuse."

82. See Roger Brubaker, "Social Theory as Habitus," in Craig Calhoun, Edward

LiPuma, and Moishe Postone, eds., *Bourdieu: Critical Perspectives* (Chicago: University of Chicago Press, 1993), pp. 212–34.

83. See Sigmund Freud, "Notes on the Mystic Writing Pad," quoted in Jacques Derrida, "Freud and the Scene of Writing," in *Writing and Difference*, trans. Alan Bass (Chicago: University of Chicago Press, 1978), pp. 222–23; and Michael J. Shapiro, "Literary Production as Politicizing Practice," in Michael J. Shapiro, ed., *Language and Politics* (New York: New York University Press, 1984), p. 227.

84. Žižek, *The Plague of Fantasies*, p. 3.

85. See Kane, "Hidden in Plain Sight: Gender and Death"; and Ferguson and Turnbull, *Oh, Say, Can You See?*, p. xiii.

86. Žižek, *The Plague of Fantasies*, p. 29. Emphasis in the original.

87. Lisa Duggan calls highlighting the heterosexist bias of ostensibly neutral laws "queering the state." See Lisa Duggan, "Queering the State," *Social Text* 39 (summer 1994): 1–14.

88. W. J. T. Mitchell, *Picture Theory* (Chicago: University of Chicago Press, 1994), pp. 1–8.

89. Ibid., pp. 11–34.

90. *The Conversation*, Francis Ford Coppola, United States, 1974.

91. *Blow-Up*, Tonino Guerra and Michelangelo Antonioni, Italy/England, 1966.

92. Cruikshank, *The Will to Empower*, pp. 104–21, emphasizes that the mythical "welfare queen" is an artifact of numbers more so than narratives because it is primarily through the accounting procedures of the stingy welfare system that women are unavoidably made out to be cheats. Both Cruikshank's analysis and mine emphasize the importance of seeing the "welfare queen" as an effect of the welfare system's machinations.

93. Mitchell, *Picture Theory*, p. 71.

94. Ernesto Laclau, *Emancipation(s)* (London: Verso, 1996), pp.14–15.

95. Slavoj Žižek, "Multiculturalism, or, the Cultural Logic of Multinational Capitalism," *New Left Review* 225 (September/October 1997): 29. For an analysis of the influence of media images on public opinion about welfare, see Gilens, *Why America Hates Welfare*, pp. 102–53. Gilens relies on Doris Graber, "Seeing Is Remembering: How Visuals Contribute to Learning from Television News," *Journal of Communication* 40 (1990): 134–55, to emphasize the power of images over text. He notes how the over-representation of African-American women in media texts and images has contributed to the public's most often exaggerating the extent to which minorities comprise the welfare population.

96. Nietzsche, *On the Genealogy of Morals*, I, 13: 45.

97. See Gillian Rose, *The Melancholy Science: An Introduction to the Thought of Theodor W. Adorno* (London: Macmillan, 1978), pp. 42–46.

98. See Judith Butler, *The Psychic Life of Power: Theories in Subjection* (Stanford: Stanford University Press, 1997), pp. 5–6.

99. Lillian Hellman was the paradigmatic case of a woman who refused to

succumb to the bullying tactics of the congressional "witch hunt" in the early 1950s that tried to get witnesses to "name other communists." In her own words, Hellman refused to "cut my conscience to fit this year's fashions." See Lillian Hellman, *Scoundrel Time* (Boston: Little, Brown, 1976), p. 93.

100. See Nancy Fraser, *Unruly Practices: Power, Discourse, and Gender in Contemporary Social Theory* (Minneapolis: University of Minnesota Press, 1989), pp. 144–60.

101. See Vobejda and Havemann, "Sanctions," p. A1. A similar picture of the woman who had been removed from welfare appeared in the *Washington Post* on March 23, 1998.

102. Cruikshank, "Welfare Queens," pp. 113–24.

103. Edin and Lein, *Making Ends Meet,* pp.172–80.

104. See Cruikshank, "Welfare Queens," pp. 113–24.

105. Vobejda and Havemann, "Sanctions," p. A1.

106. Michel Foucault, *The History of Sexuality,* Volume I (New York: Vintage Books, 1980), pp. 53–73.

107. Gilles Deleuze, "Postscript on Societies of Control," *October* 59 (January 1992): 1–7.

108. Žižek, "Multiculturalism, or, the Cultural Logic of Multinational Capitalism," p. 32. Emphasis in the original.

109. Many other parallels can be drawn to suggest that the denigrated category is needed not just to delegitimate a particular practice but also to encourage participation in practices associated with the preferred category. One unfortunate example is Paul de Man, who like others, spread anti-Semitic ideas during the Nazi period. In one instance de Man demonstrated the need for "jewish literature" as a denigrated category in order to separate and promote the superiority of European literature. De Man and others *needed* the category of "jewish literature" as a deviant other to privilege "European literature" as superior and devoid of the defects of"jewish" writings. See David Lehman, *Signs of the Times: Deconstruction and the Fall of Paul de Man* (New York: Poseidan Press, 1991), pp. 180–82.

110. Butler, *The Psychic Life of Power,* pp. 1–30.

111. Balkin, *Cultural Software,* pp. 1–41.

112. The phrase "heroes of their own lives" comes from Linda Gordon's book by that title on women and domestic violence. See Gordon, *Heroes of Their Own Lives.*

113. William M. Reddy, "Postmodernism and the Public Sphere: Implications for an Historical Ethnography," *Cultural Anthropology* 7 (May 1992): 134–68.

NOTES TO CHAPTER 3

1. See Michael B. Katz, *The Undeserving Poor: From the War on Poverty to the War on Welfare* (New York: Pantheon Books, 1996), and Herbert J. Gans *The War*

against the Poor: The Underclass and Antipoverty Policy (New York: Basic Books, 1995).

2. Jon Carroll, "Mr. Newt Explains It All for You," *San Francisco Chronicle*, November 27, 1995, p. B8.

3. See Nancy Fraser and Linda Gordon, "A Genealogy of *Dependency*: Tracing a Keyword of the U.S. Welfare State," *Signs* 19 (winter 1994): 309–36.

4. For a defense of medicalizing welfare under the guise of a "new paternalism," see Lawrence M. Mead, "The Rise of Paternalism," in Lawrence M. Mead, ed., *The New Paternalism: Supervisory Approaches to Poverty* (Washington, D.C.: Brookings Institution Press, 1997), pp. 1–38. Elizabeth Bartle notes the connection between dependency talk and a therapeutic orientation:

> Although not unique to social work, the language of dependency used by social workers includes phrases such as welfare dependency, drug dependency, chemical dependency, co-dependency, and client dependency. Having achieved the status of common usage, the meanings of these powerful phrases, along with the application of the term dependency to certain populations (namely children, the elderly, and women), are now taken for granted in social workers' literature and everyday communication.

Elizabeth E. Bartle, "Exposing and Reframing Welfare Dependency," *Journal of Sociology and Social Welfare* 25 (June 1998): 23. The parallels between welfare and medicine are evoked in Peter Passell, "Like a New Drug, Social Programs Are Put to the Test," *New York Times*, March 9, 1993, p. C1.

5. For a discussion on how welfare gains legitimacy as a therapeutic intervention, see Murray Edelman, *Political Language* (New York: Academic Press, 1977), pp. 135–49.

6. See Randy Albelda and Chris Tilly, *Glass Ceilings and Bottomless Pits: Women's Work, Women's Poverty* (Boston: South End Press, 1997), pp. 107–32.

7. On growing inequality, see Sheldon Danziger and Peter Gottschalk, *America Unequal* (Cambridge: Harvard University Press, 1995); and Charles Tilly, *Durable Inequality* (Berkeley: University of California Press, 1998), pp. 229–46. For over a decade now there has been a consistent stream of reports on declining wages, reduced benefits, the increased number of temporary positions, and a decline in permanent ones for low-skilled work. "[I]n 1982 workers in the top 10 percent—$35.16 a hour—was 4.56 times that of workers in the bottom 10 percent—$7.72 an hour. Fourteen years later, the ratio had increased to 5.43 to 1 with highly paid worker having gained $1.73 an hour and low-end workers having lost 93 cents an hour." Peter Passell, "Benefits Dwindle for the Unskilled along with Wages," *New York Times*, June 14, 1998, p. A1.

8. On the medicalization of welfare, see Miles F. Shore, "Psychological Factors in Poverty," in Mead, *The New Paternalism,* pp. 305–29.

9. J. M. Balkin, *Cultural Software: A Theory of Ideology* (New Haven: Yale University Press, 1998), pp. 74–97.

10. For a critique of the medicalization of poverty and welfare dependency that locates its roots in the middle-class emphasis on self-discipline for economic success, see David Wagner, *The New Temperance: The American Obsession with Sin and Vice* (Boulder: Westview Press, 1997), pp. 103–34.

11. See Shore, "Psychological Factors in Poverty," pp. 315–19.

12. Shore writes:

[D]ependency is regarded as a learned phenomenon whose intensity is determined by the nature of the learning situation. . . . [T]he individual's view of his or her experience . . . can be responsible, whether dependency is considered the cause of depression or its consequence. . . . Repeated experiences of loss of control lead to a state of learned helplessness that interferes with the ability to seek and make use of opportunities to exercise control. Eventually, this becomes a persistent motivational deficit and is associated with resignation and depression.

Ibid., pp. 316–17.

13. See Michel Foucault, *The Birth of the Clinic: An Archaeology of Medical Perception* (New York: Vintage Books, 1975); *Discipline and Punish: The Birth of the Prison* (New York: Vintage Books, 1979), pp. 73–103; "The Politics of Health in the Eighteenth Century," in *Power/Knowledge: Selected Interviews and Other Writings, 1972–1977* (New York: Pantheon, 1980), pp. 173–80; and *The History of Sexuality*, Volume I (New York: Vintage Books, 1980), pp. 53–73; and Nikolas Rose, "Medicine, History and the Present," in Colin Jones and Roy Porter, eds., *Reassessing Foucault: Power, Medicine and the Body* (New York: Routledge, 1994), pp. 48–72.

14. Wagner, *The New Temperance*, pp. 103–34.

15. See Peter Conrad and Joseph W. Schneider, *Deviance and Medicalization: From Badness to Sickness* (Philadelphia: Temple University Press, 1992), pp. 1–31.

16. Lawrence M. Mead, "The Rise of Paternalism," in Mead, *The New Paternalism*, pp. 1–38.

17. See Frances Fox Piven and Richard A. Cloward, *Regulating the Poor: The Functions of Public Welfare* (New York: Vintage, 1971), Epilogue.

18. "Women's Advocates Support Proposed TANF Rules," *Welfare Reform Watch*, May 1, 1998 (http://www.igc.apc.org/handsnet2/welfarereform/Articles/art .893094342.html); and Jody Raphael and Richard M. Tolman, "Trapped in Poverty/ Trapped by Abuse: New Evidence Documenting the Relationship between Domestic Violence and Welfare" (Ann Arbor: School of Social Work, University of Michigan, 1998) (http://www.ssw.umich.edu/trapped/).

19. See Rachel Swarns, "Welfare Family Advocates, Once Allies, Become Rivals," *New York Times*, March 29, 1997, p. A1.

20. Barbara Cruikshank helped clarify this point.

21. The National Institute of Mental Health has initiated a program on poverty, risk, and mental health designed in part to estimate the prevalence of mental health problems among welfare recipients and to recommend forms of treatment and programs so that recipients can get the help they need. For instance, see Ariel Kalil et al., "Getting Jobs, Keeping Jobs, and Earning a Living Wage: Can Welfare Reform Work?" (Ann Arbor: Center on Poverty, Risk and Mental Health, University of Michigan, May 1998). At the same time, in response to a mandate from Congress the U.S. Department of Health and Human Services has initiated a process to define, measure, and track welfare dependency. See *Indicators of Welfare Dependence: Annual Report to Congress* (Washington, D.C.: U.S. Department of Health and Human Services, October 1997). (http://aspe.os.dhhs.gov/hsp/indicator/front.htm).

22. Daniel Patrick Moynihan, "Toward a Postindustrial Social Policy," *Public Interest* 96 (summer 1989): 16–27.

23. *Indicators of Welfare Dependence: Annual Report to Congress*, p. 1.

24. Ibid., p. 2.

25. Ibid.

26. The data presented by the Task Force on Welfare Dependency from the Panel Study of Income Dynamics for 1968–1992 examined females in the sample born between 1954 and 1959 who lived in families that had received welfare income assistance or food stamps for all three years when they were aged fourteen to sixteen. The task force found that 35.7 percent of these women received welfare income assistance or food stamps for all three years between the ages of twenty-five and twenty-seven and 68.4 percent did so for one of those years. See *Indicators of Welfare Dependence: Annual Report to Congress.*

Other studies also indicate that growing up in a family that relied on welfare increases the probability of doing the same as an adult. See Thomas P. Vartanian, "Neighborhoods and the Intergenerational Use of Welfare," *Journal of Marriage and the Family* 61 (March 1999): 225–37; and Peter Gottschalk, "AFDC Participation across Generations," *American Economic Review* 9 (1990): 80, and Peter Gottschalk, "The Intergenerational Transmission of Welfare Participation: Facts and Possible Causes," *Journal of Policy Analysis and Management* 11 (1992): 254–72.

I would suggest that such replication of welfare use across generations often occurs for good reasons, such as residing in the same poor neighborhood and confronting the same lack of opportunities. For the argument that "much of the observed correlation in AFDC participation across generations can be explained by the intergenerational correlation of income and other family characteristics," see Phillip B. Levine and David J. Zimmerman, "The Intergenerational Correlation in AFDC Participation: Welfare Trap or Poverty Trap?" Discussion Paper # DP 1100-96 (Madison, Wis.: Institute for Research on Poverty, 1996).

The larger issue is whether intergenerational welfare dependence, if it does exist, is necessarily a bad thing—or is it perhaps laudable, even if learned and modeled, behavior that enables the children of welfare recipients to get the help they need? Lost in the quest to track the spread of welfare dependency from one generation to the next is consideration of the fact that families that use welfare may be no less deserving of our respect than other families, that families that use welfare may be doing nothing wrong, even in terms of affecting their life chances, and that families that use welfare may be just as likely to be poor as other poor families. Focusing on intergenerational welfare dependency may be a diversion from the more important, and larger issue of poverty.

27. See Rose, "Medicine, History and the Present," p. 49.

28. Ibid., p. 51.

29. Michel Foucault, "Nietzsche, Genealogy, History," in D. F. Bouchard, ed., *Michel Foucault: Language, Counter-Memory, Practice: Selected Essays and Interviews* (Ithaca, N.Y.: Cornell University Press, 1977), pp. 139–64.

30. Rose, "Medicine, History and the Present," p. 48.

31. Michel Foucault, "Questions of Method," in Graham Burchell, Colin Gordon, and Peter Miller, eds., *The Foucault Effect: Studies in Governmentality* (Chicago: University of Chicago Press, 1991), pp. 75–78.

32. Ibid., p. 79. Foucault states:

[M]y problem is to see how men govern (themselves and others) by the production of truth (I repeat once again that by production of truth I mean not the production of true utterances, but the establishment of domains in which the practice of true and false can be made at once ordered and pertinent). . . . I would like to resituate the production of true and false at the heart of historical and political critique.

33. Rose, "Medicine, History and the Present," pp. 53–57.

34. Michel Foucault, "Governmentality," in Burchell, Gordon, and Miller, *The Foucault Effect*, pp. 98–104.

35. Rose, "Medicine, History and the Present," pp. 66–70.

36. Ibid., p. 64.

37. Ibid., p. 54.

38. For an emphasis on the "medical model" as one where a medical professional is in a hierarchical relationship to other service providers and clients, see Ivan Illich, *Medical Nemesis* (New York: Pantheon, 1976).

39. Conrad and Schneider, *Deviance and Medicalization*, pp. 1–31.

40. Wagner, *The New Temperance*, p. 47.

41. Ibid., pp. 103–34.

42. Rose, "Medicine, History and the Present," pp. 53–57.

43. Wagner, *The New Temperance*, pp. 44–48.

44. Ibid., pp. 67–73.

45. On how metaphors "make themselves real," see Balkin, *Cultural Software*, pp. 211–15.

46. See Richard A. Cloward and Frances Fox Piven, "Hidden Protest: The Channeling of Female Innovation and Resistance," *Signs* 4 (summer 1979): 651–69.

47. For an analysis of how dependency has sometimes been valorized and at other times stigmatized, see Fraser and Gordon, "A Genealogy of *Dependency*," pp. 309–36.

48. Wagner, *The New Temperance*, pp. 127–30.

49. See Rebecca M. Blank, *It Takes a Nation: A New Agenda for Fighting Poverty* (Princeton: Princeton University Press, 1997), p. 152.

50. Ibid., pp. 151–52.

51. See *Personal Responsibility and Work Opportunity Reconciliation Act of 1996*, P.L 104-193, sec. 101(9)(C), 110 STAT. 2153, 42 U.S.C. sec. 601 et seq. (Supp. 1996).

52. Gwendolyn Mink, *Welfare's End* (Ithaca, N.Y.: Cornell University Press, 1998), p. 104.

53. Lawrence M. Mead, "Telling the Poor What to Do," *The Public Interest* 132 (summer 1998): 97–112.

54. Lawrence M. Mead, "Welfare Employment," in Mead, *The New Paternalism*, p. 65. Emphasis in the original.

55. Nancy Fraser and Linda Gordon have noted how welfare policy discourse has traditionally alternated between economic and therapeutic idioms, with a combination of the two being more emphasized in recent years. See Fraser and Gordon, "A Genealogy of *Dependency*," pp. 309–36.

56. "Moral hazard" is a term popular with economists implying that by pursuing your self-interest you will be undermining goals either you or others had hoped to realize. Welfare dependency has been commonly referred to by economists in particular as a moral hazard. "Moral hazard" in this light appears close to "poverty trap." Both terms suggest that welfare recipients are constrained by taking welfare, as if it had addictive properties, from doing what is in their own best interest. Both suggest that recipients are powerless before the addictive properties of welfare and must act contrary to their own best interest in spite of themselves. The economics of moral hazards and the sociology of "poverty traps" both point toward the medicalization of welfare dependency. Such is the subtext of cultural proliferation, each discourse finding a way to say the same tendentious thing, if each in its own idiom, about welfare receipt.

57. Mead, "The Rise of Paternalism," p. 21. Emphasis in the original.

58. See Sanford F. Schram, *Words of Welfare: The Poverty of Social Science and the Social Science of Poverty* (Minneapolis: University of Minnesota Press, 1995), pp. 3–19.

59. Nancy Fraser, *Unruly Practices: Power, Discourse, and Gender in Contemporary Social Theory* (Minneapolis: University of Minnesota Press, 1989), pp. 144–60.

60. For a discussion on the semantic abolition of welfare, see Richard P. Nathan, "The Newest New Federalism for Welfare: Where Are We Now and Where Are We Headed?" (Albany, N.Y.: Nelson A. Rockefeller Institute of Government, October 30, 1997); and *Report to the W. K. Kellogg Foundation: Fiscal Year 1997* (Albany, N.Y.: Nelson A. Rockefeller Institute of Government, April 8, 1998), p. 15. This latter document is the interim report of the Rockefeller Institute's "State Capacity Project," whose primary focus is welfare reform.

61. Thomas Kaplan, "Wisconsin's W-2 Program: Welfare as We Might Come to Know It," paper presented at the Midwest Political Science Association annual meeting, Chicago, April 5, 1998, pp. 26–27.

62. *Report to the W. K. Kellogg Foundation: Fiscal Year 1997*, p. 14.

63. Barbara Vobejda and Judith Havemann, "Sanctions: A Force behind Falling Welfare Rolls," *Washington Post*, March 23, 1998, p. A1.

64. *Making Welfare Reform Work: Tools for Confronting Alcohol and Drug Problems among Welfare Recipients* (Washington, D.C.: Legal Action Center, September 1997).

65. Ibid., p. 85.

66. NGA Center for Best Practices, *National Governors' Association Center for Best Practices Summary of Selected Elements of State Plans for Temporary Assistance for Needy Families as of November 20, 1997* (http://www.nga.org/CBP/Activities/WelfareReform.asp).

67. Mink, *Welfare's End*, p. 111.

68. See Andrew J. Polsky, *The Rise of the Therapeutic State* (Princeton: Princeton University Press, 1991), pp. 191–99; and Jan L. Hagen, "Income Maintenance Workers: Technicians or Service Providers," *Social Service Review* 61 (1987): 262.

69. Polsky, *The Rise of the Therapeutic State*, p. 193.

70. Mead, "Welfare Employment," pp. 61–67.

71. Kaplan, "Wisconsin's W-2 Program: Welfare as We Might Come to Know It," pp. 26–27; and *Report to the W. K. Kellogg Foundation: Fiscal Year 1997*, pp. 16–18.

72. See Kaplan, "Wisconsin's W-2 Program," pp. 26–27; and Anu Rangarajan, *Keeping Welfare Recipients Employed: A Guide for States Designing Job Retention Services* (Princeton: Mathematica Policy Research, June 1998).

73. "Technologies of the self" is from Michel Foucault. See Luther H. Martin, Huck Gutman, and Patrick H. Hutton, *Technologies of the Self: A Seminar with Michel Foucault* (Amherst: University of Massachusetts Press, 1988). On welfare's growing reliance on what she calls "technologies of citizenship," see Barbara Cruikshank, *The Will to Empower: Democratic Citizens and Other Subjects* (Ithaca, N.Y.: Cornell University Press, 1999), pp. 1–9 and 92–95.

74. *Welfare Reform and State Human Service Information Systems* (Lexington, Ky.: National Association of State Information Resource Executives, June 1998). (http://www.nasire.org/publications/welfare.html).

75. *Report to the W. K. Kellogg Foundation: Fiscal Year 1997*, p. 19.

76. Ibid., p. 17.

77. See *Personal Responsibility and Work Opportunity Reconciliation Act of 1996*, P.L 104-193 sec. 891, 110 STAT. 2153, 42 U.S.C. sec. 601 et seq. (Supp. 1996).

78. See Rose, "Medicine, History and the Present," p. 60.

79. Eugene Bardach, "Implementing a Paternalist Welfare-to-Work Program," in Mead, *The New Paternalism*, p. 259.

80. Gilles Deleuze, "Postscript on the Societies of Control," *October* 59 (winter 1992): 1–7.

81. Paul Virilio, *Open Sky*, trans. Julie Rose (London: Verso, 1997), p. 115.

82. Deleuze, "Postscript on the Societies of Control," pp. 3–4.

83. Frances Fox Piven gave me the term "damaged people."

84. Shore, "Psychological Factors in Poverty," p. 320.

85. Deborah Stone, *Policy Paradox: The Art of Political Decisionmaking* (New York: W. W. Norton, 1996).

86. See Schram, *Words of Welfare*, p. 144.

87. See Kathryn Edin and Laura Lein, *Making Ends Meet: How Single Mothers Survive Welfare and Low-Wage Work* (New York: Russell Sage Foundation, 1997), pp. 20–45.

88. Mark Carl Rom, Paul E. Peterson, and Kenneth F. Scheve, Jr., "Interstate Competition and Welfare Policy," in Sanford F. Schram and Samuel H. Beer, eds., *Welfare Reform: A Race to the Bottom?* (Baltimore: Johns Hopkins University Press, 1999), pp. 28–29.

89. Tilly, *Durable Inequality*, pp. 229–46; and Danziger and Gottschalk, *America Unequal*.

90. "Welfare and Workfare," transcript, *The NewsHour with Jim Lehrer* (New York: Corporation for Public Broadcasting, July 7, 1998).

91. Foucault, *History of Sexuality*, Volume I: *An Introduction*, p. 95.

92. Mink, *Welfare's End*, pp. 115–17.

93. "Women's Advocates Support Proposed TANF Rules"; and Raphael and Tolman, "Trapped in Poverty/Trapped by Abuse."

94. National Governors Association, *Round Two Matrix and Summary of Selected Elements of State Programs for Temporary Assistance for Temporary Assistance for Needy Families (TANF)* (March 14, 1999) (http://www.nga.org/welfare/TANF.htm).

95. Swarns, "Welfare Family Advocates, Once Allies, Become Rivals," p. A1.

96. Kalil, "Getting Jobs, Keeping Jobs, and Earning a Living Wage," pp. 25–26. Also see Rukmalie Jayakody and Herbert Pollack, "Barriers to Self-Sufficiency among Low-Income Single Mothers: Substance Abuse, Mental Health Problems and Welfare Reform," paper presented at the annual research conference of the Association for Public Policy and Management, Washington, D.C., November 1997.

97. See the discussion in Schram, *Words of Welfare*, pp. 7–8.

98. As quoted in Jason DeParle, "Project to Rescue Needy Stumbles against the Persistence of Poverty," *New York Times,* May 15, 1999, pp. A1, A10.

99. See Rukmalie Jayakody, Sheldon Danziger, and Harold Pollack, "The Effects of Substance Abuse and Mental Health Problems on the Work Efforts of Single Mothers," paper presented at the twentieth annual research conference of the Association for Public Policy Analysis and Management, New York, New York, October 31, 1998; Sanders Korenman, Jane E. Miller, and John E. Sjaastad, "Long-Term Poverty and Child Development in the United States: Results from the NLSY," *Children and Youth Services Review* 17 (1995): 127–55; and David R. Williams, Yan Yu, and James S. Jackson, "Racial Differences in Physical and Mental Health," *Journal of Health Psychology* 2 (1997): 335–51.

100. See George E. Vaillant, "Poverty and Paternalism: A Psychiatric Viewpoint," in Mead, *The New Paternalism,* pp. 283–85.

101. See Kai T. Erikson, *Everything in Its Path: Destruction of Community in the Buffalo Creek Flood* (New York: Simon and Schuster, 1976), pp. 255–56.

102. Vaillant, "Poverty and Paternalism," in *The New Paternalism,* pp. 283–85.

103. See Ronald C. Kessler, "The National Comorbidity Survey: Preliminary Results and Future Directions," *International Journal of Methods in Psychiatric Research* 5 (1995): 139–51.

104. John McKnight, *The Careless Society: Community and Its Counterfeits* (New York: Basic Books, 1995), pp. 76–77.

105. In response to an interviewer's questions about living in a poor neighborhood, Kathryn Edin stated:

> We live in East Camden, two blocks from the worst housing project in the city, and two blocks from one of the worst drug corners. . . . [Y]ou learn a lot about the disadvantaged. And just the sheer depression associated with living there. I mean *I* get depressed when I spend more than two or three days there. . . . What's really interesting about young girls is how their lives oftentimes start spinning out of control. . . . So one hypothesis you could draw is that childbearing is a form of self-medication.

See Kathryn Edin, "Welfare Queen," *Philadelphia,* March 1998, pp. 22–24. Emphasis in the original.

106. Wagner, *The New Temperance,* pp. 103–34.

NOTES TO CHAPTER 4

1. See Ed Gillespie and Bob Schellhas, eds., *Contract with America: The Bold Plan by Rep. Newt Gringrich, Rep. Dick Armey and the House Republicans to Change the Nation* (New York: Times Books, 1994), p. 125.

2. Since President Richard Nixon called for a "New Federalism" in the late 1960s, every president has echoed the theme, sometimes even reusing the same slo-

gan. See Timothy Conlan, *New Federalism: Intergovernmental Reform from Nixon to Reagan* (Washington, D.C.: Brookings Institution Press, 1988).

3. *Personal Responsibility and Work Opportunity Reconciliation Act of 1996,* 110 Stat. 2159, 42 U.S.C.S. § 601 et seq. (Supp. 1996).

4. John D. Donahue, *Disunited States: What's at Stake as Washington Fades and the States Take the Lead* (New York: Basic Books, 1997), p. 13.

5. Ibid., p. 67.

6. While in other chapters I have emphasized that cultural proliferation proceeds by way of basic categorical distinctions being adopted in one area after another, we also need to examine how individuals, organizations, state governments, and the like mimic each other in using these basic categorical distinctions. See J. M. Balkin, *Cultural Software: A Theory of Ideology* (New Haven: Yale University Press, 1998); and Charles Tilly, *Durable Inequality* (Berkeley: University of California Press, 1998). One way of studying state government emulation is to track the diffusion of innovation from state to state. For an analysis of the diffusion of mothers' pensions as an innovative social policy adopted in state after state in the early twentieth century, see Theda Skocpol, Christopher Howard, Susan Goodrich Lehmann, and Marjorie Abend-Wein, "Women's Associations and the Enactment of Mothers' Pensions in the United States," *American Political Science Review* 87 (September 1993): 686–701.

7. As quoted in Sanford F. Schram and Carol S. Weissert, "The State of American Federalism: 1996–1997," *Publius: The Journal of Federalism* 27 (spring 1997): 3–7.

8. The metaphor of a "race to the bottom" to characterize competition between subnational units in a federal system has been widely used in recent years. For instance, the following is from an unsigned article entitled "A Race to the Bottom" in the *Indian Express,* November 6, 1997 (http://expressindia.com/index.html):

> The competition among states to attract projects has touched a nadir with the Maharashtra government going to the extent of issuing tradable sales tax vouchers. The company setting the project will be able to trade sales tax vouchers with sales tax payers who will get the benefit of not paying sales tax. The neighbouring state of Gujarat has not been far behind.

9. Donahue, *Disunited States,* p. 13.

10. For an analysis of how environmental regulation in the United States in the 1990s has been emphasizing improving property values rather than reducing business restrictions, see Mary Graham, "Environmental Protection and the States: 'Race to the Bottom' or 'Race to the Bottom Line'?" *Brookings Review* 16 (winter 1998): 22–25.

11. Donahue, *Disunited States,* p. 67. Brandeis in his dissent in Liggett wrote: "The race was one not of diligence but of laxity" (*Liggett Co. v. Lee,* 288 U.S. 517, 558–59, 1933).

12. Brandeis wrote in his dissent in *New State Ice Co.*: "It is one of the happy incidents of the federal system that a single courageous State may, if its citizens choose, serve as a laboratory; and try novel social and economic experiments without risk to the rest of the country" (*New State Ice Company v. Liebmann*, 285 U.S. 311, 1932). This was eventually popularized as the term "laboratories of democracy."

13. See Donahue, *Disunited States*, pp. 32–37.

14. See the comments of Theda Skocpol in the symposium, "Welfare: Where Do We Go from Here?" *New Republic* 215 (August 12, 1996): 19–22. Skocpol suggests that the 1996 law's repeal of AFDC is not that significant in part because when it was originally created by the Social Security Act of 1935, AFDC did not radically revise the state public assistance programs that had predated it. States had substantial discretion before AFDC and continued to do so afterward. Repealing AFDC therefore still leaves intact a system that relies heavily on the states for the provision of public assistance. See Theda Skocpol, *Protecting Soldiers and Mothers: The Political Origins of Social Policy in the United States* (Cambridge: Belknap Press, 1992), pp. 525–26.

15. See Gwendolyn Mink, *Welfare's End* (Ithaca, N.Y.: Cornell University Press, 1998), p. 50; Schram and Weissert, "The State of American Federalism: 1996–1997," pp. 3–7.

16. Schram and Weissert, "The State of American Federalism: 1996–1997," pp. 3–7; and Mink, *Welfare's End*, pp. 133–39.

17. See United States Department of Health and Human Services, Administration for Children and Families (http://www.acf.dhhs.gov/news/caseload.htm).

18. See *Explaining the Decline in Welfare Receipt, 1993–1996* (Washington, D.C.: Council of Economic Advisors, May 9, 1997).

19. See James P. Ziliak, David N. Figlio, Elizabeth E. Davis, and Laura S. Connolly, "Accounting for the Decline in AFDC Caseloads: Welfare Reform or Economic Growth?" paper presented at the Association for Policy Analysis and Management annual research conference, Washington, D.C.: November 1997. This paper found that "the decline in per capita AFDC caseloads is attributable largely to the economic growth of states and not to waivers from federal welfare policies. In the 26 states experiencing at least a 20 percent decline in per capita AFDC caseloads from 1993–1996, we attribute 78 percent of the decline to business-cycle factors and 6 percent to welfare waivers."

20. Initial reports indicate that a good part of the decline in the welfare rolls since 1996 is attributable to states using their newfound discretion under welfare reform to purge the rolls. There is evidence that states are aggressively using sanctions to remove recipients from the rolls if they do not comply with newly imposed requirements of varying degrees of importance, ranging from missing appointments to refusing to accept work assignments. Barbara Vobejda and Judith Havemann, "Sanctions: A Force behind Falling Welfare Rolls," *Washington Post*,

March 23, 1998, p. A1; "CDF, New Studies Look at Status of Former Welfare Recipients," *CDF Reports* (April/May 1998); and Pamela Loprest, "Families Who Left Welfare: Who Are They and How Are They Doing?" Discussion Paper 99-02 (Washington, D.C.: The Urban Institute, Assessing the New Federalism, 1999). Additional reports suggest that roll decline is also due to state efforts to deter people from signing up for assistance. See Barbara Vobejda and Judith Havemann, "States' Welfare Shift: Stop It before It Starts," Washington Post, August 12, 1998, p. A1. Also see Robert E. Rector and Sarah E. Youssef, "The Determinants of Welfare Caseload Decline," Report #99-04 (Washington, D.C.: The Heritage Center for Data Analysis, Heritage Foundation, May 1999).

21. See Jason DeParle, "Shrinking Welfare Rolls Leave Record High Share of Minorities," *New York Times*, July 27, 1998, p. A1.

22. Richard Wolf, "States Plug Budget Gaps with Welfare Wind- falls," *USA Today*, March 24, 1997, p. A1.

23. Ibid.

24. Steve Savner and Mark Greenberg, *The New Framework: Alternative State Funding Choices under TANF* (Washington, D.C.: Center on Law and Social Policy, March 1997).

25. Ibid.; and "HHS TANF Guidelines Recognize State Flexibility," *Welfare News* 2 (February 1997): 1–2.

26. Rachel Swarns, "Welfare Family Advocates, Once Allies, Become Rivals," *New York Times*, March 29, 1997, p. A1.

27. "Women's Advocates Support Proposed TANF Rules," *Welfare Reform Watch*, (www.igc.apc.org/handsnet2/welfarereform/Articles/art.893094342.html). See 62 *Federal Register* 62124 (November 20, 1997).

28. While the welfare rolls nationwide declined 22 percent between 1993 and 1997, they increased approximately 20 percent in Hawai'i. In response to the growth in recipients, in early 1997 Hawai'i had instituted an unprecedented 20 percent cut in benefits to families receiving TANF support. See *Changes in Welfare Caseloads* (Washington, D.C.: U.S. Department of Health and Human Services, Administration for Children and Families, April 1997); William Douglas, "Welfare Caseload Down 3.1 Million," *Honolulu Advertiser*, July 6, 1997, p. A11; *Explaining the Decline in Welfare Receipt, 1993–1996*. Also see, "Clinton Boasts of Welfare Cuts," *Honolulu Advertiser*, April 11, 1997, p. A1; and Jason DeParle, "Sharp Decrease in Welfare Cases Is Gathering Speed," *New York Times*, February 2, 1997, p. A1.

29. Donald A. Nichols, "Labor Shortages in Wisconsin," *La Follette Policy Report* 8 (winter 1997): 22–24.

30. Jason DeParle, "Wisconsin's Welfare Plan Justifies Hopes and Some Fear," *New York Times*, January 15, 1999, p. A1; and Peter Edelman, "Clinton's Cosmetic Poverty Tour," *New York Times*, July 8, 1999, p. A27.

31. Francis R. David, "Working Poor Need Jobless Benefit Change," *Christian*

Science Monitor, November 22, 1996, p. 8; John Harwood, "Poor Results: Think Tanks Battle to Judge the Impact of Welfare Overhaul," *Wall Street Journal*, January 30, 1997, p. A6; and Bob Herbert, "The Artful Dodger," *New York Times*, March 10, 1997, p. A15.

32. Jason DeParle, "White House Calls for Minimum Wage in Workfare Plan," *New York Times*, May 16, 1997, p. A1.

33. Sam Howe Verhovek, "Clinton Reining in Role for Business in Welfare Reform," *New York Times*, May 11, 1997, p. A1.

34. *Personal Responsibility and Work Opportunity Reconciliation Act of 1996*, 110 Stat. 2159, 42 U.S.C.S. § 617 (1996).

35. *Personal Responsibility and Work Opportunity Reconciliation Act of 1996*, 110 Stat. 2159, 42 U.S.C.S. § 617 (1996).

36. See Jack Tweedie, "Welfare Spending: More for Less" (Denver: National Conference of State Legislatures, March 1998) (http://www.ncsl.org/statefed/welfare/spendin.htm). Tweedie writes:

In FY 1998, states maintained appropriations at least at the level of their required MOE [Maintenance of Effort], and most states appropriated more. They have decreased spending below the 1994 level (the 100 percent MOE level), but not by as much as they could without losing federal money. . . . [M]ost state appropriations for FY 1998 are below the 100 percent MOE levels. Seven states are close at the minimum 75 percent required to get the full federal block grant. Another 10 to 13 states are between 75 percent and 80 percent. Thirty states are above the 80 percent MOE, including seven that maintained their 100 percent required spending MOE levels or went above them. What is surprising is not that some states have reduced their spending to the 75 percent and 80 percent maintenance of effort levels, but that so many have continued to spend above those levels despite the large drop in caseloads.

Most states are however not spending all of their money nor doing much to help recipients after they leave welfare. See Edelman, "Clinton's Cosmetic Poverty Tour," p. A27.

37. Paul E. Peterson and Mark C. Rom, *Welfare Magnets: A New Case for a National Standard* (Washington, D.C.: Brookings Institution Press, 1990).

38. See Russell Hanson and David T. Hartman, "Do Welfare Magnets Attract?" Discussion Paper #1028-14 (Madison, Wis.: Institute for Research on Poverty, University of Wisconsin-Madison, 1994).

39. Peterson and Rom, *Welfare Magnets*, pp. 13–22.

40. See Sanford F. Schram and Gary Krueger, "'Welfare Magnets' and Benefit Decline: Symbolic Problems and Substantive Consequences," *Publius: The Journal of Federalism* 24 (fall 1994): 61–81.

41. See Irene Lurie, "Temporary Assistance for Needy Families: A Green Light for States," *Publius: The Journal of Federalism* 27 (spring 1997): 73–88. The option to pay people who had lived in the state for less than a year the benefits they would have received in their prior state of residence was quickly tied up in litigation.

42. See Helen Hershkoff and Stephen Loffredo, *The Rights of the Poor* (Carbondale, Ill.: Southern Illinois Press, 1997), pp. 32–53. Title 42 was amended to include a new Section 402(a), stating that: "A State operating a program funded under this part may apply to a family the rules (including benefit amounts) of the program funded under this part of another State if the family has moved to the State from the other State and has resided in the State for less than 12 months." By 1998 fifteen states had adopted this provision and the U.S. Supreme Court agreed to hear a Ninth Circuit decision overturning California's two-tier benefit schedule in *Saenz v. Roe*, 119 S.Ct. 1526 (1999). See Laura Meckler, "High Court Weighs Welfare Restriction on California Newcomers," *Philadelphia Inquirer*, January 14, 1999, p. A1. During the oral arguments in this case, Justice Ruth Bader-Ginsburg said that it was the "genius" of our constitutional system that "people can pick their states, but the states can't pick their people." The Supreme Court decided in May 1999 to strike down two-tier benefit schedules.

43. Hershkoff and Loffredo, *The Rights of the Poor*, pp. 32–53.

44. In its *Amicus Curiae* brief submitted to the Supreme Court in *Saenz v. Roe* the U.S. government argued that Congress had anticipated that the Personal Responsibility and Work Opportunity Reconciliation Act of 1996 could well induce migration. Unfortunately, the Solicitor General went on to write that this justified allowing states to establish two-tier benefit schedules to discourage migration. The Court rejected this argument. A better argument than that offered by the Solicitor General would have been to agree that welfare reform may well cut people off from assistance and induce migration, but that that is exactly why states should not be able to create barriers and deny access to such needed services.

45. See Stacy Milbouer, "Mass. Welfare Deadline Causes Concern: Some Could Seek Benefits in N.H.," *Boston Globe*, November 22, 1998, p. 8.

46. See Meckler, "High Court Weighs Welfare Restriction on California Newcomers," p. A1.

47. As Peterson and Rom have argued, policy makers could quickly undercut the potential for welfare migration by creating a national program offering uniform benefits in each state. See Peterson and Rom, *Welfare Magnets*, pp. 119–50.

48. Frances Fox Piven and Richard A. Cloward, *The Breaking of the American Social Compact* (New York: New Press, 1997), pp. 404–5.

49. Jill Quadagno, *The Color of Welfare: How Racism Undermined the War on Poverty* (New York: Oxford University Press, 1994); and Theda Skocpol, "African Americans in U.S. Social Policy," in Paul E. Peterson, ed., *Classifying by Race* (Princeton: Princeton University Press, 1995), pp. 129–55.

50. Joel F. Handler, *The Poverty of Welfare Reform* (New Haven: Yale University Press, 1995), p. 91. Also see Joel F. Handler and Yeheskel Hasenfeld, *The Moral Construction of Poverty: Welfare Reform in America* (Newbury Park, Calif.: Sage, 1991).

51. See Michael Walzer, *Spheres of Justice: A Defense of Pluralism and Equality* (New York: Basic Books, 1983), p. 31.

52. Handler, *The Poverty of Welfare Reform*, p. 91; and Handler and Hasenfeld, *The Moral Construction of Poverty.*

53. Karl de Schweinitz, *England's Road to Social Security, 1349–1947* (Philadelphia: University of Pennsylvania Press, 1947).

54. Douglas Lamar Jones, "The Strolling Poor: Transience in 18th-Century Massachusetts," *Journal of Social History* 8 (March 1974): 28–54.

55. Walter Trattner, *From Poor Law to Welfare State: A History of Social Welfare in America* (New York: Free Press, 1974), chapter 2.

56. Rand E. Rosenblatt, "Legal Entitlement and Welfare Benefits," in David Kairys, ed., *Politics of Law: A Progressive Critique* (New York: Pantheon, 1982), p. 265.

57. Skocpol, *Protecting Soldiers and Mothers*, pp. 139, 149.

58. Jim Baumohl, "Now We Won't Call It Lobbying: The Federal Bureau of Narcotics and the Depression-Era Maintenance Controversy in California and Washington," paper presented at the Conference on Historical Perspectives on Alcohol and Drug Use in American Society, 1800–1997, Philadelphia, Pa., May 9–11, 1997.

59. Linda Gordon, *Pitied but Not Entitled: Single Mothers and the History of Welfare* (New York: Free Press, 1994), p. 294.

60. Rosenblatt, "Legal Entitlement and Welfare Benefits," p. 266.

61. Martha F. Davis, *Brutal Need: Lawyers and the Welfare Rights Movement, 1960–1973* (New Haven: Yale University Press, 1993), p. 77.

62. See Mink, *Welfare's End*, pp. 50, 133–39.

63. See Hershkoff and Loffredo, *The Rights of the Poor*, p. 46; and Todd Zubler, "The Right to Migrate and Welfare Reform: Time for *Shapiro v. Thompson* to Take a Hike," *Valparaiso University Law Review* 31 (1997): 893–950.

64. Donahue, *Disunited States*, pp. 56–74.

65. Piven and Cloward, *The Breaking of the American Social Compact*, pp. 71–72.

66. See Sanford Schram, Lawrence Nitz, and Gary Krueger, "Without Cause or Effect: Reconsidering Welfare Migration as a Policy Problem," *American Journal of Political Science* 42 (January 1998): 210–30.

67. Richard J. Cebula, "A Survey of the Literature on the Migration-Impact of State and Local Government Policies," *Public Finance/Finages Publiques* 1 (1979): 69–84.

68. Peterson and Rom, "Welfare Magnets," pp. 50–83; and Thomas R. Dye, "The Policy Consequences of Intergovernmental Competition," *Cato Journal* 10 (spring 1990): 59–73.

69. Robert B. Moffitt, "Incentive Effects of the U.S. Welfare System: A Review," *Journal of Economic Literature* 30 (1992): 32–36.

70. Hanson and Hartman, "Do Welfare Magnets Attract?"; James R. Walker, "Migration among Low-Income Households: Helping the Witch Doctors Reach Consensus," Discussion Paper #1031-94 (Madison, Wis.: Institute for Research on Poverty, University of Wisconsin-Madison, 1994); William H. Frey et al., "Interstate Migration of the U.S. Poverty Population: Immigration 'Pushes' and Welfare Magnet 'Pulls,'" Research Report #95-331 (Ann Arbor, Mich.: Population Studies Center, University of Michigan, 1995); Phillip B. Levine and David J. Zimmerman, "An Empirical Analysis of the Welfare Magnet Debate Using the NLSY," Working Paper #5264 (Cambridge: National Bureau of Economic Research, 1995); Carole Roan Gresenz, "An Empirical Investigation of the Role of AFDC Benefits in Location Choice," Working Paper Series 97-05, DRU-1611-RC (Santa Monica: RAND Corporation, 1997); and Schram, Nitz, and Krueger, "Without Cause or Effect," pp. 210–30.

71. American Public Welfare Association, *State-by-State Welfare Reform Policy Decisions* (Washington, D.C.: September 1997), pp. 22–24. Hereafter cited as APWA.

72. For a critique of the "top-down" perspective, see Sanford F. Schram, *Words of Welfare: The Poverty of Social Science and the Social Science of Poverty* (Minneapolis: University of Minnesota Press, 1995), pp. 9–14.

73. See Sanford Schram and Joe Soss, "The Real Value of Welfare: Why Poor Families Do Not Migrate," *Politics & Society* 27 (1999): 39–66.

74. See Kathryn Edin and Laura Lein, *Making Ends Meet: How Single Mothers Survive Welfare and Low-Wage Work* (New York: Russell Sage Foundation, 1997), pp. 20–45.

75. See Schram and Soss, "The Real Value of Welfare," pp. 56–60.

76. Ibid. Schram and Soss compared the food stamps and the monthly maximum benefit in 1996 for a family of three to housing costs. See *Living at the Bottom: An Analysis of AFDC Benefit Levels* (New York: Center on Social Welfare Policy and Law, 1993, 1997). Housing cost differentials were calculated using the U.S. Department of Housing and Urban Development's Fair Market Rents. See 61 *Federal Register* 6690 (February 21, 1997). Comparisons were made between the major metropolitan areas with the most welfare recipients in each state. Simple regression analysis was used to estimate how much in additional housing costs a migrant would have to absorb for each additional dollar received in welfare benefits.

77. See Edin and Lein, *Making Ends Meet*, pp. 21–45.

78. Ibid., p. 43.

79. Carol Stack, *Call to Home: African Americans Reclaim the Rural South* (New York: Basic Books, 1996), pp. xiii–xix.

80. Paul Voss, Thomas Corbett, and Richard Randell, "Interstate Migration and Public Welfare: The Migration Decision Making of a Low Income Population," in

P. C. Jobes, W. F. Stinner, and J. M. Wardell, eds., *Community, Society, and Migration* (New York: University Press of America, 1992), pp. 111–47.

81. Edin and Lein, *Making Ends Meet,* pp. 218–35.

82. Schram, Nitz, and Krueger, "Without Cause or Effect," p. 220.

83. See National Governors' Association Center for Best Practices, *Summary of Selected Elements of State Plans for Temporary Assistance for Needy Families as of November 20, 1997* (http://www.nga.org/CBP/Activities/WelfareReform.asp). Hereafter *State Plans for Temporary Assistance.*

84. U.S. House of Representatives, Committee on Ways and Means, *Background Material and Data on Programs within the Jurisdiction of the Committee on Ways and Means, "The 1996 Green Book," WMCP: 104-14* (Washington, D.C.: U.S. Government Printing Office, 1996) (http://www.access.gpo.gov/congress/wm001.html). Hereafter *The Green Book.*

85. APWA, pp. 22–24; and *State Plans for Temporary Assistance.*

86. *The Green Book.*

87. Ibid.

88. APWA, pp. 22–24; and *State Plans for Temporary Assistance.*

89. *The Green Book.*

90. Hershkoff and Loffredo, *The Rights of the Poor,* pp. 32–53.

91. APWA, pp. 22–24; and *State Plans for Temporary Assistance.*

92. APWA, pp. 22–24; and *State Plans for Temporary Assistance.*

93. APWA, pp. 22–24.

94. Ibid. Peter Edelman, "Clinton's Cosmetic Poverty Tour," p. A27, suggests there are a few states that are being supportive of recipients who must now leave welfare while the rest of the states concentrate on simply slashing the rolls.

95. See APWA, pp. 22–24, "Welfare Reform and Postsecondary Education: Research and Policy Update," *Welfare Reform Network News* 2 (April 1998): 1–8; and Edelman, "Clinton's Cosmetic Poverty Tour," p. A27.

96. Mink, *Welfare's End,* p. 119; and William T. Gormley, Jr., *Everybody's Children: Child Care as a Public Problem* (Washington, D.C.: Brookings Institution Press, 1995).

97. Mink, *Welfare's End,* p. 119. As of March 1999, thirteen states did not guarantee child care for recipients who left welfare for work. See *Round Two Summaries of Selected Elements for Temporary Assistance for Needy Families* (Denver: National Governors' Association Center for Best Practices, March 14, 1999).

98. See APWA, *Survey Notes,* 1, 2 (1997): 5–8.

99. Vobejda and Havemann, "Sanctions," p. A1; and Rector and Youssef, "The Determinants of Welfare Caseload Decline."

100. AWPA, pp. 22–24; and *State Plans for Temporary Assistance.*

101. Mark Alan Hughes, "The Welfare Dustbowl," *Honolulu Advertiser,* October 20, 1996, p. B1.

NOTES TO CHAPTER 5

1. Mike Yuen, "Fines Possible for Christian Coalition," *Honolulu Star-Bulletin*, November 11, 1998, p. A1.

2. J. M. Balkin, *Cultural Software: A Theory of Ideology* (New Haven: Yale University Press, 1998).

3. See U.S. Congress, House of Representatives, *Congressional Record*, 105th Congress 2d sess., 1996, p. H7448. Elizabeth Schwinn, "House OKs Ban on Gay Marriage," *San Francisco Examiner*, July 13, 1996, p. A1; Carl Weiser and Kirk Spitzer, "House Rejects Gay Unions," *Honolulu Advertiser*, July 13, 1996, p. A1; and Jerry Gray, "House Passes Bar to U.S. Sanction of Gay Marriage," *New York Times*, July 13, 1996, pp. A1, A8.

4. *Baehr v. Meike*, 74 Hawai'i 530, 852 P2d 44 (1993).

5. See Gabriel Rotello, "To Have and To Hold: The Case for Gay Marriage," *Nation*, June 24, 1996, pp. 11–18.

6. See Deborah Stone, *Policy Paradox and Political Decisionmaking* (New York: W. W. Norton, 1996).

7. For a critique of same-sex marriage as "antinatal—hostile to the regenerative female body," see Jean Bethke Elshtain, "Comments," *Commonweal* 118 (November 22, 1991): 681–87.

8. See Nancy Fraser, "After the Family Wage: Gender Equity and the Welfare State," *Political Theory* 22 (November 1994): 591–618.

9. See John P. Feldmeier, "Federalism and Full Faith and Credit: Must States Recognize Out-of-State Same Sex Marriages?" *Publius: The Journal of Federalism* 25 (fall 1995): 107–26.

10. Evan Wolfson, "The Politics of Gay Marriage," Public presentation, Department of Political Science, University of Hawai'i at Manoa, September 20, 1996.

11. Robert Pear, "Shifting Where the Buck Stops," *New York Times*, October 29, 1995, p. A11.

12. Richard Nathan, "The Devolution Revolution: An Overview," Rockefeller Institute Bulletin 1996 (Albany, N.Y.: Nelson A. Rockefeller Institute of Government, 1996), pp. 5–13.

13. E. E. Schattschneider, *Semi-Sovereign People: A Realist's View of Democracy in America* (New York: Holt, Rinehart, and Winston, 1960), p. 10.

14. *Romer et al. v. Evans et al.*, 1996 U.S. LEXIS 3245, 64 U.S.L.W. 4353.

15. *Baehr v. Meike*, 91–139, 1st Cir., HI (1996); Feldmeier, "Federalism and Full Faith and Credit."

16. Schwinn, "House OKs Ban on Gay Marriage," p. A1.

17. On the distinctiveness of Hawaiian politics in the face of assimilationist pressures from colonizers and imperialists over the last two hundred years, see Lilikalā Kame'eleihiwa, *Native Land and Foreign Desires: How Shall We Live in*

Harmony—Ko Hawai'i 'Āina a me Nā Koi Pu'umake a ka Po'e Haole: Pehea lā e Pono ai? (Honolulu: Bishop Museum, 1992).

18. See Schwinn, "House OKs Ban on Gay Marriage," p. A1; and U.S. Congress, House of Representatives, *Congressional Record,* 1996, p. H7448.

19. Spelling Hawai'i with the 'okina is itself a political issue suggesting Hawaii's otherness, as a sovereign and distinct nation with its own language, culture, and political traditions. Spelling Hawai'i without the 'okina emphasizes that while it is different it ought to be incorporated into the federal system to be no more different than any other state.

20. See Ulla Hasager and Jonathan Friedman, eds., *Hawai'i: A Return to Nationhood* (Copenhagen, Denmark: IWGIA, Document no. 75, 1994).

21. See Grover Cleveland, "A Friendly State Being Robbed of Its Independence and Sovereignty," in Hasager and Friedman, *Hawai'i: A Return to Nationhood,* pp. 121–36.

22. See Edward D. Beechert, *Working in Hawaii: A Labor History* (Honolulu: University of Hawai'i Press, 1985), pp. 216–332; and Manfred Henningsen, "Die Linke und die USA: Teil II," *L'80: Zeitschrift fur Politik und Literatur* 42 (May 1987): 148–50. For a more pessimistic reading of the state of labor in Hawai'i, which emphasizes its complicity in the state's governing progrowth coalition, see Noel J. Kent, *Hawaii: Islands under the Influence* (Honolulu: University of Hawai'i Press, 1993), pp. 134–39.

23. Lawrence H. Fuchs, *Hawaii Pono—A Social History* (New York: Harcourt, Brace and World, 1961).

24. Noenoe Silva, "Ku'u Pono, Ke Kuleana a me ke Aloha 'Āina: An Attempt to Define a Methodology to Study Hawaiian Resistance to the Annexation" (Honolulu: Department of Political Science, University of Hawai'i, 1996). See Lilikalā Kame'eleihiwa, "Ua Mau Ke Ea o Ka 'Āina i Ka Pono: The Concepts of Sovereignty and Religious Sanction of Correct Political Behavior," in Hasager and Friedman, *Hawai'i: A Return to Nationhood,* pp. 34–43, for a discussion of how for the Hawaiians *ea* (sovereignty) was contingent on *pono* (living in balance or harmony, one to all, people to land) and how the *haole* consistently from the first arrival of Captain Cook on sought to translate *ea* and *pono* in ways more consistent with white, western liberal contractual discourse, resulting in the conversion of land to property, the expropriation of those lands, and the eventual stripping of Hawaiian sovereignty. This process was partly facilitated by changing *pono* to mean doing not what is right but doing what the white man wants.

25. James Mak and Marica Y. Sakai, "Foreign Investment," in Randall W. Roth, ed., *The Price of Paradise: Lucky We Live in Hawaii?* (Honolulu: Mutual Publishing, 1992), pp. 33–39; and Kent, *Hawaii: Islands under the Influence,* pp. 189–200.

26. See Kathy Ferguson, Phyllis Turnbull, and Mehmed Ali, "Rethinking the Military in Hawai'i," in Hasager and Friedman, *Hawai'i: A Return to Nationhood,* pp. 183–93.

27. See Lowell L. Kalapa, "Paternalistic Government," pp. 47–52, and Edwin T. Fujii, "Welfare," pp. 246–52, both in Roth, *The Price of Paradise.*

28. See Miliani B. Trask, "The Politics of Oppression," in Hasager and Friedman, *Hawai'i: A Return to Nationhood,* pp. 71–87; and Hawaiian Sovereignty Elections Council, "Ho'okūkulu he aupuni hou Nāu nō e koho (To Build a New Nation: The Choice Is Yours)" (Honolulu: Hawaiian Sovereignty Elections Council, 1996).

29. On the greater toleration of gays among selected Polynesian and Asian cultural groups, including Hawaiians, see Cori Lau, "Gender Equity: Should Same-Sex Couples Be Allowed to Marry?" in Roth, *The Price of Paradise,* pp. 231–37; and Kame'eleihiwa, *Native Land and Foreign Desires.*

30. See Homi Bhabha, *The Location of Culture* (New York: Routledge, 1994); and Homi Bhabha, "Remembering Fanon: Self, Psyche and the Colonial Condition," in Patrick Williams and Laura Christman, eds., *Colonial Discourse and Postcolonial Theory: A Reader* (New York: Columbia University Press, 1994), pp. 112–23.

31. See Slavoj Žižek, *The Indivisible Remainder: An Essay on Schelling and Related Matters* (London: Verso, 1996), pp. 208–31.

32. See Michel Foucault, *The History of Sexuality,* Volume 1: *An Introduction* (New York: Vintage Books, 1978), chapter 1, "Incitement to Discourse," and chapter 2, "The Perverse Implantation," pp. 17–50.

33. For a distinctive discussion of the "symbolic" character of intergovernmental relations, see Jae-Won Yoo and Deil S. Wright, "Public Policy and Intergovernmental Relations: Measuring Perceived Change(s) in National Influence—The Effects of the Federalism Decade," *Policy Studies Journal* 21 (winter 1993): 687–99.

34. Alan Matsuoka, "Farewell to Welfare," *Honolulu Star-Bulletin,* August 6, 1996, p. 1.

35. Too much Hawaiian distinctiveness is not tolerated by the state either. The state motto is "Ua Mau Ke Ea o Ka 'Āina i Ka Pono," usually translated as "the Life of the Land is Perpetuated in Righteousness." These words were uttered by King Kamehameha III when he got his kingdom back after it was taken from him by Great Britain for six months during 1843. At the time, the words were translated to mean "the Sovereignty of the Land is Perpetuated in Righteousness." The state is evidently reluctant to sanctify the sovereignty of the land, perhaps out of fear that this might help further legitimate land claims and even nationhood by indigenous Hawaiians. The politics of translation anticipate the translation of politics. See Kame'eleihiwa, "Ua Mau Ke Ea o Ka 'Āina i Ka Pono," in Hasager and Friedman, *Hawai'i: A Return to Nationhood,* p. 36.

36. Samuel H. Beer, *To Make a Nation: The Rediscovery of American Federalism* (Cambridge: Belknap Press, 1993), pp. 3, 200, 251–52.

37. See William A. Galston and Geoffrey L. Tibbetts, "Reinventing Federalism: The Clinton/Gore Program for a New Partnership among the Federal, State, Local,

and Tribal Governments," *Publius: The Journal of Federalism* 24, 3 (summer 1994): 23–25; and Paris N. Glendening and Mavis Mann Reeves, *Pragmatic Federalism: An Intergovernmental View of American Government* (Pacific Palisades, Calif.: Palisades Publishers, 1997), pp. 119–28.

38. Following Balkin, if the colon implies where the terms "contain each other," we would want to emphasize the federal:state over the federal/state as more expressive of politics of state building today. See Balkin, *Cultural Software*, p. 234.

39. An added development is the growing recognition that the federal system of intergovernmental relations includes not just the national government and states but tribal governments as well. See Galston and Tibbetts, "Reinventing Federalism," pp. 23–25.

40. Frank Pommersheim, "Tribal-State Relations: Hope for the Future," *South . Dakota Law Review* 36 (1991): 239–76.

41. On the concessionary character of hegemony, see Ernesto Laclau and Chantal Mouffe, *Hegemony and Socialist Strategy: Toward a Radical Democratic Politics* (London: Verso, 1985); and John Fiske, *Power Plays, Power Works* (New York: Verso, 1993), pp. 251–57. For the way every hegemony is haunted by specters of its alternatives, see Jacques Derrida, *Specters of Marx: The State of Debt, the Work of Mourning, and the New International* (New York: Routledge, 1994), pp. 37–38.

42. See Linda Gordon, *Woman's Body, Woman's Right: Birth Control in America* (New York: Penguin, 1990), pp. 337–474.

43. Balkin, *Cultural Software*, pp. 138–41.

44. Michael Tomasky, as quoted in Martin Duberman, "Bringing Back the Enlightenment," *Nation*, July 1, 1996, p. 27, which reviews Tomasky's critique of the left, *Left for Dead: The Life, Death, and Possible Resurrection of Progressive Politics in America* (New York: Free Press, 1995). Also see Katha Pollitt's assessment of the views of Andrew Sullivan and Bruce Bawer in Katha Pollitt, "Gay Marriage? Don't Say I Didn't Warn You," *Nation*, April 29, 1996, p. 9.

45. See Steven Hendley, "Liberalism, Communitarianism and the Conflictual Grounds of Democratic Pluralism," *Philosophy and Social Criticism* 19 (1993): 296–316.

46. Slavoj Žižek, *The Plague of Fantasies* (London: Verso, 1997), p. 70. Emphasis added.

47. See Fraser, "Women, Welfare, and the Politics of Need Interpretation," pp. 144–60.

48. See Pollitt, "Gay Marriage?" p. 9.

49. Wendy Brown, *States of Injury: Power and Freedom in Late Modernity* (Princeton: Princeton University Press, 1995), p. 169.

50. Jean-Jacques Rousseau, "Discourse on the Origin and Foundations of Inequality among Men," in Roger Masters, ed., *Jean-Jacques Rousseau: The First and Second Discourses* (New York: St. Martin's Press, 1964), part 2, as quoted in Brown, *States of Injury*, p. 169.

51. For an acute analysis of how land claims are converted into property settlements in ways that do an injustice to the original claim, see Trask, "The Politics of Oppression," pp. 71–87. Hawaiians have a related problem of incorporation, namely, their pending recognition as a nation of indigenous people under federal constitutional law. Such legislation puts them in a double bind. It would define them as an indigenous people for the first time in U.S. legal history but would deny them the ability to achieve nationhood outside U.S. constitutional law and the boundaries of the United States. See Silva, "Kuʻu Pono, Ke Kuleana a me ke Aloha ʻĀina."

52. Shane Phelan, "Queering Connections: Kinship and Citizenship," paper presented at the Western Political Science Association Annual Meeting, Seattle, Washington, March 25–27, 1999.

53. On how the classic civil rights strategy of incorporation encourages a nonlinear movement that Victor Shklovsky calls the "knight's move," with "each step forward being a step sideways as into an alternate world where new and often unforeseen relations of power come into play," see Andrew Ross, "Chicago Gangster Theory of Life," *Social Text* 35 (summer 1993): 110.

54. Lisa Duggan, "Queering the State," *Social Text* 39 (summer 1994): 1–14.

55. Foucault, *History of Sexuality*, Volume I, pp. 97–102.

56. See Gillian Rose, *The Melancholy Science: An Introduction to the Thought of Theodor W. Adorno* (London: Macmillan, 1978), p. 13.

57. See Jacques Derrida, "The Double Session," in *Dissemination*, trans. Barbara Johnson (Chicago: University of Chicago Press, 1981).

58. Judith Stacey, *In the Name of the Family: Rethinking Family Values in the Postmodern Age* (Boston: Beacon Press, 1996), p. 15.

NOTES TO CHAPTER 6

1. In the oral arguments to the landmark U.S. Supreme Court case that overturned the Communications Decency Act, lawyers for both sides and the justices offered numerous analogies for the Internet including library, public educational institution, broadcast media, private living room, street corner, park, telephone, city, and public forum. See Stuart Biegel, "*Reno v. ACLU* in the Supreme Court: Justices Hear Oral Argument in Communications Decency Act Case" (Los Angeles: University of California at Los Angeles, 1998) (http://www.gse.ucla.edu/iclp/cda.oral.arg.html). Also see *Reno v. ACLU*, 117 S. Ct. 2329 (1997).

2. J. M. Balkin, *Cultural Software: A Theory of Ideology* (New Haven: Yale University Press, 1998).

3. See John G. Gunnell, *The Descent of Political Theory: The Genealogy of an American Vocation* (Chicago: University of Chicago Press, 1993); and Edward Bryan Portis, *Max Weber: An Introduction to His Life and Work* (Chicago: University of Chicago Press, 1986).

4. Karl Marx, "Theses on Feuerbach," XI, in Robert C. Tucker, ed., *The Marx-Engels Reader*, 2d ed. (New York: W. W. Norton, 1978).

5. For a thoughtful set of essays on the relationship of social science to politics, see Alan Wolfe, *Marginalized in the Middle* (Chicago: University of Chicago Press, 1998). However, Wolfe fails to address the issue of whether this relationship is affected by the development of the Internet as a new public sphere.

6. Michael Tanner, Stephen Moore, and David Hartman, *The Work versus Welfare Tradeoff: An Analysis of the Total Level of Welfare Benefits by State*, Policy Report no. 240 (Washington, D.C.: Cato Institute, September 19, 1995).

7. Michael Tanner and Stephen Moore, "Why Welfare Pays?" *Wall Street Journal*, September 28, 1995, p. A20.

8. John Harwood, "Poor Results: Think Tanks Battle to Judge Impact of Welfare Overhaul," *Wall Street Journal*, January 30, 1997, p. A12.

9. David G. Post, "New World War: Cancelbunny and Lazarus Battle It Out on the Frontier of Cyberspace—and Suggest the Limits of Social Contracts," *Reason: Free Minds and Free Markets* 27 (April 1996): 28–33.

10. R. Scott Daniels, "Space, Cyberspace and Identity: The Politics of the New Realities," Ph.D. dissertation, University of Hawai'i at Manoa, Honolulu, 1996.

11. Sanford F. Schram, *Words of Welfare: The Poverty of Social Science and the Social Science of Poverty* (Minneapolis: University of Minnesota Press, 1995); and Helen E Longino, *Science as Social Knowledge: Values and Objectivity in Scientific Inquiry* (Princeton: Princeton University Press, 1990).

12. Lois Quinn and Robert S. Magill, "Politics versus Research in Social Policy," *Social Service Review* 68 (December 1994): 503–16.

13. Michel Foucault, *Discipline and Punish: The Birth of the Prison* (New York: Pantheon, 1977), pp. 293–308.

14. Murray Edelman, *Constructing the Political Spectacle* (Chicago: University of Chicago Press, 1988); and Michael J. Shapiro and Howard R. Alker, eds., *Challenging Boundaries* (Minneapolis: University of Minnesota Press, 1996).

15. Michael J. Shapiro, *Reading "Adam Smith": Desire, History and Value* (London: Sage, 1993), pp. 52–54; and Michael J. Shapiro, *Violent Cartographies: Mapping Cultures of War* (Minneapolis: University of Minnesota Press, 1997), pp. 20–30.

16. Schram, *Words of Welfare*, pp. xxvii–xxxi.

17. Shapiro, *Violent Cartographies*, pp. 20–30; and Shapiro and Alker, *Challenging Boundaries*, pp. xx–xxii.

18. Michel Foucault, "Of Other Spaces," *Diacritics* 16 (fall 1986): 22–27; and Edward Soja, "History: Geography: Modernity," in Simon During, ed., *The Cultural Studies Reader* (New York: Routledge, 1993), pp. 135–50.

19. Also see Post, "New World War," p. 29.

20. Ibid., pp. 28–33.

21. Daniels, "Space, Cyberspace and Identity."

22. See ibid.; Post, "New World War"; and Peter Uwe Hohendahl, "The Public Sphere: Models and Boundaries," in Craig Calhoun, ed., *Habermas and the Public Sphere* (Cambridge: MIT Press, 1992), pp. 99–108.

23. Shapiro, *Reading "Adam Smith,"* pp. 69–74.

24. Hohendahl, "The Public Sphere," pp. 105–8.

25. Judith Butler, *Excitable Speech: A Politics of the Performative* (New York: Routledge, 1997), pp. 103–26.

26. Diane Rubenstein, "The Mirror of Reproduction: Baudrillard and Reagan's America," *Political Theory* 17 (November 1989): 582–606; and Sanford F. Schram, "The Postmodern Presidency and the Grammar of Electronic Electioneering," *Critical Studies in Mass Communication* 8 (June 1991): 210–16.

27. Post, "New World War," pp. 28–33.

28. Balkin, *Cultural Software*, pp. 41–44.

29. Post, "New World War," pp. 29–30.

30. See Daniels, "Space, Cyberspace and Identity."

31. William E. Connolly, *Identity\Difference: Democratic Negotiations of Political Paradox* (Ithaca, N.Y.: Cornell University Press, 1991), pp. 158–97.

32. For considerations on why the Communications Decency Act of 1996 was passed, see *Reno v. ACLU*, 117 S. Ct. 2329 (1997).

33. Marjorie Heins, "Screening Out Sex: Kids, Computers, and the New Censors," *American Prospect* 39 (July/August 1998): 38–44. The Communications Decency Act was overturned by the U.S. Supreme Court as an unconstitutional infringement on free speech. See *Reno v. ACLU*, 117 S. Ct. 2329 (1997).

34. Daniels, "Space, Cyberspace and Identity."

35. Hohendahl, "The Public Sphere," pp. 105–8.

36. Daniels, "Space, Cyberspace and Identity."

37. Dennis R. Judd and Todd Swanstrom, *City Politics: Private Power and Public Policy* (New York: HarperCollins, 1994), pp. 176–212.

38. See Daniels, "Space, Cyberspace and Identity."

39. Hohendahl, "The Public Sphere"; and Pheng Cheah, "Violent Light: The Idea of Publicness in Modern Philosophy and in Global Neocolonialism," *Social Text* 43 (fall 1995): 163–90.

40. William M. Reddy, "Postmodernism and the Public Sphere: Implications for an Historical Ethnography," *Cultural Anthropology* 7 (May 1992): 134–68.

41. Daniels, "Space, Cyberspace and Identity."

42. See Dietrich Reuschemeyer and Theda Skocpol, eds., *States, Social Knowledge, and the Origins of Modern Social Policies* (Princeton: Princeton University Press, 1996).

43. Max Weber, "Science as a Vocation," and "Politics as a Vocation," in H. H. Gerth and C. Wright Mills, eds., *From Max Weber* (New York: Oxford University Press, 1946), pp. 77–156.

44. See William M. Epstein, *Welfare in America: The Dilemma of Social Science* (Madison, Wis.: University of Wisconsin Press, 1997).

45. Reuschemeyer and Skocpol, *States, Social Knowledge, and the Origins of Modern Social Policies.*

46. Ira Katznelson,"Knowledge about What? Policy Intellectuals and the New Liberalism," in Reuschemeyer and Skocpol, eds., *States, Social Knowledge, and the Origins of Modern Social Policies,* pp. 17–38.

47. Stanley Aronowitz, "On Intellectuals," in Stanley Aronowitz, *The Politics of Identity: Class, Culture, Social Movements* (New York: Routledge, 1992), pp. 125–74.

48. Schram, *Words of Welfare,* pp. 3–19.

49. Frances Fox Piven and Richard A. Cloward, *The Breaking of the American Social Compact* (New York: New Press, 1997), pp. 243–63.

50. On Daniel Patrick Moynihan, see Nicholas Lemann, *The Promised Land: The Great Black Migration and How It Changed America* (New York: Alfred A. Knopf, 1991), pp. 170–81.

51. Christopher Lasch, "Academic Pseudo-Radicalism and the Charade of 'Subversion'," in *The Revolt of Elites and the Betrayal of Democracy* (New York: W. W. Norton, 1995), pp. 176–92.

52. Richard B. McKenzie, "Orphanages: The Real Story," *Public Interest* (spring 1996): 100–104.

53. Matthew Crenson, *Building the Invisible Orphanage: A Prehistory of the American Welfare System* (Cambridge: Harvard University Press, 1998); and Robert H. Bremner, ed., *Children & Youth in America: A Documentary History,* 2 vols. (Cambridge: Harvard University Press, 1971).

54. Schram, *Words of Welfare,* pp. 3–19.

55. Harwood, "Poor Results."

56. Tanner, Moore, and Hartman, *The Work versus Welfare Tradeoff.*

57. Tanner and Moore, "Why Welfare Pays?"

58. Center on Budget and Policy Priorities, "The Cato Institute Report on Welfare Benefits: Do Cato's California Numbers Add Up?" (Washington, D.C.: Center on Budget and Policy Priorities, 1996).

59. See Schram, *Words of Welfare,* pp. 38–55.

60. Liberals have joined conservatives in emphasizing that there has been a proliferation of social welfare programs. This point has even been used to suggest that the retrenchment of public assistance is not that significant. See Shep Melnick, "The Unexpected Resilience of Means-Tested Programs," paper presented at the American Political Science Association annual meeting, September 3–6, 1998, Boston, Massachusetts.

61. Kris Foster, "Cato Institute Report," unpublished report (Honolulu: Hawai'i State Department of Human Services, November 16, 1995).

62. Center on Social Welfare Policy and Law, "Living at the Bottom: An Analysis

of 1994 AFDC Benefit Levels," Publication no. 210-2 (Washington, D.C.: Center on Social Welfare Policy and Law, June 1994).

63. Foster, "Cato Institute Report."

64. Barbara Sard et al., "Housing Bill Could Weaken Welfare Reform and Create Problems for the Working Poor" (Washington, D.C.: Center on Budget and Policy Priorities, July 1997).

65. Schram, *Words of Welfare*, pp. 3–19.

66. See U.S. House of Representatives, Committee on Ways and Means, *The Green Book* (Washington, D.C.: U.S. Government Printing Office, 1996).

67. Center on Budget and Policy Priorities, "The Cato Institute Report on Welfare Benefits."

68. Robert Moffitt, "Incentive Effects of the U.S. Welfare System: A Review," *Journal of Economic Literature* 30 (March 1992): 1–32.

69. Kathryn Edin and Laura Lein, *Making Ends Meet* (New York: Russell Sage Foundation, 1997), p. 218.

70. Harwood, "Poor Results."

71. Bob Herbert, "The Real Welfare Cheats," *New York Times*, April 26, 1996, p. A31. Also see Martin Gilens, *Why Americans Hate Welfare: Race Media, and the Politics of Antipoverty Policy* (Chicago: University of Chicago Press, 1999), pp. 178–203.

72. Tanner and Moore, "Why Welfare Pays?"

73. Center on Budget and Policy Priorities, "The Cato Institute Report on Welfare Benefits."

74. Bob Herbert, "Poison Numbers," *New York Times*, April 22, 1996, p. A13.

75. Michael Tanner and Naomi Lopez, *The Value of Welfare: Cato vs. CBPP*, Briefing Paper no. 27 (Washington, D.C.: The Cato Institute, June 12, 1996).

76. See Andrew Ross, *Real Love: In Pursuit of Cultural Justice* (New York: New York University Press, 1998), pp. 23–27. For a response to the problem of the growth of undigested information on the Internet, go to http://www.fieldsofknowledge .com/.

77. Slavoj Žižek, "Multiculturalism, or, the Cultural Logic of Multinational Capitalism," *New Left Review* 225 (September/October 1997): 36, 48; and Slavoj Žižek, *The Plague of Fantasies* (London: Verso, 1997), pp. 156–57.

78. Paul Virilio, *Open Sky*, trans. Julie Rose (London: Verso, 1997), p. 118. Emphasis in the original.

79. Schram, *Words of Welfare*; and Charles Lindblom, *Inquiry and Change: The Troubled Attempt to Understand and Shape Society* (New Haven: Yale University Press, 1990).

80. Longino, *Science as Social Knowledge*.

81. See Reuschemeyer and Skocpol, *States, Social Knowledge, and the Origins of Modern Social Policies*.

NOTES TO CHAPTER 7

1. On cultural proliferation, see J. M. Balkin, *Cultural Software: A Theory of Ideology* (New Haven: Yale University Press, 1998).

2. See Lawrence M. Mead, ed., *The New Paternalism: Supervisory Approaches to Poverty* (Washington, D.C.: Brookings Institution Press, 1997).

3. Ibid., p. 16. Also see Judith Stacey, *In the Name of the Family: Rethinking Family Values in the Postmodern Age* (Boston: Beacon Press, 1996), pp. 45–48.

4. Frances Fox Piven and Richard A. Cloward, *The Breaking of the American Social Compact* (New York: New Press, 1997), p. 4.

5. See Peter Passell, "Benefits Dwindle for the Unskilled along with Wages," *New York Times*, June 14, 1998, p. A1; Sheldon Danziger and Peter Gottschalk, *America Unequal* (Cambridge: Harvard University Press, 1995); and Charles Tilly, *Durable Inequality* (Berkeley: University of California Press, 1998), pp. 229–33.

6. Linda Gordon, *Pitied but Not Entitled: Single Mothers and the History of Welfare* (New York: Free Press, 1994), pp. 37–64.

7. See Stephanie Coontz, *The Way We Never Were: Family and the Nostalgia Trap* (New York: Basic Books, 1993).

8. See Linda Gordon, "What Does Welfare Regulate?" *Social Research* 55 (winter 1988): 23.

9. "CDF, New Studies Look at Status of Former Welfare Recipients," *CDF Reports* (April/May 1998); and Pamela Loprest, "Families Who Left Welfare: Who Are They and How Are They Doing?" Discussion Paper 99-02 (Washington, D.C.: The Urban Institute, Assessing the New Federalism, 1999).

10. See Rebecca Blank, *It Takes a Nation: A New Agenda for Fighting Poverty* (Princeton: Princeton University Press, 1997), pp. 191–219. Blank uses the political philosopher John Rawls to justify her social welfare policy recommendations.

11. See Amy Ansell, *New Right, New Racism: Race and Reaction in the United States and Britain* (New York: New York University Press, 1997), p. 62; and Etienne Balibar, "Is There a 'Neo-Racism'?" in Etienne Balibar and Emmanuel Wallerstein, eds., *Race, Nation, Class*, trans. Chris Turner (London: Verso, 1991), p. 43.

12. See Tilly, *Durable Inequality*, p. 224.

13. See William E. Connolly, *The Ethos of Pluralization* (Minneapolis: University of Minnesota Press, 1995), pp. 36–40.

14. Nancy Fraser, "Recognition or Redistribution? Dilemmas of Justice in a Post-Socialist Age," *New Left Review* 212 (July/August 1995): 68–93; and Iris Marion Young, "Unruly Categories: A Critique of Nancy Fraser's Dual Systems Theory," *New Left Review* 222 (March/April 1997): 147–60.

15. Martha Nussbaum, *Sex and Social Justice* (New York: Oxford University Press, 1999), pp. 29–54, provides a defense on behalf of the need to specify a foundational normative theory as the crucial first step to realizing the satisfaction of uni-

versal basic needs. She recognizes that universal standards of human needs must account for culture and identity; but she fails to address effectively the possibility that beyond the most generic conditions for survival basic human needs are socially constructed and the conditions for realizing them are politically contingent. As such, foundational normative theory is inappropriate as a first step. Barbara Cruikshank, *The Will to Empower: Democratic Citizens and Other Subjects* (Ithaca, N.Y.: Cornell University Press, 1999), pp. 2–6, argues against normative theory as a foundation that specifies what is to be done. She emphasizes that that is an issue of politics. Theory serves instead to enhance the capacity for political reflection when addressing the contingencies of politics. William E. Connolly, *Why I Am Not A Secularist* (Minneapolis: University of Minnesota Press, 1999), chapter 2, argues against relying too much on foundational theories of justice. He wants to make room for a paradoxical "politics of becoming" that allows for new identities to emerge out of unexpected energies as well as institutionally inflicted injuries.

16. Nancy Fraser, "After the Family Wage: Gender Equity and the Welfare State," *Political Theory* 22 (November 1994): 591–618.

17. See Nancy Fraser, *Justice Interruptus: Critical Reflections on the "Postsocialist" Condition* (New York: Routledge, 1997), pp. 207–23.

18. Fraser, "After the Family Wage," in Fraser, *Justice Interruptus*, pp. 59–62.

19. Ibid., p. 62.

20. For instance, see the otherwise informative analysis by Blank, *It Takes a Nation,* pp. 191–219.

21. See Theda Skocpol, "Sustainable Social Policy: Fighting Poverty without Poverty Programs," *American Prospect* 2 (summer 1990): 58–70.

22. Theda Skocpol has developed a historical institutional approach to the study of the welfare state that tries to account for the specific circumstances that give rise to the forms of social provision in each country. On the United States, see Theda Skocpol, *Protecting Soldiers and Mothers: The Political Origins of Social Policy in the United States* (Cambridge: Belknap Press, 1992). For an excellent attempt to combine the historical institutional and politico-economic approaches, see Charles Noble, *Welfare as We Knew It: A Political History of the American Welfare State* (New York: Oxford University Press, 1997).

23. "Welfare capitalism" is Gosta Esping-Anderson's term. See his *Three Worlds of Welfare Capitalism* (Princeton: Princeton University Press, 1990).

24. See Walter Korpi, "Power, Politics, and State Autonomy in the Development of Social Citizenship: Social Rights during Sickness in Eighteen OECD Countries since 1930," *American Sociological Review* 54 (June 1989): 309–28; and Piven and Cloward, *The Breaking of the American Social Compact,* pp. 17–31.

25. Piven and Cloward, *The Breaking of the American Social Compact,* p. 4.

26. Ibid., pp. 17–31.

27. See Frances Fox Piven and Richard A. Cloward, "The American Road to Democratic Socialism," *Democracy* 3 (summer 1983): 58–69.

28. Piven and Cloward, *The Breaking of the American Social Compact*, p. 65.

29. Judith Butler, *The Psychic Life of Power: Theories in Subjection* (Stanford: Stanford University Press, 1997). If power has a psychic life, welfare probably does as well.

30. The historical role of establishing innocence to legitimize access to assistance was clarified for me by Jim Baumohl. For disabled populations, the concept of innocence has been critical in separating the deserving disabled, such as those with physical conditions, from the nondeserving, such as alcoholics. See Deborah Stone, *The Disabled State* (Philadelphia: Temple University Press, 1984), pp. 15–20.

31. Young, "Unruly Categories," pp. 147–60.

32. For the argument that we do need to specify a priori norms in order to know how to build a system of social provision, see Fraser, *Justice Interruptus*, p. 4. For an alternative perspective, see Connolly, *Why I Am Not a Secularist*, pp. 47–71.

33. Simon Critchley, *The Ethics of Deconstruction: Derrida & Levinas* (Cambridge: Blackwell, 1992). For intimations of such a postmodern, nonfoundational ethic, see Michael J. Shapiro, *Violent Cartographies: Mapping Cultures of War* (Minneapolis: University of Minnesota Press, 1997).

34. For a helpful discussion of both the potential and limits of compensation, see Andrew Ross, *Real Love: In Pursuit of Cultural Justice* (New York: New York University Press, 1998), pp. 189–216.

35. For an explication of the ethic of alterity as offered by the Hebrewist, philosopher, and literary theorist Emmanuel Levinas, see Shapiro, *Violent Cartographies*, pp. 171–209.

36. See ibid., pp. 181–82.

37. Homi Bhabha, "DissemiNation: Time, Narrative, and the Margins of the Modern Nation," in Homi Bhabha, ed., *Nation and Narration* (New York: Routledge, 1995), p. 301.

38. For attempts to contrast but not deconstruct the distinctions between a work ethic and a care ethic, see Joan Tronto, *Moral Boundaries: Toward of Political Ethic of Care* (New York: Routledge, 1993).

39. Barbara J. Nelson, "The Origins of the Two-Channel Welfare State: Workmen's Compensation and Mothers' Aid," in Linda Gordon, ed., *Women, the State, and Welfare* (Madison: University of Wisconsin Press, 1990), pp. 123–51. Also see Joe Soss, "Lessons of Welfare: Policy Design, Political Leaning, and Political Action," *American Political Science Review* 93 (June 1999): 363–80.

40. For a sound analysis that still refers to Social Security as an insurance program even though its obligations are underfunded and its Trust Fund is in treasury bonds, see Dean Baker, "Nine Misconceptions about Social Security," *Atlantic Monthly* (July 1998): 34–39.

41. Robert Kuttner, "Rampant Bull: Social Security and the Market," *American Prospect* 39 (July/August 1998): 30–36.

42. Helen Hershkoff and Stephen Loffredo, *The Rights of the Poor* (Carbondale: Southern Illinois Press, 1997), pp. 41–98.

43. See Nelson, "The Origins of the Two-Channel Welfare State," pp. 123–51; and Gordon, *Pitied but Not Entitled,* pp. 299–306.

44. Jill Quadagno, *The Color of Welfare: How Racism Undermined the War on Poverty* (New York: Oxford University Press, 1994); and Robert C. Lieberman, *Shifting the Color Line: Race and the American Welfare State* (Cambridge: Harvard University Press, 1998).

45. Piven and Cloward, *The Breaking of the American Social Compact,* p. 65.

46. See Tilly, *Durable Inequality,* pp. 203–4.

47. Gwendolyn Mink, *Welfare's End* (Ithaca, N.Y.: Cornell University Press, 1998).

48. See Stone, *The Disabled State,* pp. 15–20.

49. See Theodore Marmor and Jerry Mashaw, "The Case for Social Insurance," in Stanley B. Greenberg and Theda Skocpol, eds., *The New Majority: Toward a Popular Progressive Politics* (New Haven: Yale University Press, 1997), p. 103.

50. The point that Social Security's own fictitious status as an insurance program consonant with American individualism and capitalism has made it vulnerable to attack for not living up to these ideals is made by Michael J. Sandel, *Democracy's Discontent: America in Search of a Public Philosophy* (Cambridge: Harvard University Press, 1996), pp. 281–86.

51. In recent years, the rumors about Social Security's insolvency have been pushed by advocates for the privatization of the system. The Cato Institute has been at the forefront of this multimillion dollar, corporate-sponsored campaign. See Kuttner, "Rampant Bull," pp. 30–36.

52. See Robert Eisner, *Social Security: More, Not Less* (New York: Twentieth Century Fund, 1998).

53. See Kuttner, "Rampant Bull," pp. 30–36. Like most other analysts, Kuttner admits that Social Security has an emerging shortfall but states (p. 32): "A return in the rate of real economic growth to levels normal for most of this century would eliminate the shortfall entirely."

54. Baker, "Nine Misconceptions about Social Security," p. 36.

55. See Quadagno, *The Color of Welfare,* p. 157.

56. See Martha Derthick, *Agency under Stress: The Social Security Administration and American Government* (Washington, D.C.: Brookings Institution Press, 1990).

57. See Kuttner, "Rampant Bull," p. 33, on how the American Association of Retired Persons and other supposedly pro-Social Security lobbies have failed to defend the program during the push for privatization in the 1990s.

58. Even Robert Kuttner, one of the most vocal supporters of Social Security, while ardently and intelligently defending it, includes proposals to transform it into an all-purpose insurance program of "wealth endowments" that people can use for

education, training, and retirement over the course of the adult lifespan. Kuttner feels that while Social Security is basically fiscally sound, politically it is not, and intergenerational conflict is likely to ensure its demise if it is not converted into the kind of program he suggests. See Kuttner, "Rampant Bull," pp. 35–36.

59. U.S. House of Representatives, Committee on Ways and Means, *Background Material and Data on Programs within the Jurisdiction of the Committee on Ways and Means, "The 1998 Green Book"* (Washington, D.C.: U.S. Government Printing Office, 1998) (http://www.access.gpo.gov/congress/wm001.html): "Although the UC system covers 97 percent of all wage and salary workers, table 4-2 shows that on average only 36 percent of unemployed persons were receiving UC benefits in 1996. This compares with a peak of 81 percent of the unemployed receiving UC benefits in April 1975 and a low point of 26 percent in June 1968 and in October 1987."

60. See Ralph Waldo Emerson, "Compensation," in *Essays and Lectures* (New York: Library of America, 1983), pp. 285–302 (http://www.jjnet.com/emerson/essays1.html). Also see Thomas L. Dumm, *A Politics of the Ordinary* (New York: New York University Press, 1999), pp. 71–89; and Ross, *Real Love,* pp. 189–216.

61. See Fraser, "After the Family Wage," pp. 591–618.

62. Sanford F. Schram, "Against Policy Analysis: Poststructural Resistance vs. Critical Reason," *Policy Science* 28 (fall 1995): 375–84.

63. The problem of creating marginal and underfunded insurance pools for those who do qualify for participation in the primary pool has already been well established in state health insurance programs for those who do not receive private health insurance. See Deborah Stone, "When Patients Go to Market: The Workings of Managed Care," *American Prospect* 13 (spring 1993): 109–15 (http://epn.org/prospect/13/13ston.html).

64. Elaine Sorensen and Robert Lerman, "Welfare Reform and Low-Income Noncustodial Fathers," *Challenge* 41 (July/August 1998): 101–16.

65. Balkin, *Cultural Software,* pp. 1–41.

66. William Julius Wilson, *When Work Disappears: The World of the New Urban Poor* (New York: Knopf, 1996), pp. 183–206; and Skocpol, "Sustainable Social Policy," pp. 58–70.

67. Robert Greenstein, "Universal and Targeted Approaches to Relieving poverty: An Alternative View," in Christopher Jencks and Paul Peterson, eds., *The Underclass* (Washington, D.C.: Brookings Institution Press, 1991), pp. 437–59.

68. Wendy Sarvasy, "Transnational Citizenship through Daily Life," paper presented at the annual meeting of the Western Political Science Association, Seattle, Washington, March 25–27, 1999.

69. André Gorz, *A Strategy for Labor: A Radical Proposal* (Boston: Beacon Press, 1964), pp. 6–8.

Index

About the Author

Sanford F. Schram teaches social policy and social theory in the Graduate School of Social Work and Social Research at Bryn Mawr College. He is the author of *Words of Welfare: The Poverty of Social Science and the Social Science of Poverty*, which won the Michael Harrington Award from the American Political Science Association.